BEYOND
REVENGE

BEYOND
REVENGE

The Evolution
of the Forgiveness Instinct

Michael E. McCullough

JOSSEY-BASS
A Wiley Imprint
www.josseybass.com

Published by Jossey-Bass
A Wiley Imprint
989 Market Street, San Francisco, CA 94103-1741—www.josseybass.com

Jossey-Bass books and products are available through most bookstores. To contact Jossey-Bass directly call our Customer Care Department within the U.S. at 800-956-7739, outside the U.S. at 317-572-3986, or fax 317-572-4002.

Jossey-Bass also publishes its books in a variety of electronic formats. Some content that appears in print may not be available in electronic books.

Three case descriptions labeled case nos. 059, 534, and 165, as they appear on p. 172 of Kubrin, C. E., & Weitzer, R. (2003). Retaliatory homicide: Concentrated disadvantage and neighborhood culture. Social Problems, 50, 157–180. Published by University of California Press. © 2003 by Society for the Study of Social Problems.

Library of Congress Cataloging-in-Publication Data

McCullough, Michael, date.
    Beyond revenge : the evolution of the forgiveness instinct / Michael McCullough.—1st ed.
      p. cm.
    Includes bibliographical references and index.
    ISBN-13: 978-0-7879-7756-6 (cloth)
      1. Revenge. 2. Forgiveness. I. Title.
  BF637.R48M43 2008
  155.9'2—dc22

                                          2007050225

Printed in the United States of America
FIRST EDITION
HB Printing   10 9 8 7 6 5 4 3 2 1

Contents

To Billie

ACKNOWLEDGMENTS

I'm a lucky man. I have a job that enables me to interact with people who are smart, interesting, nice, and enthusiastic about learning more about people and why they do what they do. My thinking about forgiveness, and therefore this book, have benefited immeasurably from research collaborations with a wonderful group of such people, including Jack Berry, Giacomo Bono, Bob Emmons, Julie Juola Exline, Frank Fincham, Bill Hoyt, Shelley Dean Kilpatrick, Steve Sandage, Jo-Ann Tsang, Charlotte vanOyen Witvliet, and Ev Worthington.

I've also had the privilege of advising some of the best graduate students in the world. Without them—Anna Brandon, Sharon Brion, Adam D. Cohen, Marcia Kimeldorf, Courtney Mooney, Emily Polak, Chris Rachal, Lindsey Root, and Ben Tabak—it would have been impossible to conduct the original research that I describe in this book. Ditto for the army of undergraduates who have worked in my laboratory over the years.

My research on forgiveness and revenge has been generously sponsored by grants from the John Templeton Foundation, the Campaign for Forgiveness Research, the Fetzer Institute, and the National Institute of Mental Health. I can't thank you enough for your faith in me and the work that I've been trying to accomplish. The views and opinions expressed herein, of course, are solely my own.

This book is a story of scientific progress—a story that I couldn't have told without the help of many scholars who shared their ideas, their hunches, their unpublished papers, their impressions of where the science stands today, and their recollections of the past. Thanks especially to Bob Axelrod, Chris Boehm, Adam B. Cohen, Martin Daly, Doug Fry, John Haidt, Dan Hruschka, Th. Emil Homerin, Tim Ketelaar, Brian Knutson,

Graeme Newman, Don Parker, Harry Reis, Arlene Stillwell, Frans de Waal, David Sloan Wilson, and Paul Zak.

My colleagues at the University of Miami exemplified everything that is good about the modern university. John Fitzgerald, John Kirby, David Kling, Phil McCabe, Bryan Page, Greg Simpson, and Ashli White helped me to avoid trouble when I was deep in intellectual terra incognita. Thanks also to Michael Halleran for his encouragement.

This would have been a very different book had Benjamin Lee, who has a fierce love both for science and for the English language, not taken an early and active interest. Josh Nowlis provided useful guidance on some of the early chapters from an ecologist's perspective. Bob Emmons, Juliette Guilbert, and Stephen Post also furnished me with important feedback at critical junctures in the book's development. Last but not least, my wife, Billie, read every word in this book—many of them two or three times—and I'm deeply grateful that she was willing to let me know what she thought of each and every one of them.

Susan Arellano, my superhumanly patient and infinitely knowledgeable literary agent, played a vital role in shaping the direction of this book and in counseling me through the writing process. *Beyond Revenge* also benefited greatly from the efforts of Julianna Gustafson, my editor at Jossey-Bass, whose enthusiasm about the book was a great encouragement to me. Naomi Lucks is the best development editor one could hope for. Catherine Craddock and Sheryl Fullerton from the Jossey-Bass team also played important roles in keeping the wheels turning, especially in the home stretch.

I received very useful feedback on some of the ideas presented in this book while giving lectures on forgiveness and revenge at the Institute for Research on Psychology and Spirituality at Rosemead School of Psychology (January 2004), a conference sponsored by the Metanexus Institute and the Institute for Research on Unlimited Love at Villanova University (May 2004), the 6th Annual Meeting of the Society for Personality and Social Psychology in New Orleans (January 2005), the Positive Psychology Summit in Washington, D.C. (September 2005), The University of Oxford's Centre for Anthropology and Mind (November 2006), the Center for the Study of Law and Religion at Emory University

(April 2007), and the Department of Psychology at the University of Florida (October 2007).

My work on this book was supported in part through the generosity of the Institute for Research on Unlimited Love, the Center for the Study of Law and Religion at Emory University, and the John Templeton Foundation. A special thank you is reserved for Stephen Post, who was a constant source of encouragement.

I reserve my most profound words of thanks for Billie, Joel, and Madeleine, who understood that there were days when I needed to work on this book, even when we all would have preferred to be at the beach.

Introduction:
Three Simple Truths
About Revenge and
Forgiveness

Early on the morning of October, 26, 2001, twenty-five-year-old Chante Mallard was driving home along Interstate 820, just southeast of Fort Worth. It had been a long night of partying, and she was drunk and high and ready to be back in her own house. Fatigue, combined with the many substances in her bloodstream—alcohol, marijuana, ecstasy—had impaired her judgment and slowed her reaction time, so there was no way she could have reacted quickly enough to prevent what happened next. As she rounded the horseshoe-shaped curve to merge onto Route 287, Mallard drove her car straight into a man who had been walking along the dark highway. Gregory Biggs, an out-of-work bricklayer, was only thirty-seven-years old. Greg was catapulted onto the hood of Mallard's car. His head and upper body went crashing through the windshield until they came to rest on the passenger-side floorboard. His legs remained trapped inside the windshield.

With all of the drugs and the noise and the broken glass, Mallard was so disoriented at first that she didn't even know that a human being was stuck in her windshield. When she realized what had happened, she took the Village Creek exit off of Route 287 and stopped the car. She got out and went around to try and help, but as soon as she touched Greg's leg, she panicked. In her drug-addled state, she couldn't figure out what to do next. So with Greg still immobilized in the windshield, she drove the final mile back to her house, pulled into the garage, and closed the garage door behind her. Mallard let Greg bleed to death right there in the garage. Over and over, Greg begged Mallard to help him, but Mallard, a nurse's aide, insisted that there was nothing she could do for him. So she left him to die. Medical examiners would later testify that Greg almost certainly would have survived the crash had he received prompt medical attention.

Later that morning, Mallard entertained a boyfriend inside the house while the car and Greg's lifeless body sat in her garage. When darkness fell, Mallard and two friends dumped the body in a nearby park. An informant told the police that she joked about the incident later.

It was several months before police received the tip that would lead them to Mallard. After her arrest, Mallard was tried and convicted of murder. She was sentenced to fifty years in prison. At her sentencing hearing, Greg's son Brandon had the opportunity to make a victim impact statement. Instead of using this opportunity to request the harshest possible sentence, Brandon said to the court and to Mallard's family, "There's no winners in a case like this. Just as we all lost Greg, you all will be losing your daughter." Later, Brandon would go on to say, "I still want to extend my forgiveness to Chante Mallard and let her know that the Mallard family is in my prayers."[1]

An act of forgiveness like this is certainly astonishing, but Brandon Biggs is hardly unique. In April 1995, twenty-three-year-old Julie Welch was killed when Timothy McVeigh bombed the Murrah Federal Building in Oklahoma City. For months afterward, Julie's father Bud craved nothing more than revenge. "Three days after the bombing, as I watched Tim McVeigh being led out of the courthouse, I hoped someone in a high building with a rifle would shoot him dead. I wanted him to fry. In fact, I'd have killed him myself if I'd had the chance."

For months, Bud tried to assuage his grief and slake his thirst for revenge with alcohol, but it just wasn't working. Then one day in January 1996, while nursing a terrible hangover, Bud returned to 200 Northwest 5th Street in downtown Oklahoma City where the Murrah Building once stood. There, his epiphany began: "For the next few weeks I started to reconcile things in my mind, and finally concluded that it was revenge and hate that had killed Julie and the 167 others. Tim McVeigh and Terry Nichols had been against the U.S. government for what happened in Waco,

Texas, in 1993 and seeing what they'd done with their vengeance, I knew I had to send mine in a different direction."

He recalled an interview with Timothy McVeigh's father, Bill, that he'd seen on television a few weeks after the bombing. "[Bill] was working in his flowerbed," Welch writes. "The reporter asked him a question, and when he looked into the television camera for a few seconds, I saw a deep pain in a father's eyes that most people could not have recognized. I could, because I was living that pain. And I knew that some day I had to go tell that man that I truly cared about how he felt."

During a visit to New York State, Bud initiated contact with Bill McVeigh and his daughter Jennifer—Timothy's sister—with a brief visit to their home.

> [W]e spent the first half-hour in that garden getting to know one another. Then we went into the house, and spent an hour visiting at the kitchen table. His twenty-three-year-old daughter Jennifer was there. As I walked in, I noticed a photograph of Tim above the mantelpiece. I kept looking at it as we were sitting at the table. I knew that I had to comment on it at some point, so finally I looked at it and said, "God, what a good-looking kid." Bill said, "That's Tim's high school graduation picture." A big tear rolled out of his right eye, and at that moment I saw in a father's eyes a love for his son that was absolutely incredible.
>
> After our visit I got up, and Jennifer came from the other end of the table and gave me a hug; we cried, and I held her face in my hands and told her, "Honey, the three of us are in this for the rest of our lives. And we can make the most of it if we choose. I don't want your brother to die. And I will do everything in my power to prevent it."

This wasn't forgiveness (yet), but forgiveness would eventually arrive. "About a year before the execution I found it in my heart to forgive Tim McVeigh. It was a release for me rather than for him."[2]

This book is about people like Brandon Biggs and Bud Welch—people who seem to transcend the urge for revenge and, instead, find a way to forgive. But it's not just a "book about forgiveness." It's also a "book about revenge." It's about a grieving father who murders the air traffic controller whom he blames for his family's tragic death. It's about men and women living outside of the protection of the law who use revenge as their first line of defense against victimization. It's about heads of state who use tough talk of retaliation to deter aggression by other nations, thereby boxing themselves into corners in which they're sometimes forced to back up the tough talk with lethal military force. It's about people whose desire for vengeance against what they view as an unjust foreign occupation leads them to capture Westerners, behead them, and incinerate their bodies for the world to see. It's about a disenfranchised loner who, feeling abused by the system, takes a giant bulldozer, converts it into an assault vehicle, and then razes the homes and workplaces of the people who have caused him pain. It's a book about every outrageous, despicable, tragic story of revenge you have ever heard or read.

In a broader sense, it's also a book about a species called *Homo sapiens.* It's about us. You might be tempted to assume that people like Brandon Biggs and Bud Welch possess some special trait that enables them to be more forgiving than the average person would be in their shoes, but I'm going to take that assumption to task. Brandon Biggs and Bud Welch are regular human beings just like the rest of us. I wrote this book not because I want to tell you what makes "super-forgivers" like Brandon Biggs and Bud Welch unique but, rather, because I want to show you how you can change the world to enable more of us to behave more like them.

I'm also going to challenge the idea that people who feel the urge to seek revenge are somehow defective, sick, or morally misshapen. Sure, some avengers are troubled by severe mental illness, but most aren't. We might intuitively assume that we're somehow different from the types of people who commit the horrible acts of vengeance that we read about and hear about every day, but the people who lash out in revenge aren't fundamentally different from you and me. Mostly, what makes them different from us is the circumstances in which they live and the tools they perceive to be at their disposal for defending their interests. In another place, at another time, under different circumstances, the guy in the bulldozer might have been any of us.

I wrote this book for people who want to understand where human beings' inspiring capacity for forgiveness and their hair-trigger propensity for revenge come from. It's for people who want to bypass all of the pious-sounding statements about the power of forgiveness, and all of the fruitless sermonizing about the destructiveness of revenge. It's for people who want to see human nature for what it really is.

It's also a book for people who want to make the world a better place.

These two goals—understanding the world and improving it—are connected, of course. If you're really committed to making the world a better place—a place in which forgiveness is more plentiful and revenge is increasingly rare, you have to learn three simple truths about forgiveness and revenge.

TRUTH #1: THE DESIRE FOR REVENGE IS A BUILT-IN FEATURE OF HUMAN NATURE

A century of research in the social and biological sciences reveals a crucial, unsettling truth about the place of revenge in human nature: though we might wish it were otherwise, the desire for revenge is normal—normal in the sense that every neurologically intact human being on the planet has the biological hardware for experiencing it. Few of us, if any, are strangers to the desire for revenge. Its potential destructiveness and apparent senselessness can blind us to this fact. But by viewing the scientific research on revenge through the lens of evolutionary theory, we'll arrive at the conclusion that a readiness to seek revenge served important functions for ancestral humans, and that it's still capable of serving many of those important functions today. We'll also see that the propensity for revenge isn't strictly confined to humans: revenge takes place throughout the animal kingdom, and the reasons why we find it in other animals are similar to the reasons why we find it in humans. What's more, thanks to brand-new scientific research, we're now in a position to describe what a brain in pursuit of revenge is really trying to accomplish, and we're in a position to understand the cultural, social, and ecological factors that make revenge more likely and more violent. If we can better appreciate the naturalness of revenge, the functions revenge arose to serve, and the factors that elicit the motivation

to seek revenge, we'll be better equipped to change the world so
that revenge becomes less destructive and less common.

TRUTH #2: THE CAPACITY FOR FORGIVENESS IS A BUILT-IN FEATURE OF HUMAN NATURE

The claim that revenge is an authentic, standard-issue, bred-
in-the-bone feature of human nature doesn't imply that forgiveness is a thin veneer of civility that we slap on top of an unwilling,
brutish, fundamentally vengeful core. Nothing could be further
from the truth. In fact, when you use the conceptual tools of evolutionary science as a lens through which to view the past century
of research on forgiveness, you can't help but conclude that our
capacity for forgiveness is every bit as authentic as is our capacity
for revenge. The human capacity for forgiveness, like the human
capacity for revenge, solved critical evolutionary problems for
our ancestors, and it's still solving those problems today. And the
capacity for forgiveness, like the capacity for revenge, isn't even
a uniquely *human* characteristic. Many animals—including most
primates, dolphins, hyenas, goats, and even fish—do some very
forgiving-esque things. The evolutionary lens also helps us make
sense of the things that the human mind needs in order to forgive—the cultural, social, and ecological factors that can activate
the brain systems that make forgiveness happen. Evolutionary
thinking can also help us envision new ways of putting the
"forgiveness instinct" to work to help us solve some of the personal, social, and even geopolitical challenges that humanity
faces today.

TRUTH #3: TO MAKE THE WORLD A MORE FORGIVING, LESS VENGEFUL PLACE, DON'T TRY TO CHANGE HUMAN NATURE: CHANGE THE WORLD!

Human nature is what it is: the outcome of billions of years of
biological evolution, the details of which are managed by a
genetic cookbook. In other words, it's pretty well locked in.

But there's a hopeful paradox waiting in the wings: our fixed, evolutionarily shaped, genetically superintended human nature is flexible, multifarious, and exquisitely sensitive to context. The nature of human nature is to help people change their behavior to suit their changing circumstances! An implication of this flexibility and context-sensitivity is that it's possible to make the world a less vengeful, more forgiving place even when we're forced to work with a fixed human nature. How do you do that? By making the social environments in which humans reside (homes, neighborhoods, communities, nations, hemispheres, planets, and so forth) less abundant in the factors that evoke the desire for revenge, and by making those environments more abundant in the factors that evoke forgiveness. Helping humans adapt to the contingencies that present themselves is one of the things that human nature is for. Change those contingencies in one way, and more revenge results. Change them in another way, and more forgiveness results. So if you master the contingencies governing the human desire for revenge and the human propensity to forgive, then you can go back to your home, your school, your workplace, or your community and make it a less vengeful, more forgiving place.

I hope to challenge you to think more deeply about who we are as a species, about the prospects for changing ourselves and our society, and about the possibilities for using forgiveness to improve our lives on this little planet. To get started on this venture, let's first think a bit more carefully about what it means to say that there is such a thing as human nature—a set of psychological and behavioral dispositions that are shaped and refined by natural selection, nurtured and evoked by the environments in which we live, and deeply influential in determining our thoughts, feelings, and actions. Our propensities for revenge and forgiveness aren't created anew in each individual by the forces of culture, parenting, and good (or bad) life experiences: they're part of our birthright as a species.

BEYOND
REVENGE

CHAPTER ONE

PUTTING VENGEANCE
AND FORGIVENESS
BACK INTO HUMAN
NATURE

There seems to be no end to people's appetite for debating the big questions about human nature. Do humans have free will, or are we hopelessly pushed back and forth by forces that are essentially out of our control? To what extent is our behavior a product of culture and to what extent does it emerge from the basic biological realities of human existence? How would people behave if we removed the civilizing influences of parenting, religion, culture, and government? Are we just very smart animals, or is there something more to what makes us distinctively human? Best of all: Are people basically good or basically evil?

A pair of books published in 1996 renewed my interest in the endless debate surrounding the are-we-basically-good-or-are-we-basically-evil question. They sparked my curiosity in part because they addressed the question by looking not at humans, but at some of our closest living primate relatives. In *Good Natured,* primatologist Frans de Waal uses case studies and decades of his own research to argue that humans have inherited not only greed, deceit, and the love of power from the long-extinct species from which we descended, but also the capacity for a variety of highly moral behaviors: setting and enforcing rules that benefit the group, sharing with the needy, sympathizing with those that suffer, offering consolation to the vanquished, and returning favors to the generous. By de Waal's lights, our biological heritage has resulted in a human nature that's both "fundamentally brutish" and "fundamentally noble."[1]

Case closed? Not so fast. For sure, de Waal's depiction is an important and novel installment on the age-old debate, but the book right next to *Good Natured* on my shelf shows that there's something very important still to be said about the "fundamentally brutish" side of humanity's moral repertoire. In *Demonic Males,* Harvard anthropologist Richard Wrangham and his writing partner Dale Peterson acknowledge that chimpanzees have the cooperative and moral streak that de Waal writes about, but what strikes Wrangham and Peterson about chimpanzee morality is that it's very much an "ingroup" morality.[2] Chimpanzees seem to have a certain set of rules for how to treat members of their own living groups and a very different—and more cold-blooded—set of rules for how to treat chimpanzees from other groups.

After many years of believing that chimpanzees were mostly peace-loving and docile (save for petty squabbles, protests over unfair treatment, and rowdy competitions for leadership within the community), naturalists began to publish case after case in which chimpanzees from one community went out of their way to seek out the members of other chimpanzee communities, and then to maim and kill them. As primatologists began to put the disturbing clues together—clues such as the chimpanzee corpses left in the bloody aftermath of these encounters—they came to the conclusion that bands of adult and adolescent chimpanzee males occasionally gather in something like "war parties" for the purpose of patrolling the borders of their territories and killing males from other communities. These killings usually seem opportunistic—if you find a strange chimpanzee male that you can overpower with force of numbers, get him—but on occasion the attacks seem more calculated, more sinister.

Here's a grisly example of what can happen. In the early 1960s, when Jane Goodall began studying the community of chimpanzees in Tanzania's Kasekela region, the community was already getting too large. Fifteen boisterous adult males were just too many for a single group to manage comfortably. Eventually, the Kasekela community splintered and a new Kahama community was formed, with roughly equal numbers of males in each. The individuals in these two emerging communities were once close associates, of course, but after the split, relations between the Kasekela group and the new Kahama group gradually became more distant and more tense. Eventually, relations between the two groups became downright hostile, and later, deadly. Raids and opportunistic attacks ensued over the course of several years. One by one, the Kahama males (and many of the females) began to disappear. Then one day, Kahama was no more. Their former friends from Kasekela had annihilated them.

Blame it on male bonding. Wrangham and Peterson argue that at some point back in chimpanzees' evolutionary history, males began to develop strong positive psychological attachments (called *coalitional bonds*) to other males within the community. Coalitional bonding developed, they argue, precisely because it helped the group to function better, but with its benefits for group cohesiveness came hostility and an attack-on-sight ethic toward individuals from other communities.[3] Male bonding helped ancestral apes preserve their own territories and look after their own relatives and associates, but it also generated antipathy toward members of other groups.

It's hard to resist comparing the Kasekela and Kahama communities to the Jets and the Sharks of *West Side Story,* or to the stranded boys in *Lord of the Flies* who splinter into two mutually hostile groups under the leadership of Jack the hunter and Ralph the guardian of civility. Like us, it seems, chimpanzees have a coalitional psychology—a tendency to form tightly structured ingroups that foment hostility toward outgroups. Scores of studies in social psychology now show that human beings maintain a certain set of moral rules for kith and kin, and a very different set for outsiders.[4]

The realization that chimpanzees divide their social worlds into Jets and Sharks with so little cognitive effort—just as we do—came home for me one crisp October day in 2003 when I was touring the field station of the Yerkes National Primate Research Center, part of Emory University. The Center includes two separate communities of chimpanzees—the very communities that Frans de Waal has been studying for many years. Even though I had read about chimpanzee aggression, I was surprised to learn that the two colonies of chimpanzees at the Center are completely isolated from each other, and that they probably don't even know of each other's existence. The researchers at Yerkes aim to keep it that way: they house the two colonies on opposite sides of the Center's large wooded property. When I asked my tour guide what would happen if the two colonies got together one afternoon for a "mixer," she shot me a look: "Let's just say that it wouldn't be pretty."

Having read *Demonic Males* some years previously, I didn't press for details, but I got some details to mull over a couple of years later. In a newspaper article, I read how Buddy, age sixteen, and Ollie, age thirteen—two male chimpanzees living at an animal sanctuary called "Animal Haven Ranch" near Bakersfield, California—escaped from their cages and attacked a human male visitor, chewing off most of his face and tearing off his testicles and a foot before they were shot by the owners' son-in-law.[5]

De Waal's titular implication that chimpanzees (and maybe we) are "good natured," and Wrangham and Peterson's suggestion that they (and maybe we) are "demonic," gets us right into a critical point about the place of forgiveness and revenge in human nature: Maybe they're both natural. But this assertion is a major departure from the way that most social scientists, and in fact, most people, think about revenge and forgiveness today.

Is Revenge a Communicable Disease? Is Forgiveness the Cure?

Most people view the desire for revenge as something decidedly abnormal—something like a disease that invades a hapless host, replicates, and then infects other poor souls. This view is, in fact, the orthodox view of revenge in Western society: revenge is an infection that invades a vulnerable host (perhaps one whose resistance to the infection has been weakened by a poor constitution or a bad childhood), releases a toxin that poisons the host morally, physically, and psychologically, and then wreaks destructive effects on the avenger and the objects of his or her vengeance—sometimes spreading from one host to another until the outbreak reaches epidemic proportions. I call the orthodox Western view of revenge the *disease model* of revenge.

Because revenge is seen as dirty, dangerous, and communicable, talking about it has become taboo. Even when we're really angry, resentful, and filled with a desire for retribution, we dare not use the name revenge to justify our own behavior toward our attackers for fear of seeming petty, base, immoral, immature, or just plain evil. As Susan Jacoby writes in *Wild Justice*—one of the few books that has questioned the disease model of revenge— "We are more comfortable with the notion of forgiving and forgetting, however unrealistic it may be, than with the private and public reality of revenge, with its unsettling echoes of the primitive and its inescapable reminder of the fragility of human order."[6]

The disease model of revenge has been standard fare in Western thought for millennia. Part of its appeal comes from the most influential Western religious traditions. Scriptures and popular piety in Christianity and Judaism both stress the notion that forgiveness is a good thing to do (they've got their own ways of praising and motivating vengeance, too, but I'm saving that for Chapter Ten).[7] The Western world's greatest dramatists, essayists, and novelists have also made the disease model of revenge their stock-in-trade. Many of the tragedies of antiquity, as well as the poetry and drama of the Elizabethan era, for example, are soaked in bloody revenge that spreads like the Ebola virus.[8]

If Western religion and Western literature set the disease model of revenge in motion, Western society's therapeutic mindset raised the disease model of revenge to the exalted place it enjoys today. The influence of the mental health profession was once restricted to preventing and treating mental disorders, identifying and nurturing intellectual talent, and assisting veterans in their transitions from the battlefield to civilian life. But mental health professionals now claim authority over the entire range of human behavior—revenge included. The mental health profession, which models itself after the field of medicine, conceptualizes many undesirable behaviors as illnesses, so mental health professionals were in a very good position to promulgate the disease model of revenge during the twentieth century.

Actually, psychiatry didn't have much to say about revenge until 1948, when Karen Horney, an influential psychoanalyst, published an essay titled "The Value of Vindictiveness." Horney describes how the desire for revenge could absorb people for a moment in time, or for life—becoming, effectively, a chronic illness: "This drive can be the governing passion of a life-time to which everything is subordinated, including self-interest. All intelligence, all energies, then, are dedicated to the one goal of vindictive triumph."[9] Horney goes so far as to argue that people prevented from exercising their vengeful impulses may exhibit symptoms such as headaches, stomachaches, fatigue, and insomnia—in short, the desire for revenge produces such a powerful psychological toxin that it literally makes you sick.

Horney's ideas were warmly received—hardly surprising given that the ideas were familiar to anyone acquainted with the great works of Western literature (which Horney cites aplenty). The notion that vindictiveness is evidence that something has gone awry in the sufferer, who therefore should be treated for a disorder, is now so well established that we rarely think about it. Even mental health professionals have tended simply to assume its veracity rather than to test this link empirically.

For example, a paper in the *British Journal of Psychiatry* titled "Psychiatric Problems Following Bereavement by Murder or Manslaughter" described "obsessive revenge seeking," along with post-traumatic stress disorder, major depression, and anxiety disorders, as one of the common "diagnostic categories" that people experience after the murder of a loved one.[10] In another study, scientists who examined the mental health of Kosovar Albanians during some of most intense violence of the war in Kosovo thought it was important to measure their subjects' hatred and feelings of revenge toward the Serbs.[11] I'm not saying that it's *not* important to measure the hatred and feelings of revenge of a victimized group, or that obsessive revenge-seeking is *not* a common characteristic of people who have had a loved one murdered. To the contrary, such reactions are typical, if not universal. Nevertheless, the assumption that the desire for vengeance is a symptom or, even more strongly, a cause of illness or disease is just that—an assumption.

Horney and other proponents of the disease model of revenge are correct to link the desire for revenge with mental illness: vindictiveness is a feature of many of the mental disorders that psychiatrists call "personality disorders."[12] And, of course, some of the most outrageous acts of revenge-motivated violence that we see in the real world are committed by people who really are suffering from some form of mental disorder. Seung-Hui Cho—the Virginia Tech undergraduate who killed twenty-seven fellow students and five professors before killing himself one morning in April 2007 during a rampage that he attributed, incomprehensibly, to a desire for vengeance—was surely hobbled by a severe mental illness that compromised his reality-testing, his moral judgment, and his ability to empathize with others.[13] But not even this means that the desire for revenge makes people crazy: an equally plausible (and in Seung-Hui Cho's case, more plausible) explanation is that mental disorders and emotional problems make people sensitive to interpersonal injury, and then make it difficult for them to resist the natural vindictive impulses that arise when they perceive that they've been injured.[14]

More recent studies show that when people think vengeful or vindictive thoughts about someone who harmed them in the past, they experience increases in blood pressure and heart rate.[15] Such findings suggest that holding a grudge for years or decades could contribute to wear and tear on the cardiovascular system, which in turn could be one of the physiological mechanisms by which hostile thoughts and feelings cause people to die prematurely.[16] But none of this evidence makes the desire for revenge itself a disease either. For me, thinking about cleaning out the garage increases cardiovascular arousal and negative emotion, but nobody would argue that gearing up to clean out the garage is a disease or some form of pathology for which we need a cure. Still, the power of the disease model is such that when problems get framed as diseases, well-meaning people often go off in search of cures.

Revenge as "Illness" and Forgiveness as "Cure": Thank the Standard Social Science Model

Looking through the lens of the disease model, many contemporary mental health professionals see forgiveness as the best "treatment" for vindictiveness and resentment—like a cure for a disease, an antidote for a poison, or a balm for a wound. One psychiatrist recently endorsed a colleague's work on forgiveness by saying that it "may be as important to the treatment of emotional and mental disorders as the discovery of sulfa drugs and penicillin were to the treatment of infectious diseases."[17] Another recent book title dubs forgiveness "the greatest healer of all."[18] But the "cure" model of forgiveness is as erroneous as is the disease model of revenge.

The idea that the desire for revenge is a disease, and that forgiveness is its cure, sounds so right to so many people because it fits so well with the reigning paradigm in the social sciences— what John Tooby and Leda Cosmides have called the "Standard Social Science Model."[19] The Standard Social Science Model is based on the proposition that everything that exists in your mind was put there by forces acting on your mind from the outside— the reinforcements and punishments you receive throughout life, your interactions with caregivers and role models, and the norms and folkways of your particular culture. According to the Standard Social Science Model, your emotions, thoughts, preferences, and perceptual biases are cultural products. Sure, maybe chimpanzees can be characterized as "good natured" or "demonic," but humans? The Standard Social Science Model says, "no way."

The Standard Social Science Model has many conceptual roots. The first is the radical behaviorism that preoccupied psychologists from the 1920s until well into the 1960s, when the field of "cognitive science" gained greater control over psychology. The second is the cultural relativism (that is, the conviction that human culture is created entirely in response to local conditions) that preoccupied anthropologists in the first half of the twentieth century. The third is the belief that culture, rather than biology, is the predominant cause of human behavior, which continues to preoccupy sociologists right up to the present day. Social scientists have labored under the influence of the Standard Social Science Model for decades, and the model has blinded them to profound realities about human nature.[20]

Most critically, the Standard Social Science Model would have us believe that there aren't any universal human psychological characteristics. According to the Standard Social Science Model, I as an American could not tell if an Andaman Islander were experiencing joy just because I happened to see a certain type of smile on his face, because there is no universal facial expression for joy. There are also no universal human tendencies to fear snakes, to care for our own children better than the children of strangers, or to deepen our friendships with people by eating with them. None of these traits is universal, according to the Standard Social Science Model, and none could be: human beings think, feel, and act the way they do solely because of the experiences they've had, and because every culture is different, the people that emerge from those cultures will be different too. Even though there is a universal human anatomy—every properly developed human has a circulatory system, a four-chambered heart, a liver, and a giant brain sitting atop his or her nervous system—there is no universal human psychology. Humans, as a species, can't be "good-natured" or "demonic" or anything else because there's no "human nature" there about which we might make such generalizations in the first place.

Putting Revenge and Forgiveness Back into Human Nature

Despite the pervasiveness of the Standard Social Science Model and the safe harbor it provides for the "revenge is a disease/forgiveness is the cure" conceit, I don't believe that the desire for revenge is "out there," like a virus waiting to get inside vulnerable human beings. The scientific evidence against such an idea is overwhelming, as we'll soon see. And it's beginning to look like the Standard Social Science Model has one foot in the grave as well.[21]

So perhaps there really are human universals after all. And if there are, should the desire for revenge and the ability to forgive be counted among them? I believe the answer is yes, and if I'm correct, it has profound implications for how we understand the desire for revenge, control its devastating effects, and help people forgive old grievances and move on with their lives in a peaceful, constructive way. This seems like a good time to restate the first basic truth about revenge and forgiveness that we're going to be exploring: *The desire for revenge isn't a disease to which certain unfortunate people fall prey. Instead, it's a universal trait of human nature, crafted by natural selection, that exists today because it was adaptive in the ancestral environment in which the human species evolved.*

I'm hardly the first writer to suggest that the desire for revenge is part of human nature. The ethical theorist Joseph Butler made a similar point nearly three hundred years ago,[22] as did the philosopher-cum-economist Adam Smith.[23] Butler, Smith, and their ilk used theological and philosophical arguments to bolster their claims, but to make a case today that revenge is a built-in feature of human nature, we have two resources that Butler and Smith didn't have.

First, we have a set of conceptual tools from evolutionary theory that can explain the universal psychological and behavioral features of human nature as well as it can explain the universal physical features of human nature. When Charles Darwin published *The Origin of Species* in 1859, seeds were planted in the biological sciences that would eventually germinate into a theory that made the concept of human nature scientifically plausible. Indeed, the application of evolutionary theory to human behavior and mental processes has begun to supplant the Standard Social Sciences Model. I'll have a lot more to say about evolutionary theory in the chapters to come.

Darwin didn't have a great deal to say about the desire for revenge, but he didn't exempt this desire from his theory of natural selection either. For Darwin, the capacity for revenge was, in fact, characteristic of *all* humans and at least some other vertebrates. In *The Descent of Man* he writes, "It has, I think, now been shewn that man and the higher animals, especially the Primates, have some few instincts in common. All have the same senses, intuitions, and sensations—similar passions, affections, and emotions, even the more complex ones, such as jealousy, suspicion, emulation, gratitude, and magnanimity; they practise deceit and are revengeful. . . ."[24]

Let me be clear: there's no single "evolutionary hypothesis" about revenge. Evolutionary theory provides many potential explanations for why revenge exists in the human behavioral repertoire, but the explanation that I'll pursue in this book is a straightforward one: that the capacity for revenge is a universal human trait because natural selection specifically crafted it for its ability to help humans' ancestors to solve social problems that threatened their survival and their ability to produce descendants.

For this story about the origin of revenge to be correct, two important things need to have happened during human evolution. The first is that the desire for revenge must have been effective in helping organisms to solve specific *adaptive problems:* challenges in their environment (including the social environment) that, if not surmounted, would have detracted from reproductive success. The second is that individual differences in the motivation to seek revenge must have been transmittable through some mechanism (evolutionary theorists traditionally assume, as do I, that the primary mechanism of transmission is genetic, but the process of cultural transmission has its own role to play, too) [25] If those two conditions—selection and transmission—hold over many generations of reproduction, the capacity for vengeance could become typical of a species, even a species such as ours. The science writer Robert Wright aptly describes the orthodox (and quite possibly correct) genetic-evolutionary view on the place of resentment in human nature: "It evolved not for the good of the species, or the good of the nation, or even for the good of the tribe, but for the good of the individual. And, really, even this is misleading; the impulse's ultimate function is to get the individual's genetic information copied. . . . Its origin is no more heavenly than that of hunger, hatred, lust, or any of the other things that exist by virtue of their past success in shoving genes through generations."[26]

Today, we may view revenge as a problem (and, as we'll see in the next chapter, it is), but through the lens of evolution, it's also a solution (as we'll see in Chapters Three and Four). Echoing

Wright's take on resentment, the emotion theorist Nico Frijda wrote of revenge, "[B]y itself it is tailored to be for the individual's benefit. Revenge is a natural thing to desire, and sometimes it is a natural thing to take."[27]

The second resource we have to understand the place of revenge in human nature is a massive database of scientific evidence that tells a remarkably consistent story. Thanks to legions of social scientists, biological scientists, and computer scientists who have examined revenge over the years (some working from an evolutionary point of view, others not), we really don't need theistic or stoic presuppositions, as Joseph Butler and Adam Smith did, to explain why the desire for revenge might be an intrinsic part of human nature. Instead, we can evaluate established scientific facts and then interpret them through the lens of an evolutionary theory that has become ever more sophisticated during the past century and a half.

THE "IS" AND THE "OUGHT" OF REVENGE

You might be starting to worry that an evolutionary explanation for revenge could be used to justify our species' penchant for revenge. After all, evolutionary theory has been used to justify everything from male infidelity to genocide. But the proposition that revenge is the way things *should be* because it's the way things *are* is called the "naturalistic fallacy": it's just not possible to derive "ought" exclusively from "is."[28] Just because human nature includes a tendency toward a certain behavior, this doesn't mean that the behavior is morally justified or that the tendency should be indulged. For example, even if rape were a sexual strategy that arose in some species due to natural selection, as two evolutionary theorists recently speculated,[29] this wouldn't—and logically, it couldn't—provide a moral justification for rape.

Similarly, if we conclude that the capacity for revenge is a fundamental characteristic of human nature that exists in every healthy human being from every culture, this fact could not serve as a moral justification for taking revenge. I am not going to suggest that we suddenly discard millennia of ethical and legal thought, not to mention the heartbreaking lessons of history, that counsel us to find ways of disciplining our vengeful impulses (and no one would listen to me even if I did). But if it's true that the desire for revenge is deeply embedded in human nature, we need to know about it. We're not going to improve humanity's lot by ignoring the true state of the human nature.

FORGIVENESS IS ALSO AN EVOLVED FEATURE OF HUMAN NATURE

By misunderstanding an evolutionary take on revenge, we could also fall prey to a second fallacy: if it turned out that revenge really were an evolved feature of human nature, we could begin to believe that revenge is somehow more "real" or authentically human than is the capacity for forgiveness. For years, many biologists and social scientists alike viewed positive human characteristics—love, friendship, faithfulness, gratitude, honesty, altruism, cooperation, forgiveness, and so forth—as exceptions to the rule of human nature, as self-delusions, or as a whitewash that we've brushed on top of humanity's ruthless, competitive, aggressive, authentic nature.[30] Marty Seligman and Mihaly Csikszentmihalyi recently addressed this blinkered scientific view of the human virtues: "It has been a common but unspoken assumption in the social sciences that negative traits are authentic and positive traits are derivative, compensatory, or even inauthentic, but there are two other possibilities: that negative traits are derivative from positive traits and that the positive and negative systems are separate systems."[31]

Seligman and Csikszentmihalyi are right. Forgiveness, like other positive human attributes, isn't a pretty façade that we use to mask the ugly reality that we're vengeful brutes. The capacity to forgive is every bit as authentic, every bit as intrinsic to human nature, and every bit as much a product of natural selection as is our penchant for revenge. Frans de Waal's "good-natured" primates are no less authentic, no less biologically grounded, no less a product of evolutionary forces than are Wrangham and Peterson's "demonic males." Which takes us back to the second basic truth that we'll be exploring: *The capacity for forgiveness, like the desire for revenge, is also an intrinsic feature of human nature—crafted by natural selection—that exists today because it was adaptive in the ancestral environment in which the human species developed.*

When people have been harmed by family members, romantic partners, good neighbors, or close friends, they often feel the urge to reconcile. Sometimes this urge conflicts with urges to engage in other potentially useful responses, including the desire to avoid the harmdoer and the desire to retaliate. But often the urge to reconcile wins out, and people therefore let go of their desires to avoid or retaliate against the wrongdoer. In other words, people forgive, and when they do so, valuable relationships can continue, often better and stronger than they were before the harm occurred.

Such everyday acts of forgiveness are so commonplace that we scarcely take notice. Until recently, scientists didn't take much notice either. In fact, because scientists have been toiling under the influence of the disease model of revenge, we think of forgiveness as the cure for a disease or the balm for a wound. Yet in daily life, forgiveness is often more like a Band-Aid on a scrape, and at first glance, perhaps only slightly more interesting.

But of course uninteresting does not mean unimportant. These mundane instances of forgiveness in our close relationships are the glue that keeps society from coming apart at the seams. The social institutions that make our society work are predicated upon the fact that people have a motivation and an ability to rid themselves of resentments and anger when they're harmed by their close relationship partners. People we care about are inevitably going to harm us, and we're inevitably going to harm them. We can't repair all of these breaches, but we repair many of them. We have to: *Homo sapiens* is a collaborative species that survives and thrives through bonds of affection, trust, and mutual aid. To forgive a friend is to salvage a vital resource. Preserving a relationship of trust and goodwill is much more efficient than developing a new one out of thin air.

It may come as no surprise, then, that humans, many non-human primates, and even domestic goats experience anxiety and tension in the aftermath of interpersonal transgressions—especially in relationships with relatives and close associates.[32] For these species, post-conflict anxiety appears to prompt individuals to reestablish positive contacts with each other as a way of moving forward with their damaged, but still valuable, relationships. The reason such mechanisms exist today is because as these species were evolving many millions of years ago, those individuals who could "forgive" their closest relationship partners did better on the evolutionary treadmill than those who couldn't forgive, and thus the capacity to get over resentments and reestablish important relationships became typical of the species. Natural selection is also how forgiveness became typical of *our species*—how it became part of human nature.

Human Nature Can Be Made to Do "Unnatural" Things

In "Jerusalem," William Blake wrote that "It is easier to forgive an Enemy than to forgive a Friend," but the scientific data show that Blake had it backwards. Forgiving someone you don't like, or who is different from you, or to whom you don't feel very close, is much more difficult than forgiving a friend, or someone to whom you're similar, or someone to whom you do feel close.[33] But sometimes people actually pull it off. In such cases, the relational distance between the victim and the harmdoer, not to mention the sheer magnitude of the harm done, makes forgiveness seem like a miracle rather than the outgrowth of the laws of human nature.

When grieving parents forgive a physician for the grave medical error that resulted in their child's death, they're forgiving someone whom they'll likely never see again. The physician clearly benefits (he or she is relieved of some of his or her guilt, or can feel reasonably certain that a lawsuit has been averted), but it seems like the grieving parents have to absorb all of the cost (they can't get any satisfaction that might come from retaliating; perhaps they waive their right to sue). When a grieving father like Bud Welch forgives his daughter's murderer—and even fights to have him spared the death penalty—he's behaving in a way that, at first glance, might seem hard to explain using evolutionary thinking. During (and after) World War II, many Americans instantly hated anyone of Japanese or German descent whom they encountered. Today, few Americans of my generation feel anything special at all toward people of Japanese or German descent. The old hatred is gone. The fact that the United States managed to stay together as a nation, despite all the damage that our union suffered before, during, and after the Civil War, still amazes me at times.

Is it too much of a stretch to say that Americans managed to "forgive" the Japanese and Germans for the horrors of World War II? Or that the American North and South have (more or less) forgiven each other? I don't think it is. But even if these instances really do show that forgiving our enemies is possible, why would ideas developed over 150 years ago by an English naturalist who studied barnacles and orchids be the proper way to explain them?

A superficial understanding of evolutionary theory—one that emphasizes truisms such as "survival of the fittest" and so on—would cast doubt on the idea that evolution could lead to mental mechanisms that could produce forgiveness of our enemies. If that's your understanding of how evolution works, then you're right to think that perhaps I'm barking up the wrong tree if I'm expecting evolutionary theory to explain forgiveness. But it can. Thus we come back to the third basic truth about revenge and forgiveness that will propel this book along: *To forgive a stranger or a sworn enemy, we have to activate the same mental mechanisms that natural selection developed within the human mind to help us forgive our loved ones, friends, and close associates. To encourage more forgiveness in our communities, and on the world stage, we must create the social conditions that will activate those mechanisms.* Whenever we forgive a bitter enemy, members of a warring faction, or even the insensitive jerk in the next cubicle, the same processes that developed in the human mind to help us forgive our close relationship partners must be activated. When forgiveness occurs, it's often because we've managed to get human nature to do "unnatural" things. This might sound like wishful thinking, but it isn't. In fact, we make nature do "unnatural" things all the time.

New Tricks with Old Dogs: Creating the Conditions for Forgiveness

Primatologist Frans de Waal tells of a strange zoo exhibit he once saw in Lop Buri, Thailand. In this exhibit, three large tigers and two dogs were living together in the same enclosure. As the tigers lazed idly in the enclosure, the dogs walked over the tigers' heads with no apparent fear of being devoured by the giant cats, even though the tigers outsized them severalfold, and even though tigers' favorite prey are all four-legged mammals.

De Waal explains that the tiger cubs had been orphaned or abandoned by their birth mother, so the zookeepers had enlisted the help of a surrogate dog mother to raise the three tiger cubs along with her own puppy. This social experiment was a tremendous success. The tigers thrived. The mother dog and her puppy did well, too. The five of them lived as one bizarre, happy, blended family.[34] Indeed, the practice of using dogs and even domestic pigs to provide maternal care for infant tigers has become quite common.

A dog or a pig that suckles and rears tiger cubs is engaging in a behavior that, on the surface, seems to make no evolutionary sense. The dogs and pigs gain nothing—in fact, there are tremendous metabolic costs associated with raising three tigers to maturity—and the tigers gain everything. Dogs and pigs have no genetically inherited tendency to take care of infant tigers. Similarly, tigers have no genetically inherited tendency to treat dogs with benevolent indifference, much less filial loyalty. If anything, tigers are genetically prone to view dogs as meals. However, when presented with helpless tiger cubs, a nursing mother dog's natural childrearing instincts kick in and she treats them as her own. And because the tigers were reared by their surrogate mother from early in their lives, they developed a strong attachment to her that prevented them from doing anything to harm her. Who could raise a paw against dear old mom?

Such unusual family arrangements work out because human beings put these creatures together in the right place, and at the right time, so that behavioral inclinations they inherited through thousands of generations of evolutionary history—the mother dog's childrearing instinct and the tigers' attachment to their caregivers—can be used to solve problems that evolution did not select them to address. The mother dog was acting on evolutionarily acquired capabilities that were triggered by a twist of fate: being presented with cute, helpless tiger cubs at the same time she was rearing her own puppy. She perceived these creatures as in need of maternal care, so she absorbed them into her sphere of concern. The mere presence of the infant tigers, which clearly were no threat to her at that young age, was sufficient to trigger her evolutionarily honed instincts to provide care to small and helpless creatures. Likewise, the tigers' natural tendencies to develop bonds of attachment to their caregivers are not so carefully designed that they discriminate between tiger mothers and dog (or pig) mothers. Instead, "be nice to whomever is supplying you with milk" seems to be the rule at work. This instinct prevented the tigers from viewing their canine foster mother and new sibling as food.

This bringing together of orphaned tigers and a pregnant dog wasn't an environmental accident. Human beings *designed* it, but it only worked because the nature of pregnant dogs and the nature of (infant) tigers provided the right stuff for the human designers to work with. Another animal story shows just how eagerly nature will often go along with such man-made schemes. While pregnant with her own puppies, Mademoiselle Giselle, a papillon, began to show an unnatural interest in the young squirrel named Finnegan that Debby Cantlon (the papillon's human owner) had been nursing back to health after it had fallen out of a tree in the neighborhood. Days before Giselle was to give birth to her own puppies, she began dragging Finnegan's cage over to her own bed on the floor. Repeatedly, Debbie would move the cage away from Giselle's bed, but each time she did so, Giselle would just drag it back over. Eventually, Debbie let Giselle have her way. After giving birth, the papillon continued to show nearly as much interest in the six-week-old Finnegan as in her own pups, so Debbie decided to open the cage and see what would happen. Finnegan emerged and slowly joined the new litter of puppies. He fit right in. After two days, Giselle allowed Finnegan to nurse alongside her five puppies. He began sleeping among, and playing with, his new littermates as if he had belonged there from the start. As if Giselle didn't have enough on her plate with five new pups, it seemed as though she went out of her way to adopt a sixth.[35]

If humans can design environmental conditions in which a dog's evolutionarily crafted instinct to care for its young can be directed toward other animals (even a natural predator like a tiger), why can't we do something similar to ourselves? Why can't we tinker with society so that people are motivated to forgive, even when the default setting on their evolutionarily crafted social-problem-solving software would motivate them in such a situation to seek revenge instead?

Even though our basic behavioral inclinations are shaped by natural selection, we humans aren't slaves to our instincts. From the perspective of natural selection, it's in our best interests to eat, but people occasionally starve themselves to death because of their loyalty to a compelling idea or an ideal of beauty. Likewise, it would be in our best evolutionary interests to rear many children to maturity, but many couples voluntarily go childless so that they can invest their energies in other pursuits.[36] Because our large brains enable us to reflect on our own condition, to view things from the perspectives of other people, to reason about the causes of our behavior and the behavior of others, to exert control over our appetites and emotions in the service of higher ideals, and to inspire and persuade others to do the same, there is every reason to believe that we can construct social institutions that will encourage forgiveness rather than revenge.

But before we get too far into this exploration of revenge, forgiveness, and human nature, we need to stop briefly to better understand the destructive power of revenge in the modern world. Some of us are so unfamiliar with revenge in our personal lives—we know the feeling but never act on it in any significant way—that we may be seduced into believing that revenge is a problem that plagues other people, in other societies, or at other points in history, but not us. Not so: the desire for revenge is alive and well, and it's still making problems for our species.

CHAPTER TWO

REVENGE
IS A PROBLEM
Counting the Costs

Marvin John Heemeyer was a fifty-two-year-old mechanic who lived in Granby, Colorado. His friends described him as easy-going, happy-go-lucky, compassionate. He liked snowmobiling. The owner of the bar that he frequented with a group of other snowmobilers called him "pleasant" and "jovial." But Heemeyer had suffered some setbacks that had left him feeling victimized and bitter. He was still smarting from a dispute with town officials over a re-zoning ordinance that permitted a concrete plant to be built next to his muffler repair shop. He had spent vast sums of time, money, and energy to fight the re-zoning decision (which he believed would have an adverse impact on his own business), but his efforts had failed. He had also incurred $2,500 in fines that the town had forced him to pay late in 2003 for his own city code violations.

Heemeyer made no secret of his bitterness, but he success-fully concealed an elaborate plan for revenge that took eighteen months of hard work to execute. He compiled an extensive list of targets: the concrete plant that he blamed for his failing business, a utility company, a warehouse, a hardware store, a bank, a home owned by the city's former mayor, and a municipal building that also contained a library. All of the targets were linked in some way to people against whom he held grudges, including the members of the town council that had unanimously voted in favor of the re-zoning, and even people associated with the local newspaper that had published editorials in favor of the council's decisions.

Heemeyer, an expert welder, set about converting a fifty-three-ton, thirty-foot-long bulldozer with a 410-horsepower diesel engine into an assault vehicle. He built a bulletproof coat of armor for the dozer that consisted of two layers of thick steel with a layer of concrete between them. He installed seven cameras that relayed images to three television monitors inside the cab. He also mounted three rifles to the bulldozer. The bulldozer became a killdozer.

On Friday, June 4, 2004, Heemeyer got into his killdozer, used a homemade crane to lower the armored hull over himself, and made his way out into the streets of Granby. For nearly two hours, Heemeyer cut a swath of destruction through the little town. He slowly crashed through thirteen different buildings, starting with the concrete plant next to his shop. He also destroyed sidewalks, trees, lampposts, and some city-owned vehicles. All the while, police and other authorities tried to stop him, firing hundreds of rounds of ammunition at the armored vehicle with no apparent effect.

After the killdozer stopped working and the rampage came to an end, Marvin Heemeyer took his own life with a semiautomatic pistol. It took hours for the authorities to figure out a way to remove the armor from the vehicle so that his body could be retrieved. Amazingly, no one but Heemeyer himself was seriously injured.[1]

"Revenge," if I can be technical for a moment, is any attempt to harm someone or some group of people "in response to feeling that oneself has been harmed by that other person or group, whereby the act of harming that person or group is *not* designed to repair the harm, to stop it from occurring or continuing in the immediate confrontation, or to produce material gain."[2] Marvin Heemeyer's campaign of vengeance fits this definition to a tee: he wanted to harm people who had harmed him, period. Heemeyer's actions suggest that the desire for vengeance can be a powerful motivator of human destructiveness. Still, most of us recoil from the idea that the desire for revenge is a typical human response—*our* typical response—to injustice. Thanks to the disease model of revenge into which we've been indoctrinated, we prefer to think of revenge as the prerogative of people who are evil or insane, but not us.

In two national surveys, researchers asked representative samples of American men and women to rank-order a list of eighteen personal qualities (for example, "courageous," "honest," "cheerful," and "self-controlled") to indicate how much they valued each of them. In both surveys, people ranked "forgiving" as their fourth most highly valued personal quality (beaten out only by "honest," "ambitious," and "responsible").[3] More recently, researchers asked 1,030 American adults to indicate how they behaved when "you feel that someone has deliberately done something wrong to you." Of these respondents, 42 percent indicated that they try to "overlook" the offense, and 45 percent indicated that they "try to forgive" the offender. In contrast, only 8 percent of Americans indicated that they "try to get even in some way."[4] Other studies show that people from other countries, such as France and Congo, also see themselves as forgiving rather than vengeful.[5]

These survey results really don't come as any surprise, of course. People around the world learn the disease model of revenge from their parents, their kindergarten teachers, their religions, and the other keepers of the norms of decent society. People also learn that as good citizens, they too should try to forgive people who hurt them. This would lead you to think that maybe revenge is no big deal in the social problems that plague us as a species, but when you look the facts in the eye (as we'll do in this chapter), you can see that the desire for revenge is one reason (among others) why normal, well-adjusted people try to hurt each other, why murderers murder, why nations go to war, and even why terrorists terrorize.

Scratch Forgiveness and See Vengeance Bleed

If you catch people when they're motivated to look at themselves realistically, they'll often admit just how difficult forgiveness can be and just how easily the desire for revenge can surface. In 1999, *Time* magazine asked 1,049 American adults to think about a variety of transgressions, and to indicate whether they would forgive someone who had committed those transgressions against them. As Figure 2.1 shows, most people say that they'd be willing to forgive low-stakes transgressions such as being lied about or having their money stolen, but it's only the saintliest—or the most self-deluded—who believe they could forgive their daughter's rapist or their son's murderer.[6] Most people's forgiving self-images evaporate under the searing heat of extreme violence and trauma.

So when we ask people to be specific about how they think they'd feel if they were seriously traumatized, they readily admit that forgiveness would be extremely difficult. In fact, most people do admit that they experience the desire for revenge from time

FIGURE 2.1. PERCENTAGE OF AMERICAN ADULTS WHO WOULD FORGIVE AND WOULD NOT FORGIVE A VARIETY OF HYPOTHETICAL TRANSGRESSIONS.

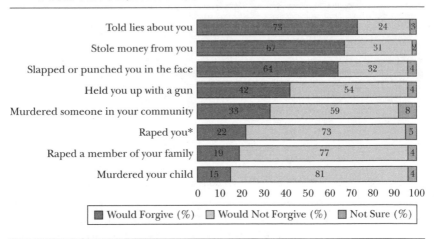

	Would Forgive (%)	Would Not Forgive (%)	Not Sure (%)
Told lies about you	73	24	3
Stole money from you	67	31	2
Slapped or punched you in the face	64	32	4
Held you up with a gun	42	54	4
Murdered someone in your community	33	59	8
Raped you*	22	73	5
Raped a member of your family	19	77	4
Murdered your child	15	81	4

Note: *Asked only of women.

to time. Researchers asked a sample of American adults to recall a time in the past month when they became angry at someone. They were then asked to choose from a list of possible responses to the situation, selecting all that applied to them—for example, trying to think about the situation in a different way, having a drink or a pill, talking to the person they were angry at, talking to someone else about the situation, and so on. When asked whether they "thought about how to get revenge," 6 percent of the sample answered affirmatively.[7]

Six percent is pretty low, but you have to remember that we're talking here about six percent within a single month. What percentage of people feel the desire for revenge in the course of a single year? When researchers asked 513 Dutch students whether they could recall a specific instance in the past year when someone did something hurtful to them for which they felt a desire to get even, 64 percent said "yes."[8]

THE DESIRE FOR REVENGE IS ONE THING; ACTING ON IT IS ANOTHER

So maybe most of us really can relate to Marvin Heemeyer's desire for revenge after all. But still, we don't all *become* Marvin Heemeyer. Only about one-third of people report that they act on their desires for revenge in any way.[9] Still, when you're hurt profoundly, the temptation to seek revenge can become very strong indeed. Barbara Cardozo and colleagues interviewed Kosovar Albanians who had been displaced during the ethnic cleansing that took place in Kosovo between 1998 and 1999. By the end of the violence, many of these people had received some truly horrible treatment. Four out of five had been displaced from their homes. Two-thirds had been deprived of food or water. Three out of five reported having been close to death at some point. One-half reported having suffered torture or abuse of one kind or another. One-quarter experienced the murder of a friend or a loved one.[10]

Given this level of traumatic exposure, it's not surprising that about half of the men and two out of every five women reported that they experienced very strong feelings of revenge—that is, they reported experiencing the desire for revenge "all the time" or "a lot of the time"—toward the Serbs. Of those who reported such frequent feelings of revenge, 44 percent of the men and 33 percent of the women indicated that they would have acted on those feelings if they had had the chance. Only 17 percent of the men and 26 percent of the women indicated that they definitely would *not* have acted act on those feelings. One year later, when the researchers repeated the survey, people's feelings of revenge and their desires to act on those feelings had not declined substantially.[11]

These survey results start to undermine the idea that the desire for revenge is something exceptional or out of the ordinary. Fortunately, feeling vengeful is not an everyday thing for most of us: when we organize societies in a way that protects people's rights and welfare, human beings tend to be good natured, law-abiding, and, yes, forgiving. It's easy to have family values when your family's interests are being protected. But if you push these generally good-natured human beings—threaten their way of life, wrench away from them what they prize most highly, or harm their loved ones—the desire for revenge comes to the fore. If you get harmed in just the right way, and society doesn't provide you with any means of redress, it's not primarily your sanity that's going to prevent you from seeking your own Hecmcycrian revenge but, rather, your lack of skill with a welding torch.

COUNTING THE COSTS OF REVENGE

Revenge gets blamed for a lot of bad things—just read the news-papers: arson, gossip, school bullying, urinating in the coffee maker in the break room at work, taking a long time to leave a parking space after someone has honked at you, road rage, World War I, World War II, workplace shootings, the bombing of a Tel Aviv pizza parlor, stealing stuff from work, giving away national secrets, the Hatfield-McCoy feud, the Alexander Hamilton–Aaron Burr duel, sports-related violence, voting against a colleague's promotion, vandalism, having an affair, shooting an unfaithful husband or wife, gang warfare, intentionally infecting someone with HIV, shoplifting, procrastinating, assassinations, and invad-ing foreign nations. Is revenge getting blamed for more than its fair share of human mischief and misery? I don't think so. In the remainder of this chapter, we'll explore just how much of the human destructiveness we see around us and read about in the newspapers has the desire for revenge at its core.

REVENGE AND GARDEN-VARIETY AGGRESSION

Scientists define human aggression as behavior that's motivated by the desire to harm another human being (masochists excluded). Social psychologists prefer to study aggression by examining people's behavior in well-controlled laboratory settings. It would be unethical for scientists to cause, or even permit, a research subject to seriously harm another person, so laboratory scientists usually study relatively mild forms of aggression. For example, a social psychologist who wanted to study your aggressive behavior might examine whether you'll deliver an unpleasant blast of loud noise to someone who has just humiliated or insulted you.

Although such forms of aggression might seem to bear little resemblance to the types of aggression that we typically care about in the real world—assaults and murders, for instance—the same factors that make people aggressive in such laboratory situations also tend to make people aggressive out in the real world. Therefore, these laboratory measures of aggression turn out to be good models for studying why people harm each other intentionally in real life.[12]

Over the years, social psychologists have learned that it's not so easy to get people to voluntarily harm another human being whom they've never met. Unlike our chimpanzee relatives, who will attack a stranger for no apparent reason at all, human beings are inclined to treat strangers with respect, tolerance, and a spirit of cooperation, unless given a reason not to. In fact, when social psychologists *want* people to behave aggressively so that they can study aggression, they often have to provoke their research participants by insulting them, humiliating them, shocking them, providing them with unflattering feedback about their personalities, taking away money they've just earned, or otherwise making them feel betrayed, neglected, or hard done by.

Thus most aggression in the laboratory is "provoked" aggression, or aggression after one has been harmed oneself.

Could it be that a lot of this aggression taking place in social psychologists' laboratories over the years has been, in fact, revenge-motivated? Maybe, but just because somebody behaves more aggressively after provocation doesn't demonstrate that he or she is trying to get revenge. People could become more aggressive after being provoked just because they want to make themselves feel better by blowing off a bit of steam. To determine whether aggression in response to harm is motivated by the desire for revenge or by simple frustration, we need to see whether the amount of aggression that people direct toward their provokers exceeds the aggression they direct toward innocent bystanders—third parties who didn't provoke them in any way.

Some people simply tend to be nastier than others, even when they're not provoked. Let's say we rank one hundred unprovoked people according to how much aggression (an unpleasant blast of loud noise, in this case) they direct toward someone who hasn't provoked them. We'll rank the person who gives the mildest noise blasts at the bottom of the class, and the person who gives the loudest noise blasts at the top. So we say that the least aggressive person is at the first *percentile* (one percent of people were as aggressive or less aggressive than this person) and the most aggressive person is at the ninety-ninth percentile (99 percent of people were as aggressive or less aggressive than this person).

To get a sense of how provocation affects aggression, let's compare the aggressive behavior of someone who has been provoked to the percentiles for our group of unprovoked people. As the left side of Figure 2.2 shows, the average person in our group of one hundred unprovoked people is, by definition, at the fiftieth percentile. He or she directs an "average" level of aggression toward the target. As the center bar of the figure shows, when someone has been provoked, his or her level of aggressiveness toward a person who wasn't the provoker—*an innocent bystander*—will climb only to the fifty-fourth percentile for the unprovoked people. That means that the subject's level of aggression is just barely above the average level of aggression

FIGURE 2.2. PERCENTILE SCORES FOR AMOUNT OF AGGRESSION DIRECTED
TOWARD ANOTHER PERSON AS A FUNCTION OF PROVOCATION AND TARGET TYPE.

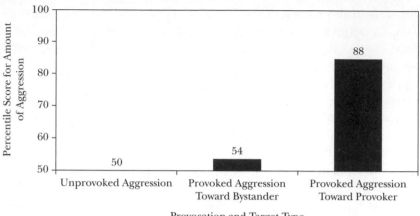

that's seen for the average unprovoked person. In other words, if you're provoked, you aren't going to suddenly go berserk and start trying to harm innocent bystanders.

Instead, you're going to try to go after your provoker. The right side of the figure shows that the average person who is provoked by someone will behave more aggressively (that is, *toward his or her provoker*) than will 88 percent of the unprovoked people who are given the opportunity to behave aggressively toward a target who didn't provoke them.[13] This is a *huge* increase in aggressive behavior. In fact, the effect of provocation on aggression toward the provoker is one of the most powerful effects in the entire field of social psychology.[14]

The bottom line of these findings is this: there's no better way to ensure that someone is going to harm you than to harm him or her first. Provocation rarely creates berserkers who are driven mad by an indiscriminate desire to harm others—that's the disease model of revenge talking. (Keep in mind that even Marvin Heemeyer was focused on hurting a relatively small group of people by whom he felt he had been personally injured.) Instead, provocation that is perceived as painful and unjust creates avengers who have specific targets in their sights.

Dial "R" for Murder

Anthropologists tell us that people have been killing each other for tens of thousands of years, if not longer.[15] There are good reasons to believe that avenging such killings by killing the offender is a cross-cultural universal—at least in societies with the most elementary forms of social organization, which lack institutional mechanisms for controlling homicide.[16] Bullies, despotic leaders, and sorcerers, in addition to people who killed someone intentionally or unintentionally, have also been common targets for lethal revenge in societies around the world throughout history.

Despite the cross-cultural prevalence of revenge-motivated homicides, more complex societies have a great stake in controlling them. When revenge runs rampant in society, governments have a hard time maintaining social stability. This undermines their credibility in the eyes of their citizens—who wants to support a government that can't keep the streets safe? For this reason, the kings of Western and Northern Europe began trying to stamp out revenge-motivated homicides more than a millennium ago. After the Norman Conquest of England in 1066, it was William the Conqueror who formally outlawed blood revenge as a response to homicide, but the powerful kings who sought to unite England under a feudal system had begun to enact laws to curtail the free expression of blood revenge as early as 602 A.D.[17] These laws, coupled with societal changes that gave people more freedom from the sacred obligation to defend the honor of their families and communities, were probably responsible in part for the extraordinary declines in European homicide rates during the past six or seven hundred years. During the Middle Ages, homicide rates in Europe ranged from twenty to forty people killed per one hundred thousand each year; by the middle of the twentieth century, these rates had fallen to less than one person per one hundred thousand per year.[18]

But the fact that homicide is twenty times rarer than it was seven hundred years ago doesn't mean that revenge as a motive for homicide is a thing of the past. In fact, the desire for revenge is still an important reason why people kill each other.

According to the FBI, 16,692 people were murdered (that is, willfully killed by another person) in the United States during

2005. Approximately 40 percent of those murders occurred during "arguments" or during the commission of other felonies (for example, robbery, crimes involving narcotics, and sex offenses). About 5 percent were attributed to juvenile gang killings, and a few hundred more were spread out over circumstance categories such as "romantic triangle," "child killed by babysitter," and "brawl due to the influence of alcohol or narcotics." For about one-half of the murders, circumstances were either unknown or designated only by the frustrating category "other—not specified."[19]

NOT FINDING REVENGE AS A MOTIVE FOR MURDER BY NOT LOOKING FOR IT

How many of these murders were motivated by revenge? FBI statistics can't help us there. "Gangland killing" doesn't tell us *why* someone was willfully killed any more than "Child killed by babysitter" does. *Why* did the gangster want to kill his victim? *Why* did the babysitter want the child dead? We need to ask questions about *motive* if we want to estimate the role of revenge in murder.

Martin Daly and Margo Wilson, biologists who have pioneered the Darwinian study of homicide, make the point that prosecutors don't really care about the specifics of killers' motives. Prosecutors only need to know whether the crime was committed in cold blood or in the heat of the moment.[20] If it's the former, they can go to trial seeking a conviction for first-degree murder. If it's the latter, the worst crime they can prosecute is second-degree murder. For this reason, crime investigators focus on establishing *premeditation* rather than the specifics of motive. As a result, the categories that they use can provide insight into the premeditation question generally, but they don't help address the motive question specifically.

Fortunately, some social scientists have looked more seriously at revenge as a cause of murders in contemporary society, and at first blush, the proportion of murders attributable to revenge seems to hover around 9 percent. An analysis of all homicides in Ireland from 1992 to 1996 put the rate of revenge-motivated homicides at 9 percent.[21] Between 1989 and 1996, approximately 9 percent of Australian murders committed by people age twenty-five or older were precipitated by revenge.[22] About 8 percent of all murders in Hong Kong between 1972 and 1992 with a known motive were revenge-motivated.[23] But upon closer inspection, this 9 percent estimate turns out to be too low by half, at least for murder in the United States.

BETTER ESTIMATES

When many people think of revenge—including, I suspect, officials and researchers who assign motives to murders—they probably have in mind a careful plan that unfolds over days, weeks, months, or even years. This type of revenge is "served cold" and executed with a steady hand. But recall that revenge is much broader than that: it encompasses all aggressive acts that are "*not* designed to repair the harm, to stop it from occurring or continuing in the immediate confrontation, or to produce material gain."[24] Thus revenge probably motivates a lot of murders beyond those that arise from cold-blooded plans that are designed expressly to settle a score. When we broaden our definition of revenge to include all cases of retaliation (including hot-blooded murders that occur during or as the ultimate conclusion to an argument or trivial quarrel), revenge-motivated murder starts to look even more common.

Using a classification system specifically designed to identify the substantive issues that motivate murder, Wilson and Daly reviewed all of the homicides that took place in Detroit, Michigan, in 1972. Among these 512 criminal homicides, Wilson and Daly discovered that 95 (19 percent) of them could be classified as acts of "retaliation for previous verbal or physical abuse."[25] Of the 212 homicides defined as taking place in the context of "social conflict" among nonrelatives, 95 (45 percent) of them were acts of retaliation. These cases no doubt included many instances of cold-blooded revenge—the sorts that other taxonomists of murder have captured in the past under the category "revenge"—but also all hot-blooded acts of lethal retaliatory violence.

In a more recent effort, criminologists Charis Kubrin and Ronald Weitzer tried to estimate the number of retaliatory homicides that occurred in St. Louis, Missouri, between 1985 and 1995. Of the 1,731 homicides for which Kubrin and

Weitzer could identify a motive, approximately 20 percent were "retaliatory," meaning that they involved "at least two time points: an initial disputatious interaction, in which an affront to one party remained unanswered or unresolved, which prompted a subsequent encounter during which the offended party exacted deadly retribution for the earlier offense."[26]

We should take the Detroit and St. Louis figures seriously because these two studies are the only thorough studies on cities in the United States in which researchers operationally defined retaliation and worked hard to look for it. With these results as a guide, we can estimate that about 20 percent of homicides nationally are revenge-motivated.[27] Were we to extrapolate to the United States overall, we might conclude that more than 3,300 of the 16,692 murders that occurred in the United States during 2005 were motivated by the desire for vengeance. To put this figure in perspective, revenge-motivated killing probably took more lives in 2005 than did the terrorist attacks on September 11, 2001. (Incidentally, the place on earth where revenge is the most frequent motive for murder probably isn't even in the United States: in Medellín, Colombia, 45 percent of the murders with known motives that were committed between 1990 and 2002 were motivated by revenge.[28])

The following three narratives, which Kubrin and Weitzer reconstructed from the St. Louis case reports, illustrate how revenge-related murders often unfold:

> The suspect liked to bully the neighborhood youths and order them around. On the day in question, the victim had apparently had enough. When the suspect told the victim to go to the store for him, the victim refused. The suspect then called the victim a "punk." The victim punched the suspect once in the mouth and the suspect hit the ground. The victim told the suspect to get his nine [gun], calling the suspect a punk because the suspect needed a weapon to be tough. Friends of the suspect later told police that the suspect was "in shock" that the victim would hit him; the suspect said that he thought the victim was afraid of him. The suspect said he would "take care of business" and his friends knew he would shoot the victim, because the suspect was no fighter and would only settle things with a gun. As the victim was sitting in a car with friends, the suspect shot into the car, then fled the area.

The suspect drove at a high speed, hitting an officer who was writing a parking ticket. The victim was thrown into the air and landed on the hood of the suspect's car. The car carried the officer approximately fifty feet down the street and he rolled off the car. Suspect then walked to the victim, searched him, and kicked him repeatedly in the face. The suspect said, "He'll think twice before he gives me another ticket," and "That'll teach him to embarrass me in front of my grandchildren," and "You don't know how much hate I got in me." The suspect had gotten a parking ticket that day, but there was no evidence that this officer had written it. It appears that the suspect was so angry over the ticket, he simply went looking for a police officer. He told police he wasn't sorry and would do it again.

The suspect accused the victim of blocking his entrance to a doorway, called the victim a name, and ordered the victim out of his way. The victim and suspect then got into a fistfight. Victim and suspect exchanged threats before leaving. Later, the suspect drove up in a car and said something to the victim, who responded, "Go ahead and shoot me," which the suspect did.[29]

As these narratives show, revenge-motivated murders are often precipitated by seemingly trivial offenses—name-calling, parking tickets, and insults to one's manly honor. By revealing the banality of the slights and minor altercations that often precipitate revenge-motivated murder, these cases also illustrate just how overwhelming the desire for revenge can become.

REVENGE AS A MOTIVE FOR SCHOOL-BASED KILLINGS

Revenge is a big contributor to one type of murder in particular: the type that takes place in schools. During the past decade, we've witnessed a spate of killings in middle schools, high schools, and universities all over the United States—schools in towns with names like Paducah, Kentucky, Littleton, Colorado, and Blacksburg, Virginia, where Seung-Hui Cho killed thirty-two people at Virginia Tech before taking his own life.

There's no single cause for school killings like these. True, school killers are more likely than their peers to be depressed, suicidal, and marginalized. They also tend to have experience with firearms and access to them. In addition, they often attend schools that are tolerant of violence and bullying. But none of these risk factors goes very far in explaining why adolescents take guns or knives to their schools with the intention of killing their peers or teachers. Most school killers are *not* depressed or suicidal, and most people who are depressed and suicidal are not violent toward others, even if they know how to get hold of a gun. To understand why kids go to school to kill, we have to take the desire for revenge into account.

When Eric Harris and Dylan Klebold went on their killing spree at Columbine High School in Littleton, Colorado, killing more than a dozen people and injuring dozens more, a witness claimed that they shouted, "this is revenge."[30] But revenge for what? Most likely, bullying. Severe bullying is surprisingly common for many students. Forty-one percent of middle school and high school kids in the United States report that they were bullied at least once during their current school term. About 11 percent of boys report that they are bullied once per week or more. Of the boys who report being bullied, nearly 18 percent of them are "hit, slapped, or pushed" once per week or more.[31] (I focus on boys because males do 93 percent of the school killings.[32])

People who kill other people in schools tend to be the victims of bullying, not the perpetrators. The best study of school-based killings in the United States found that nearly 20 percent of students who killed other students in their schools had a prior history of being bullied, as compared with only 9 percent of their victims.[33] That's 20 percent of *all* school-based killings, including killings that take place during other criminal activity (which make up about 40 percent of the circumstances in which someone was killed at school and for which bullying was presumably not an issue). Ignore these crime-motivated killings and the proportion for which bullying was an issue climbs to one-third.

But the role of revenge in school-based shootings is probably even greater than these figures let on. To get a better feel for the role that revenge plays in promoting school killings, we should look just at "targeted school violence" (that is, crimes in which the perpetrator attacks the victim with lethal means, having chosen the school as the setting for the violence). In the most comprehensive study on this topic, researchers affiliated with the United States Secret Service (an organization with lots of experience in assessing threats of violence) analyzed every incident of targeted school violence in the United States between 1974 and June 2000.[34] Of the forty-one attackers responsible for these thirty-seven incidents, twenty-nine (71 percent) had a history of being "persecuted, bullied, threatened, attacked, or injured by others prior to the incident" (p. 21). What's more, revenge was judged to be a motive for twenty-five, or 61 percent, of the forty-one perpetrators. Bullying, followed by a desire for revenge, may therefore be a key dynamic behind many targeted school killings.

Even so, we need to bear in mind that bullying is very common and that the desire for revenge is a common response. Remember that 41 percent of American high school students have been bullied at least once during their current school term. Also, one study of schoolchildren aged nine to fourteen found that 43 percent of boys who had been bullied felt a desire for vengeance in response. So even though the desire to seek revenge against bullies might be an ingredient in many school killings, it's not sufficient. It takes more than being bullied, along with a desire for revenge, to make students kill their teachers and classmates. Being bullied is common, and feeling vengeful in response is common. It's killing your classmates that's abnormal. Those students that react to bullying with vengeful action, and not just vengeful feelings, tend to have other risk factors such as school problems; psychological or behavioral problems; gang involvement; troubled home lives; or histories of preoccupation with guns, violence, or violent media. But without the desire for revenge, it's hard to imagine that these troubled, gang-involved, gun-obsessed teens would respond to bullying with lethal violence. Ignore the desire for revenge and you miss a big part of the puzzle. In many cases, the biggest part.

DOES THE DESIRE FOR REVENGE CAUSE WAR?

Violent intergroup conflict is a fact of life in most traditional societies. The large majority of societies that anthropologists have examined show some evidence of war in their histories.[35] There have been exceptions,[36] but these exceptions largely prove the rule: under enough ecological pressure (for example, the threat of starvation) or social pressure (such as other groups of people who want to steal from you or kill you), most societies have been willing (albeit reluctantly) to go to war to settle things.

One widely accepted theory of the origins of war posits that societies' motives for war become more complex as the societies themselves become more complex.[37] In the simplest foraging societies, which organize in bands (small kin-based groups of sovereign households), people don't own any possessions worth fighting over, so when these band-level societies go to war, it's usually for defensive purposes such as retaliating for a homicide against a member of the band or defending the band against retaliatory raids. In societies that organize in tribes, people also go to war to steal resources from other groups, as well as for the retaliatory purposes that motivate war in band-level societies.

In even more complex societies with more centralized forms of government—chiefdoms, for instance—people go to war for prestige or social status, as well as for resources and retaliation. And when societies are organized at the level of states, the theory goes, people also go to war to gain control over their neighbors, as well as to gain prestige, to garner resources, and to retaliate. So in this cultural-evolutionary model of war, new motivations for going to war get stacked onto the old ones as societies become more complex. As a result, revenge becomes less prominent with increasing societal complexity. But even in very complex societies, the role of the desire for revenge in motivating war doesn't go away. It just recedes into the background.

Does the desire for revenge cause war in our present age of mega-states? Scholars of modern war don't give it much attention.[38] But perhaps they should.

The sociologist Thomas Scheff gives a gripping account of the small but indispensable role that the desire for revenge played in spawning two world wars. Prior to World War I, the French were bitter about the outcome of the Franco-Prussian War, during which France lost the provinces of Alsace and Lorraine. This bitterness led to a postwar public sentiment known as *revanche*, a preoccupation with regaining the lost provinces and wreaking vengeance against Germany. *Revanchism*, Scheff argues, enticed

France into joining with Russia to defend the Serbians against the Central Powers following the crisis created by the assassination of Archduke Franz Ferdinand. This Franco-Russian alliance emboldened the Russians to move forward with their war preparations. The tinderbox eventually ignited, and most of Europe was drawn into the conflagration.

World War I ended with a defeat for the Central Powers. Through the treaty of Versailles, Germany was forced to accept full responsibility for the war. Germany was disarmed, stripped of much of her territory and her colonies, excluded from membership in the League of Nations, and blockaded for ten months. Germany's humiliated rage over the suffering and shame it was forced to endure after Versailles led to a German desire for vindication and retaliation on the world stage. This public sentiment helped pave the way for a strong nationalist leader like Adolf Hitler to rise to power and, eventually, plunge Germany into a second world war.[39]

Revenge's ability to motivate war isn't just a European problem. One sociologist recently examined every major American war from the Spanish-American War in 1898 to the war in Afghanistan following the September 11, 2001, terrorist attacks.[40] In the run-up to each of these wars, he discovered, American presidents had swayed public opinion toward support for war by creating the public perception that the nation had been victimized by unprovoked sneak attacks, and that swift retaliatory action with overwhelmingly destructive force was the only rational and self-interested course the country could take.

When you stop to consider it, the "revenge script" has indeed been weirdly ubiquitous. Could there have been a Spanish-American War without the sinking of the *Maine?* Could there have been a World War I without the sinking of the *Lusitania* and the supply ships the United States was using to send weapons to Great Britain, France, and Russia? Would the United States have had the will to enter World War II without Pearl Harbor? Would the United States have allowed itself to become mired in Vietnam without the Gulf of Tonkin attack? Probably not: public opposition to war entry in most of these cases was overwhelming. But by emphasizing the need for retaliation, our leaders succeed in obtaining broad public support for wars that are virtually guaranteed to be long, expensive, and bloody. The language of retaliation helps give the governed the stomach to bear those costs.

REVENGE AND TERRORISM

Revenge isn't "the reason" for war among modern nation-states, but it still seems to be an indispensable way to create public support for war. Likewise, terrorism isn't mainly about getting revenge. At a strategic level, terrorism seems to be largely about trying to break the will of an oppressor or a foreign occupier.[41] However, you can clearly hear the revenge motif if you listen carefully to what the major actors in international terrorism tell us about why they do what they do.[42] One need look no further than bin Laden's "Letter to America," which he published in November 2002:

> Some American writers have published articles under the title "On what basis are we fighting?" These articles have generated a number of responses, some of which adhered to the truth and were based on Islamic Law, and others which have not. Here we wanted to outline the truth—as an explanation and warning— hoping for Allah's reward, seeking success and support from Him. While seeking Allah's help, we form our reply based on two questions directed at the Americans: (Q1) Why are we fighting and opposing you? (Q2) What are we calling you to, and what do we want from you? As for the first question: Why are we fighting and opposing you? The answer is very simple: (1) Because you attacked us and continue to attack us. . . . The blood pouring out of Palestine must be equally revenged. You must know that the Palestinians do not cry alone; their women are not widowed alone; their sons are not orphaned alone.[43]

One social scientist recently reported the results of her interviews with 653 people who had been traumatized in some fashion by the war in Chechnya. She discovered a disturbing trend: people who had suffered the highest levels of trauma no longer adhered to the cultural rules that govern the expression of revenge in traditional Chechnyan society. Most important, these war victims no longer believed, in accordance with Chechnyan custom, that revenge could only be exacted upon the perpetrator of a crime; instead, they came to believe that any member of the ethnic group whose members were responsible for an act of aggression against one's own family member could be attacked in revenge.[44] Most likely, this broadened conception of revenge made them ripe for recruitment into terrorist organizations.

Never has Al Qaeda or any other modern terrorist group cited "revenge" as their raison d'être. Their primary goals are always political. However, terrorists are made, not born. Would-be terrorists find terrorism appealing in part because of the perception that getting involved would give them an outlet for their desires to harm the nations, factions, or ethnic groups that have harmed them, their families, and their communities. It follows that if we could find ways to reduce the desire for revenge, the stock of would-be terrorists would shrink as well.[45]

THE DESIRE FOR REVENGE IS A CONDUIT FOR PAIN

Most people *want* to see themselves as tolerant and forgiving, but the desire for revenge easily comes to the surface when they feel that they've been victimized, ostracized, criticized, or antagonized. Marvin John Heemeyer died on June 4, 2004, but a little part of him lives on because the desire for revenge when mistreated is a sentiment we all share. You can see that part of Marvin Heemeyer in the social psychology laboratory, in crime statistics, and on the front page of every major newspaper. You can hear the voice of Marvin Heemeyer in the back of your mind when our leaders begin trying to drum up political support for their decisions to go to war. The desire for revenge probably motivates a dozen other forms of human destructiveness too, but we just don't know it yet because scientists haven't yet bothered to find out.[46]

The fact that the desire for revenge is an important cause of human violence and destructiveness shouldn't blind us to another important fact about revenge: it's also a solution. Of course revenge creates pain and misery, and that's why we need to understand it better. The irony is that the better you understand how revenge works, the better you can appreciate all of the important problems that revenge has actually managed to solve for the human species. Evolutionary thinking gives us the vantage point from which we can appreciate exactly what those problems are and how revenge might have arisen as a tool for solving them.

CHAPTER THREE

REVENGE IS A SOLUTION
Three Evolutionary Hypotheses

On July 1, 2002, Bashkirian Airlines Flight 2937 took off from Russia for Barcelona. There were seventy-one people aboard, including fifty-two children. Swiss air traffic controllers working for a company called Skyguide were in charge of air traffic control as the aircraft passed through German airspace. A single controller named Peter Nielsen was left in charge while the only other controller on duty that night was taking a break. Suddenly, and with less than a minute to spare, Nielsen realized that the Russian airliner was coming perilously close to a DHL cargo jet. In a colossal error of judgment, Nielsen ordered the Russian plane to descend, even though the on-board collision-avoidance system was instructing the pilots to climb. Following Nielsen's instructions, the pilots of the airliner flew headlong into the cargo plane. All seventy-one people aboard the Russian plane were killed. The wreckage from the crash was scattered for twenty miles.

At the moment of the crash, Vitaly Kaloyev, a Russian from the town of Vladikavkaz in the north Caucasus, had been waiting for the Bashkirian flight to arrive at the Barcelona Airport. His wife and two children were coming to join him for a vacation. Kaloyev, an architect who was working in Spain at the time, received the news of the crash and immediately left the airport for the crash site. When he got there, he convinced the police officers in charge of the site to let him search for his family's remains. "I spent 10 days searching for the remains of my dear wife and children. My life stopped on that tragic date, July 1, 2002," he later wrote for a Russian Website commemorating the crash and its victims. "I am left to live with only memories. The only consolation I have is my daily visit to their grave in the cemetery at Vladikavkaz."

In July 2003 Kaloyev flew back to Switzerland to attend a memorial service on the one-year anniversary of the disaster. The next day, he attended a meeting with officials in which he expected to be debriefed on the final moments of the flight. Kaloyev asked over and over to be told who was responsible for the crash. "The air traffic controller is a villain and in the Caucasus we talk to villains in our own way," he reportedly said before ending the meeting.

In February 2004, Kaloyev flew back to Zurich again in search of an official apology from the director of Skyguide. Kaloyev's hopes for an apology were in vain.

On the 24th, Kaloyev went to the town of Kloten in the Zurich suburbs where Peter Nielsen lived. Kaloyev found Nielsen at home and the two men talked privately. Still seeking an apology, Kaloyev showed Nielsen some pictures of his children and asked Nielsen, "What would you feel if you saw your children in coffins?" Whatever Nielsen's response was, it wasn't enough for Kaloyev. Kaloyev snapped: "I only remember that I had a very disturbing feeling, as if the bodies of my children were turning over in their graves," he said later at trial. Kaloyev doesn't remember what happened next (though a Swiss radio station reported that someone overheard him saying, "You killed my family—and I am going to kill you"). Kaloyev proceeded to kill Nielsen with repeated knife stabs to the chest, abdomen, and throat.

Kaloyev was apprehended the next day. On October 27, 2005, Kaloyev was found guilty of premeditated murder and was sentenced to eight years in prison.[1]

Was Kaloyev's desire for revenge something unique to his own psyche—something borne of mental illness, terrible parenting, bad karma, or backwards Caucasus cultural practices? Something unique to Kaloyev that would allow us to rest easy in the belief that we could never do something like that? Or was his revenge borne of the same propensity for revenge that all human beings carry around?

In this chapter, we'll begin to explore the possibility that the same desire for revenge that motivated Vitaly Kaloyev resides in all of us, courtesy of natural selection. The scientific evidence I discussed in the previous chapter shows that the desire for revenge is in fact quite common, and that it's a very important motivator of much of the pain and violence that human beings experience (and inflict). But in this chapter and the next, I'll argue that a readiness to seek revenge when wronged is a general characteristic of human nature—a trait possessed by every neurologically normal human being.

What We Are and How We Got That Way

How did we get the universal traits that characterize us as a species? Why do we have two arms, two legs, two eyes, and two sexes, instead of one or three? For that matter, why arms and legs at all? Why not tentacles or wings instead? The only scientific account of human nature that can provide a satisfying explanation for how the human species got to be in its current form is an evolutionary account. As one evolutionary biologist famously put it, "Nothing in biology makes sense except in the light of evolution."[2]

In this chapter, I'm going to challenge you to engage in what the evolutionary biologists Martin Daly and Margo Wilson have called "selection thinking." We'll try to envision the functions that revenge might have served in the ancestral environment to which human beings are adapted.[3] The "ancestral environment to which human beings are adapted" is clearly not our modern world, with its rapid communication, highly differentiated division of labor, small families, and well-developed cultural institutions. Instead, it's a world that existed a hundred thousand or more years ago. It's a world with few cultural institutions and very little social organization beyond the extended kinship network. It's a slow world without private property, police, courts, jails, or formal codes of law. It's a world in which your wits, your relatives, and maybe a few good friends were your best (and perhaps only) sources of help when you got into serious trouble. When we engage in selection thinking, we try to envision the functions that revenge might have served in an environment like *that,* rather than in an environment like our own (even though revenge may still at times serve similar functions for us today).

Those "functions" of revenge that we as selection thinkers want to understand are its social effects that influenced our ancestors' abilities to survive, reproduce, and see their offspring to reproductive maturity. In other words, the ultimate causes for humanity's vengeful predisposition today, according to selection thinking, are the ways in which it helped our ancestors to have a lot of grandkids. But selection thinking needs to be consistent with empirical evidence if it's going to survive the scientific gantlet. As we proceed through this chapter and those that follow, we're going to consider that evidence in detail.

To do selection thinking, we need to start with three concepts: variation, inheritance, and selection.[4]

Variation provides the raw materials upon which natural selection operates. If you think about the people you know, you'll no doubt be struck by the variation in physical traits, behavioral dispositions, and personality. Much of this variation is created by differences in the individuals' genetic constitutions. These genetic constitutions are heritable, meaning they are passed from one individual to his or her offspring through reproduction.

This genetic variation between individuals is the stuff that natural selection selects. Put simply, natural selection is a process by which the genes that give rise to traits that make organisms better at creating copies of themselves (through reproduction) are precisely the genes that are more likely to show up in the organisms' next generation of offspring. As a result, the traits that provided a reproductive advantage to one's forebears (and the genes that give rise to those traits) become more prevalent in successive generations.

If, for example, normal genetic variation causes an individual animal from a given species to develop strong, sharp claws that enable it to feed itself and its offspring better than individuals that lack the genes for those strong, sharp claws, the bearer of the "strong, sharp claws" genes is likely to have more offspring (that is, to make more genetic copies of itself) than will the individuals with the more typical claw genes. In the next generation, therefore, the species will have a slightly larger proportion of individuals with strong, sharp claws than it did in the previous generation, and those individuals with strong, sharp claws will go on to out-reproduce the individuals with the more typical claws. And so it goes: compete, replicate, repeat. As this selection process unfolds over many generations of reproduction, a trait that confers a selective advantage can become species-typical.

Does natural selection operate upon psychological or behavioral traits in the same way that it operates upon physical traits? Well, why wouldn't it? We now know, for example, of a gene that's partially responsible for the evolution of the capacity for speech, and experts believe that this gene was specifically selected for its role in creating this uniquely human adaptation.[5] We also know that many behavioral and psychological traits—even rather complex ones such as dimensions of personality and intelligence— that differ among contemporary humans are caused to varying degrees by genetic differences among individuals.[6] So given that some genes that are responsible for universal adaptations such as speech are more or less species-typical, and given that variation in other genes is responsible for psychological traits on which people currently vary, it seems close to inconceivable that the genes that lead to personality and behavioral traits (including the propensity for revenge) might somehow have been impervious to natural selection during human evolution.

WHAT IS AN ADAPTATION?

"Adaptation" is one of the most basic and important concepts in evolutionary biology. It is also one of the most frequently misunderstood concepts in evolutionary biology. The evolutionary psychologist David Buss defined an adaptation as "an inherited and reliably developing characteristic that came into existence through natural selection because it helped to solve a problem of reproduction during the period of its evolution."[7] The writer Robert Wright defined adaptations as "mechanisms that are here because they have in the past contributed to your ancestors' fitness. And all are species-typical."[8]

Humans, like all species, possess lots of interesting adaptations. Language is an adaptation for communication when living groups get very large and, consequently, there is a lot more that needs to be communicated.[9] Pregnancy sickness is an adaptation for avoiding teratogens (toxins that affect fetal development) during gestation.[10] Concealed ovulation is an adaptation for managing the reproductive trade-offs that occur when individuals receive reproductive advantages both from procuring lots of mating opportunities and from providing paternal care for their offspring.[11]

But let me be clear: not everything that exists in human nature is an adaptation.[12] The evolutionary biologist George Williams noted that "adaptation is a special and onerous concept that should be used only when it is really necessary."[13] Every human being on the planet has a belly button, but the belly button itself is not an adaptation. Instead, the belly-button is the by-product of an adaptation—it's the interface that connects the umbilical cord to the fetus. Our search for the adaptive value of the belly-button will certainly be fruitless, because it didn't arise because of its adaptive value. It's an inevitable but purposeless consequence of a true adaptation—intrauterine fetal development.[14] In recent years, social scientists have claimed that art and music may be similar cross-cultural universals that arose even though they serve no known adaptive purpose.[15]

Other adaptation-irrelevant traits might become species-typical through a process known as genetic drift (or neutral selection). In genetic drift, a trait produced by a genetic variant can spread and become species-typical through sheer luck rather than because of any fitness benefits that the trait confers. So we have to keep something in mind: hypothesizing that the ubiquity of the desire for revenge is due to its co-occurrence with a *bona fide* adaptation (à la the belly button–umbilical cord relationship), or hypothesizing that it is due to genetic drift, are reasonable things to do. However, we aren't going to give these non-adaptationist hypotheses very much attention henceforth because the scientific evidence that we'll get into in the next few chapters will vindicate the adaptationist point of view resoundingly.

How Could the Desire for Revenge Possibly Be an Adaptation When It's So Maladaptive?

How could revenge possibly be an adaptation (in the evolutionary sense) when it's so destructive and seemingly pointless—when it seems so *maladaptive*—in the world in which we live? What could possibly be the evolutionary advantage of killing Vietnamese women and children because of casualties your platoon suffered the day before? What gain comes from killing the man who killed your son for spreading rumors about his daughter's chastity? Who benefits when a man whose family was killed in an airplane crash murders the air traffic controller whom he blames for the crash? If revenge is an adaptation, we have to explain the evolutionary gains that our ancestors might have acquired by possessing a willingness to take revenge, even if revenge doesn't serve those functions in the modern world (or, for that matter, even if it does). To think about revenge as an evolutionary adaptation, we won't concern ourselves so much with whether it's "adaptive" today—what will concern us is whether it was adaptive before humans existed in their contemporary form.

It might seem, then, that evolutionary scientists who deal with human behavior have a tough row to hoe, and they do. Because they want to explain not only *how* things work but also *why they work* the way they do and *how they came to work the way they do,* they often have to seek out sources of data that more conventional social scientists do not.[16] In this, their endeavor is a bit like astronomers' efforts to understand how the universe began by studying things that they can observe today. Evolutionary researchers excavate ancient burial sites and scrutinize dried-out skeletons. They isolate specific genes and figure out what they do. They watch the behavior of infants. They study the behavior of college freshmen in the social psychology laboratory. They watch nonhuman primates in the wild and in captivity. They interview people from hunter-gatherer societies who haven't yet had much contact with modern civilization.[17] None of the bits of data they gather from any single one of these sources proves definitively that a given behavior is an adaptation, but all of the data put together should tell a consistent story one way or the other. First and foremost, if a behavioral or psychological trait really is an adaptation, the data should give us a consistent story about the adaptive problem (or problems) that the trait helps to solve.

WHAT ADAPTIVE PROBLEMS DOES REVENGE SOLVE?

Some emotional states serve obvious functions that give evolutionary theorists confidence that those emotions are part of the solution to an adaptive problem. For example, fear prompts us to escape potential threats in the environment. It also makes us more cautious and avoidant of risk in general.[18] But some fears are easier to develop than others. For instance, primates learn to fear snakes the first time they see an individual looking fearful in a toy snake's presence; the same sort of automatic learning doesn't occur when primates see an individual looking fearful in the presence of toy rabbits or flowers. In the laboratory, humans can be conditioned to fear snakes even when they aren't consciously aware that they've even seen a snake (this is also an effect that doesn't occur when researchers try to "teach" people to fear innocuous objects such as mushrooms and flowers). Moreover, fears of snakes are extremely difficult to unlearn. All of this evidence, when put together with an understanding of the general psychological and behavioral effects of fear and the survival threat that snakes and reptiles played during human evolution, suggests that fear of snakes is a *bona fide* psychological adaptation.[19]

Some social scientists have tried to discover the functionality of revenge by studying the justifications that people provide for their own vengeful behavior. On this basis, some have proposed that people seek revenge because they want to balance a moral ledger that has become lopsided, or because they're interested in teaching a transgressor a moral lesson, or because revenge feels good and raises the avenger's self-esteem.[20] All of these statements could well be true, and from certain perspectives it might be correct to view them as "causes" of revenge, but such explanations can't help us understand *why* we have a capacity for revenge or *where that capacity came from in the first place.* The social scientists who generated these hypotheses about revenge weren't using selection thinking.

To conceptualize revenge as an adaptation, we have to know what social problems it helped our ancestors to adapt *to.* There are three very good possibilities. First, the propensity for revenge may have been selected because it helped to deter individuals who aggressed against ancestral humans from harming them a second time. Second, revenge may have deterred would-be aggressors from committing acts of aggression against our ancestors in the first place. Third, revenge may have been useful for punishing (and reforming) members of the social groups to which our ancestors belonged when those members failed to "pitch in" and make appropriate contributions to the common good. Let's look at these three possibilities and some of the evidence behind them.

THE FIRST ADAPTIVE FUNCTION: REVENGE DETERS AGGRESSORS FROM AGGRESSING A SECOND TIME

The first possible adaptive function of revenge is its ability to deter an aggressor from harming you a second time. When somebody harms you, you're obviously motivated to prevent it from happening again, so one thing you can do is simply stay out of the aggressor's way in the future. In highly mobile modern societies such as ours, often we can simply end relationships in which we've been betrayed and form new relationships in their place. But in the close societies in which our earliest hominid ancestors lived, moving away wasn't always a good option. Indeed, ostracism from the group was often a severe punishment that carried the risk of death. Therefore, our ancestors often had to find more direct ways to cope with the despots and bullies in their midst.

One way to cope with someone who wants to take advantage of you is to make it less profitable for that person to do so. If a bully determines that, by taking advantage of you, he can gain access to resources (for example, food, shelter, a good tool, a good mate, or a bump up the social ladder) that will improve his own well-being by x, but he knows that he'll incur a transaction cost (for example, in the form of wounds, or in the loss of status if he actually loses the fight) that equals, say, 50 percent of x, then taking advantage of you will produce, on average, a net benefit of only $.5x$. Would the bully try to steal your mate for a benefit of x? Perhaps. For $.5x$? Perhaps not. Revenge turns x into $.5x$.

Revenge of this nature, which evolutionary biologists define as the "retaliatory infliction of a fitness reduction," is actually quite prevalent in animal societies. For example, if a rhesus macaque finds a source of a highly valued food, but fails to issue one of the "food calls" that are used to alert others to the big discovery, the animal is likely to be attacked when others realize what he's done. In a scenario like this, you can almost see the evolutionary logic at work: if you don't want to share your food with us, then we're going to make it less fitness-enhancing for you to try and be sneaky about it. Theoretical biologists have gone on to show that the social impulses that motivate individuals to harm others who take advantage of them can become "evolution-arily stable." In other words, the math works out right for revenge to evolve precisely because of its ability to teach our aggressors that crime doesn't pay.[21]

When we look at modern-day data on revenge and its effects, we can see that revenge seems to perform a similar deterrent function in human relations. A social psychologist examined this deterrent function over twenty-five years ago in a simple experiment.[22] Male undergraduate students were asked to write an essay, which was then evaluated by another person (who was actually working for the researcher). All participants received insulting evaluations of their essays, regardless of their actual quality.

The participants were brought back to the psychologist's lab twenty-four hours later and given the opportunity to give ten shocks of varying intensities to the very person who wrote the insulting reviews of their essays the day before. (In reality, no shocks were delivered, but participants were led to believe that they would be.) Recall from the previous chapter that this is the very sort of setup that typically leads people to behave vengefully: insult me and I'll more readily shock you in the lab. The intensity of the supposed shocks was controlled by a panel of seven buttons.

One-half of the participants were also led to believe that after they administered shocks to their evaluator from the previous day, they would then switch roles with their evaluator and receive the shocks themselves. The other half of the participants weren't told anything about receiving shocks later. People who believed that they could harm their insulting evaluators without the threat of retaliation gave stronger shocks to the evaluators than did people who thought that the evaluators would have an opportunity to retaliate. Thus the fear of retaliation deterred aggression. In another study, people refrained from harming the interests of their opponent in an economic bargaining game when they knew that the opponent had a strong ability to retaliate—especially when the opponent had shown an aversion to starting trouble in the first place.[23] What these two studies show is that believing that the target of your aggression will have the opportunity to retaliate against you severely reduces how much harm you're willing to do to him or her in the first place.

THE SECOND ADAPTIVE FUNCTION: REVENGE WARNS WOULD-BE HARMDOERS TO BACK OFF

A second candidate for an adaptive function of revenge—and perhaps even a more important one—is its ability to deter people who mean to harm us from doing so in the first place. Ancestral humans were group-living creatures that lived, worked, and ate in the presence of others. Thus the outcomes of their aggressive encounters with other individuals quickly became public knowledge.

Many social primates, including humans, are savvy political actors who observe each others' behavior and then use that information to make calculated, strategic decisions about how to interact with each other. Any information I might gain about your inner disposition—how fearful you are, how easy-going you are, how generous you are, how vengeful you are—could be useful as I try to negotiate my own social world. Any insights I can gather about what you are made of could turn out to be useful as I try to determine whether I ought to befriend you, cooperate with you, take advantage of you, kowtow to you, or simply stay out of your way. For this reason, I'm very interested in what you do after someone else tries to take advantage of you. If you let somebody harm you without seeking your revenge, then I'll know that you're an easy mark and I might consider trying to take advantage of you myself.

Don't kid yourself by thinking that the ancestral human beings I'm describing were too stupid to engage in such sophisticated political thinking. We modern humans can do it, of course, and our modern-day primate relatives, most notably the chimpanzees, are endowed with cognitive abilities that enable them to engage in such score-keeping and perhaps even to make inferences *about other individuals' inferences*.[24] So it's reasonable to assume that our hominid forebears were outfitted with similar cognitive abilities.

Social psychologists have shown in the laboratory that a victim will retaliate more strongly against his or her provoker when an audience has witnessed the provocation—especially if the audience lets the victim know that he or she looks weak because of the abuse he or she suffered or if the victim knows that the audience is aware that he or she has suffered particularly unjust treatment. In fact, when people find out that bystanders think less of them because of the harm they've endured, they'll actually go out of their way—even at substantial cost to themselves—to retaliate against their provokers.[25] Moreover, when two men have an argument on the street, the mere presence of a third person doubles the likelihood that the encounter will escalate from the exchange of words to the exchange of blows.[26]

The effect of third parties on revenge can also help to explain a couple of puzzles about cultural differences in violence. First off, why do white men in the modern American South have higher levels of gun violence than do white men in the Northeast? Social psychologists Richard Nisbett and Dov Cohen say it's because the Europeans who originally settled in the Old South were sedentary herders rather than farmers.[27] (Stay with me; this story gets pretty good.)

Sedentary herders are highly vulnerable to theft and exploitation. The lands they occupy are usually not very good for more intensive agriculture. Grazing land is often in short supply, which creates a chronically high level of social tension. Moreover, herders gamble their entire livelihood on a commodity that is both very expensive and highly portable (cattle, sheep, and goats, after all, have hooves). Therefore, as a herder you have to be on guard to make sure no one steals your herd while you sleep. By comparison, it's awfully hard to steal someone's barley crop overnight, and it's the land rather than the harvest that holds long-term value for the farmer anyway.

For this reason, according to Nisbett and Cohen, it makes good sense for herders to cultivate honor—reputations as the type of people whom you can't slight without facing certain, violent retaliation. Indeed, in his book *Cohesive Force,* the anthropologist Jacob Black-Michaud documented extensively the self-protective functions that honor (backed up by feuding and vengeance) served among the traditional herding societies of the Mediterranean and Middle East.[28] Honor is of such value to people from a herding culture that they'll kill or be killed to defend it: once your honor is lost, it's just a matter of time before your neighbors begin to take advantage of you.

So, where did the Europeans who originally settled the American South come from? You guessed it: they came from Ireland, Scotland, and Wales, where livestock herding was the traditional agricultural activity. Once in the United States, they went on after several decades to farm tobacco, rice, indigo, and cotton,[29] but even then they were reluctant to give up the herder's honor mentality. Old mental habits, enshrined in a thousand different cultural edifices and passed from father (and mother) to son, die hard. The need for honor—backed up by a proneness for revenge—might have been particularly acute in the frontier South of the seventeenth and eighteenth centuries, where institutions for law enforcement were often meager or nonexistent. People had to take care of their own affairs. In contrast, the Europeans who settled the American Northeast came predominantly from places such as England, Germany, and Holland, where intensive farming was the traditional way of life—a way of life that didn't require people to be so obsessed with honor.[30]

Studies show that Nisbett and Cohen are on to something. They had Northern and Southern undergraduate men at the University of Michigan participate in several experiments in which they were bumped and then cursed at by someone who was surreptitiously working for the experimenter. In this situation, the Southern males became angrier, more hostile, and more prepared for aggressive action than did their Northern counterparts. They also had higher increases in cortisol (a stress hormone) and testosterone (a hormone that's associated with dominance and aggression) than did the Northern males.

In addition, when the Southern males were unwittingly put into a "chicken game" (they were asked to head down the hall for an appointment, but as soon as they set out, they encountered a six-foot-three, 250-pound young man who was coming down the hall from the opposite direction), those who had previously been jostled and cursed at waited longer before giving way to the big guy. This didn't happen with the Northern males. The jostled and insulted Southern males also gave firmer handshakes, and they were rated by evaluators as seeming more "dominant" than were the Northern males who had been jostled and insulted. Finally, when the Southern males were bumped and insulted in front of a witness, they believed that the witness thought less of their manliness, courage, and toughness. The Northerners didn't think the witness thought any less of them in this situation. In other words, being insulted and sworn at seemed like a violation of manly honor to those young Southern gentlemen, but no similar thoughts seemed to cross the minds of the Northern men. These results reinforce the assertion that white Southern men are more prone to retaliatory aggression than are Northerners— precisely because of their preoccupation with manly honor.[31]

The deterrent value of revenge also helps make sense of the high rates of retaliatory violence in the disadvantaged neighborhoods of America's inner cities. In his marvelous book *Code of the Street*, the sociologist Elijah Anderson contrasts two codes for regulating social interaction in contemporary urban communities.[32] The first is a code of decency that's characterized by relaxed, friendly, tolerant social interaction: this is a code for well-maintained, well-lit, multiethnic neighborhoods where there are job opportunities and safe public spaces. The second is a "code of the street" that's characterized by a preoccupation with acquiring and protecting one's honor (or "respect," or "props") and projecting an image of self-confidence, nerve, skill, and an ability to look out for oneself. In the burned-out inner-city neighborhoods in which poverty and crime are high, police protection is unreliable, and opportunities for an honest living are scarce, young black men learn from an early age to regulate their behavior according to the code of the street. These sorts of neighborhoods are magnets for retaliatory homicide.[33]

Anderson argues that inner-city black men's reliance on the code of the street results in large measure from their lack of trust that the criminal justice system will be there to defend their interests for them. Developing "respect," therefore, becomes such a preoccupation in these neighborhoods because it works as an insurance policy against victimization—just as it did (and maybe still does) among Mediterranean herders, the Scots-Irish settlers of the Old South, and their descendants. As Anderson describes, the readiness and willingness to retaliate for real or imagined slights is a key part of the code of the street—primarily because of how it helps people to obtain respect and to defend it: "For young people this means being prepared to meet challenges with counteractions. When they are hit or otherwise violated, they may hit back. Or they may even 'pay back' later on by avenging transgressions. An important part of the code is not to allow others to chump you, to let them know that you are 'about serious business' and not to be trifled with. The message that you are not a pushover must be sent loudly and clearly."[34]

A substantial body of research evidence supports the idea that adherence to the street code predisposes young people to lives of retaliatory violence. For example, a nationally representative, three-year longitudinal study of more than nine hundred adolescent males found that boys who endorsed street-code beliefs (for example, that it's okay to get into a fight to uphold your honor or to retaliate against someone who's called you a name) went on one year later to engage in more violence, including greater participation in gang fights and attacks in which their goal was to seriously injure or kill someone.[35]

One African-American man nicknamed "Stub," who sells heroin on the streets of St. Louis, explained to some researchers the logic of deterrence that was behind his decision to kill a man who once shot him and then robbed him:

> See, you have to realize if I didn't get back at him, you and him could say [Stub]'s a punk. Everybody can go take [Stub's] shit. So if he [gets] hurt, everybody knew who hurt him. . . . So if you handle your business you ain't got to even worry about it cause they gonna say that time [so-and-so] robbed [Stub], and shit he came up missing. So that gonna give them the fear right there not to fuck with you. . . . That's very important if you gonna live that lifestyle. You need to let it be known you not gonna take no shit, you know what I'm saying? Fuck no, you would be out of business . . . or dead you know what I'm saying, cause you would have people, little kids, coming up trying to rob you [thinking] he ain't gonna do nothing, he's a punk. . . . People just know . . . don't fuck with me [because of my] reputation.[36]

THE THIRD ADAPTIVE FUNCTION: REVENGE COERCES FREE RIDERS TO COOPERATE

A third function of revenge that was probably adaptive for ancestral humans is its value in coercing people to cooperate who would otherwise take advantage of other people's hard work without pitching in themselves. Cooperation is widespread in the animal kingdom. Predatory animals cooperate in tracking and bringing down prey; chimpanzees form alliances to steal power away from more powerful, but socially isolated, alpha males; male dolphins cooperate to isolate females so they can mate with them; pairs of fish from several species cooperate in checking out predator fish to determine whether they're hungry; and wasps, ants, and bees divide labor in exquisitely elaborate ways.[37] But cooperation among humans has a distinctive feature: we readily cooperate with nonrelatives and even perfect strangers without promise of special consideration in the future. Indeed, human societies are built upon this sort of cooperation. Without cooperation, agriculture, conservation of natural resources, and warfare (not to mention writing, the Internet, and international trade) would have been impossible.[38] Thus civilization as we know it would have been impossible.

The evolution of large-scale human cooperation has puzzled scientists for quite some time. Jean-Jacques Rousseau understood the nub of the problem: suppose twenty of us pledge that we're going to make sacrifices so that we can achieve some grand goal that none of us could accomplish alone. We're all going to sacrifice a bit of our individual time and energy (in the evolutionary sense, our "fitness") in the short run to create something that will yield gains for all of us in the long run. Perhaps this group endeavor is large-game hunting. If we're all willing to take time out of our schedules to hunt deer, we'll be much more successful in the endeavor of deer hunting than we would have been otherwise, and therefore there will be more meat for us and our families than if we'd all stayed close to home and fended for ourselves.

But deer hunting is not a risk-free enterprise. It takes time, its outcome is uncertain, and there's a real possibility that you'll run into a dangerous animal in the woods. Given the potential costs of deer hunting, large-scale cooperative endeavors such as group hunts are vulnerable to cheaters or "free riders." What's to stop someone in the hunting party from loafing so as to avoid injury or inconvenience? Meat is often shared among the group rather than owned by any specific hunter, so hypothetically a free rider could benefit from the hunt without making any personal sacrifice.

Or, what's to stop one of our hunters from breaking faith with his comrades if the opportunity to kill a hare presents itself? Rabbit hunting is relatively easy and safe, and it carries a higher probability of personal payoff to the hunter. So wouldn't everybody go after the rabbit if given the opportunity?[39] As Rousseau rightly perceived, it's hard to see why someone would remain faithful to a social contract that required him or her to give up short-term personal gain in service of the common good. It's easier to be a free rider on the bus and let everyone else pay to keep it maintained. So how does large-scale cooperation emerge at all? Not surprisingly, philosophers and social scientists call this problem the "free-rider problem."

When we think of the free-rider problem not as a problem about individual organisms but rather as a problem about gene frequencies within a population of replicating organisms, it gets even knottier. Let's say that there are genes that favor group cooperation and genes that favor free riding. The individuals with the genes that favor group cooperation are the people who will be inclined to do the work of cooperating, and this reduces their fitness slightly relative to the fitness of individuals with the free-rider genes who gain the benefits of group cooperation without the costs associated with all the extra work. As a result of the fitness advantage that free-riding genes seem to enjoy generation after generation, it's hard to see how the proportion of cooperative genes in the gene pool could do anything but decline with each successive generation, just as it's hard to see how the free-rider genes could do anything except increase. Thus the free-rider problem makes large-scale cooperation look like an evolutionary nonstarter.

One possible solution to the mystery of large-scale cooperation in light of the free-rider problem is punishment, more specifically, a form of punishment that goes by the name "altruistic punishment" or "moralistic enforcement."[40] Altruistic punishments might include humiliating the free rider, physically injuring him, fining him, socially ostracizing him, or taking away some other resource that steeply reduces his fitness. We call this sort of punishment "altruistic" because it comes with a cost to the punisher—if you decide to punish a free rider, you do so at some metabolic cost to yourself. Still, research with modern-day humans has shown that people willingly incur considerable costs to themselves in order to punish free riders,[41] and that they do so in order to prevent free riders from parasitically benefiting from the cooperative effort of other group members.[42] Altruistic punishment occurs even when the punisher gets no personal benefit from punishing the noncooperator and even when the punisher doesn't have the opportunity to engage in any more interactions with the uncooperative partner: people punish free riders, it seems, just because they feel like it. And actually, the psychological mechanism that promotes altruistic punishment is even more specific than that: people freely and gladly punish free riders because free riders make people angry, and because harming them in kind makes people feel good.[43]

Research on modern human behavior shows that regularly punishing free riders can indeed establish and maintain large-scale group cooperation. In one study, the individuals within four-person groups were each given an endowment of twenty monetary units (for simplicity's sake, I'll call them dollars) by the investigators. Then the groups played repeated rounds of an investment game in which the four individuals could contribute whatever amount they desired from their personal accounts into a joint account that was shared by all four members. When you put a dollar into the common account, that dollar is subtracted from your personal account, and $1.60 (or 40 cents per group member) is placed in the joint account. At the end of each round, the earnings in the joint account are distributed evenly among the four group members. In the short run, making contributions to the joint account is a bad deal for you as an individual group member (you lose 60 cents for every dollar you contribute), but if all four of your group's members make a one-dollar contribution on each round, you'll all get 4 × .40 = $1.60 per round, for a 60-cent gain per round.

This is the classic dilemma of cooperation, monetized: if you're cooperative but no one else is, you get screwed. If everybody cooperates, everybody benefits. If everyone except you cooperates, you get to be a free rider, benefiting from everyone else's cooperative spirit without taking on any personal risk.

To test whether retaliation deterred free riders and encouraged better group outcomes, the researchers gave half of the four-person groups the ability to punish group members who didn't make solid financial contributions to the joint account on each round. If you wanted to punish a member of your group whom you viewed as a free rider, you could make a "punishment" decision that would cost that person three dollars, but to enact your decision to punish the free rider, you had to pay a dollar from your personal account (hence the "altruism" in "altruistic punishment"). For the other half of the four-person groups, punishing other group members simply wasn't an option.

The effect of the ability to punish free riders on contributions to the joint account was staggering. Individuals within groups that could punish free riders readily deposited huge proportions of their individual endowments into the joint account, and the sizes of their contributions increased with each new round. By the end, about 40 percent of players in the groups that could punish were contributing *all* of their personal endowments into the joint account during each round. By contrast, in the groups that couldn't punish free riders, contributions *declined* with every successive round.[44]

In another study, researchers had participants play a similar type of investment game, but the researchers gave the participants the freedom to choose what kind of group they wanted to join—a group that could punish free riders or a group that couldn't. If people didn't like their outcomes in one kind of group, they could switch to the other kind of group whenever they wanted. Initially, only about one-third of the participants chose to belong to a punishing group, but because the free riders hobbled the effectiveness of these nonpunishing groups so dramatically, most people in the nonpunishing groups eventually realized that joining the punishing groups was worth the trouble. In fact, after thirty rounds of play, about 93 percent of people had moved into a group that could punish free riders. By that time, cooperative behavior in the punishment-free groups had collapsed completely: large-scale group cooperation simply can't be sustained without the ability to punish free riders.

Experience is a hard teacher. In this study, she taught participants that they'd have better individual outcomes in the long run if they belonged to a group that could reward cooperation and punish cheating—even though their intuition told them that they'd do better by free riding or by belonging to a nonpunishing group. The fact is that when enough cooperators who are willing to retaliate against free riders get together in a group, the fitness disadvantage associated with bearing the costs of punishment is spread out among so many potential punishers that its actual effects on fitness are quite trivial. By the end of thirty rounds of play, the high contributors who were willing to punish defectors were getting 98 percent of the payoffs that the high contributors who were unwilling to punish were receiving. With more rounds of play, the differences in their payoffs would likely have disappeared completely. This is because nearly everyone eventually comes to play by the rules nearly all the time within the punishing groups, so no one has to punish anyone else very often.[45]

The conclusion looks clear: without the ability to punish, large-scale group cooperation is probably an evolutionary nonstarter. With the ability to retaliate against free riders, however, it begins to look like an evolutionary no-brainer.

REVENGE: THE PROBLEM THAT IS A SOLUTION

To the outside observer, revenge looks pointlessly destructive. And when we count the costs of revenge from a nonselectionist vantage point, it is. As we saw in the previous chapter, the desire for revenge motivates aggression, murder, and perhaps even international conflict. Marvin Heemeyer built his killdozer and then used it to destroy a lot of property and upset a lot of people, but he accomplished very little else. In the end, his rampage on Granby, Colorado, seemed like nothing so much as a very destructive temper tantrum. Vitaly Kaloyev got his revenge against the air traffic controller Peter Nielsen, but the only thing he really managed to do was to make more widows and orphans.

But when we use selection thinking, we can appreciate the evolutionary logic that might lie behind the human propensity for revenge. Selection thinking leads one to suspect that humans' propensity for revenge exists because of how it protected our ancestors from aggressors and because of how it protected their efforts to benefit from large-scale cooperative behavior. With these potential adaptive functions in mind, it gets easier to accept the idea that revenge is a built-in feature of human nature, despite its awful effects in the world today. We might rightly view revenge as a modern-day problem, but from an evolutionary point of view, it's also an age-old solution.

In this chapter we've explored some of the functions that revenge might have served in our evolutionary past, but so far we've only come part way in this endeavor to understand why revenge evolved and what it's really all about. We need to take a closer look at how revenge is actually practiced in real human lives and real human societies—and some nonhuman ones as well.

CHAPTER FOUR

THE RETRIBUTION SOLUTION
The Evidence for Adaptation

It's a minor miracle that we know anything at all about the fifty-seven-year-long feud between the families of Earl Uhtred of Bamburgh and Thurbrand the Hold. The only written record was discovered on two leaves of a pamphlet that an anonymous cleric, perhaps a monk, wrote at the end of the eleventh century. The original is long gone, but against all odds a single twelfth-century copy survived its nine-hundred-year journey to the present day. The writer's main interest was not in documenting Anglo-Saxon political history. His task was to detail the history of six northern estates whose ownership was in dispute (the church leaders at Durham believed the estates were the church's rightful property), presumably in preparation for an upcoming lawsuit. But even though our cleric's account of the feud was a digression from his main purpose, we find in the bare facts he did record on those two sheets of vellum a gripping testimony to the captivating power of the desire for revenge.

The feud was prosecuted, from start to finish, in Northumbria, England's northernmost province. It began in the spring of 1016. Earl Uhtred was the head of the house of Bamburgh—the most powerful family in Northumbria and one of the most powerful families in all of England. You couldn't rule England effectively if you didn't have cooperation, or subjugation, from the House of Bamburgh in the North. Uhtred was strongly allied with the West Saxon King, Ethelred II (in fact, he was married to Ethelred's daughter—his third wife). At the time, Ethelred was locked in an intense struggle with the Danes for England's throne. Under the leadership of Canute, the Danes were gaining ground, and eventually, Ethelred was killed. Uhtred saw the writing on the wall: England was destined to have a Danish king, and his name was Canute. It was time for Uhtred to switch allegiances.

A time and a place were set for a formal public ceremony in which Uhtred would submit to King Canute and negotiate the terms of peace. It was to take place in a village known as Wiheal, which may be the modern village of Wighill, near Tadcaster in North Yorkshire. Unfortunately for Uhtred and the forty "chief men" he brought with him on that blustery spring day, Canute had conspired with another Northern magnate called Thurbrand the Hold—one of Uhtred's long-standing enemies—to have Uhtred assassinated. As soon as Uhtred and his escort arrived and assembled before Canute—unarmed and utterly vulnerable—they were slaughtered, to the man, by Canute's soldiers, who had been lying in wait.

The assassination of Uhtred ignited a vengeful sequence of ripostes and counterattacks that would, in the end, consume four generations of men from the houses of Uhtred and Thurbrand. Like many feuds, this one unfolded slowly and deliberately. Uhtred's son Ealdred killed Thurbrand approximately a decade after Uhtred was assassinated. A decade later, probably in 1038, Thurbrand's son Carl killed Ealdred while Carl was showing Ealdred around his estate in the village of Rise. This was a searing betrayal: some time previously, after years of setting ineffective ambushes for each other in "Spy vs. Spy" fashion, Carl and Ealdred had made peace and had sworn a solemn oath of brotherhood. Ealdred's murder was the third in the sequence.

It would be another thirty-five years before a fourth and final act of blood vengeance would bring the feud to an end. Earl Waltheof, who was Ealdred's grandson (and Uhtred's great-grandson), wasn't even born when Carl killed his grandfather in Rise Wood. But something reignited the animosity between the two families, and it fell to Waltheof to pick the feud back up in the winter of 1073–1074. Waltheof orchestrated a surprise attack on the sons and grandsons of Carl (they were Thurbrand's grandsons and great-grandsons) while they were feasting at Settrington, near York. Three of Carl's sons were killed along with a number of unnamed grandsons.

Two years later, Waltheof was executed for unrelated acts of rebellion. He left no male heirs behind, and thus no one for the surviving sons and grandsons of Carl to kill in vengeance for the slaughter at Settrington. When Uhtred's last male descendant died, the feud died too.

It would be oversimplifying things to say that a feud is merely an extended cycle of revenge between families. Feuds are governed by conventions—conventions about the types of affronts that require retaliation, conventions about who can kill whom, conventions about where and when one can find temporary sanctuary, conventions about making peace, and so forth. Moreover, feuds like the feud between the families of Uhtred and Thurbrand are often motivated by political goals that are quite distinct from vengeance. But feuds run on flex-fuel: a combination of political goals and vengeance goals provides them with maximum power. As Richard Fletcher, the British historian who has pieced together the story of Uhtred and Thurbrand, observed, "You hit me, I'll hit you back: the primal, instinctive satisfaction of such a remedy dates from long before *Homo* became remotely *sapiens*. It is from this primordial response that what we call the bloodfeud has developed."[1] Even working with the skeleton of facts that history has preserved about the feud of Uhtred and Thurbrand, it takes little effort or imagination to recognize that the vengeful sentiments that animated their feud a millennium ago continue to animate the avengers of our own age.

Revenge has been a human social reality for a long time—perhaps, as Professor Fletcher supposes, "long before *Homo* became remotely *sapiens*." In Chapter Three, I used selection thinking to identify three adaptive functions that the propensity for revenge likely played during human evolution. Describing those functions—and marshalling evidence to show that revenge continues to work in the ways I've suggested it did while humans were evolving—is an indispensable first step in developing an evolutionary account of revenge, but anyone can come up with a "just-so story" about how this or that behavior might have arisen through natural selection. Rudyard Kipling made up just-so stories that provided fanciful explanations for why enormous whales eat only tiny animals, why camels have humps, and why leopards have spots. But Kipling's just-so stories were made to entertain children, not to teach them evolutionary biology.

So we need to be wary of just-so stories. Attention Deficit Hyperactivity Disorder (ADHD) has its own modern just-so story that is interesting, memorable, widely discussed, and profoundly wrong. ADHD is a prevalent disorder, and its prevalence has led some theorists to postulate that the propensity for ADHD might be a psychological adaptation (albeit a disregulated one). When our species was evolving into its present form, these theorists surmise, perhaps it would have been a good thing to have people with ADHD-like traits in your group because their quickly shifting attention, impulsivity, and motor hyperactivity would have made them good hunters.[2]

The problem with this proposal is that it's hard to see how a disorder characterized by self-control deficits, an inability to focus, and poor planning could help people become better hunters.[3] Anybody who's ever done any hunting (at least, any successful hunting) knows that you have to be able to tolerate boredom, stay focused on a single goal for hours on end, suppress all manner of bodily impulses (from hunger to the desire to sneeze), move across the terrain without making a sound, and stand ready to fire your weapon neither a millisecond too soon nor a millisecond too late. Needless to say, these traits are not the strong suit of people with ADHD. We need much more than a compelling just-so story to prove that something like ADHD was adaptive for ancestral humans.

Likewise, to prove that revenge really is an adapted feature of the human psyche, we need more than a good just-so story about function. But what other kinds of evidence should we seek? Here are some good places to start. First, we should be able to identify the environmental input that activates the desire for revenge. That is, the desire for revenge should be a reliable response to a specific kind of input to the human brain—a "thin slice" of human experience. Second, we should find that revenge exists among peoples from all cultures. If revenge is a universal feature of human nature, it shouldn't be limited to people from some cultures but not others. Third, we should find evidence for revenge in other extant species that face the same kinds of adaptive problems in their social interactions that ancestral humans did. Fourth, the mathematics of revenge should work out: computer-based simulations of evolutionary processes (which are the stock-in-trade of a field called theoretical biology) should show that vengeful organisms tend to out-survive and out-replicate organisms that aren't prone to vengeance. We're going to dive head-first into this evidence.[4]

IS THE DESIRE FOR REVENGE A RESPONSE TO A THIN SLICE OF EXPERIENCE?

There are no all-purpose adaptations. Specific adaptations evolve because they help specific organisms respond to specific problems that arise in the course of their evolution. Consider your sensory organs—for example, your nose. It's actually a transducer—a device that converts one form of information (the chemical signature of an airborne substance) into another form (electrochemical activity in your brain that leads, perhaps, to the perception, "This tuna smells funny") that you can then use for decision making ("I think I'll make chicken salad instead."). A transducer such as the human nose is sensitive to one form of input from the environment (molecules) but completely unresponsive to other types of environmental input (for example, pressure waves, some of which our hearing systems can process). You can try all day long to smell the difference between middle A and middle C, but it's just not possible because sounds are for hearing rather than for smelling. The nose only transduces a thin slice of reality. This "thin slice" principle is, of course, also true of the electronic sensing devices that humans have developed. Radio receivers that operate on the basis of frequency modulation (FM) are completely insensitive to signals sent from radio stations that use amplitude modulation (AM).

THE HUMAN HEARING SYSTEM'S "THIN SLICE"

A closer look at the human hearing system illustrates how understanding the thin slices of experience that activate particular human traits can help us evaluate adaptationist hypotheses about those traits. The human hearing system is sensitive to compression waves in the frequency range of 20 to 20,000 cycles per second. This is a pretty impressive dynamic range—the thin slice that the hearing system processes looks pretty thick. But even so, there are a lot of compression waves out there that simply fall on deaf ears. Compression waves that are slower than 20 cycles per second don't sound like tones to humans, even though elephants regularly communicate with sound waves below this threshold. Human hearing is also insensitive to compression waves that are faster than 20,000 cycles per second, but bats and dolphins use such "ultrasonic" waves for communication and navigation. Dogs' ears are also sensitive to ultrasound, as anyone who has ever watched a dog's response to a dog whistle knows.

So our hearing system ignores a lot of the information out there that it could be taking in, but nestled within this limited system there is a curious region of sensitivity. Because of its design, the auditory canal has a natural resonance in the range of 2,000 to 5,000 cycles per second.[5] As a result, sounds in this frequency band end up sounding much louder than do other sound waves of equal sound pressure. Why does this pocket of sensitivity exist? An answer can be found by considering the spectral distribution of background noise in the three habitats that primates inhabit— rain forests, savannas, and forests that surround rivers in otherwise arid areas. The only habitat in which animal activity makes a substantial contribution to background noise is the rain forest, where the contributions of insect noise and bird calls to total background noise are easily identifiable. The noise made by bugs, birds, and other animals in the rain forest is in a frequency band ranging from approximately 2,000 to 4,000 cycles per second.[6]

Perhaps it's no coincidence, then, that the ears of some of the living rain forest primates that have been studied—as well as those of human beings—have a built-in sensitivity to the frequency band that critters use to make their noise in the rain forest! Our ears, therefore, aren't all-purpose compression wave transducers. They seem more like "animal detectors"—very useful if you're concerned about where your next meal is coming from or you're trying to prevent something from making a meal out of you. This sort of tight fit between the human hearing system and types of sounds that it's really good at transducing seems too advantageous to have arisen by mere coincidence: a selection thinker sees natural selection at work.

THE HUMAN REVENGE SYSTEM'S "THIN SLICE"

Now if the motivation to seek revenge is an adaptation like hearing, it also needs to be sensitive to a thin slice of input from the world out there. But which thin slice? We generally don't wake up in the middle of the night full of wrath toward nobody because of the spontaneous firing of a few errant neurons. We don't feel vengeful when our three-year-old children tell us they hate us, or when we hit our thumbs with hammers, and only the nuttiest among us feel vengeful when a waiter accidentally brings us spaghetti with marinara sauce instead of the alfredo sauce we ordered. Neither does the desire for revenge arise from generic psychological pain. People don't feel vengeful toward cancer when it takes a loved one. Sure, such a loss often produces overwhelming grief and even anger, and such losses might even cause a few people to change careers and devote their lives to finding a cure for cancer, but even then it would be stretching things to say that such people were seeking revenge against cancer.

So what does activate the desire for revenge? Humans desire revenge when they perceive that they've been harmed significantly and intentionally by another person. The more severe and intentional the injury, the more intense the desire for vengeance. For instance, a survey of Dutch men who had been the victims of violent crimes and property crimes showed that the extent to which they wanted to retaliate against their perpetrators was related to the seriousness of the crimes they encountered and the extent to which those crimes led to lasting physical consequences (for the victims of violent crimes), or personal financial loss (for the victims of property crimes).[7] Moreover, many studies have shown that when people perceive that someone is responsible for a harm they've suffered—particularly when they perceive that the person who harmed them acted intentionally—anger and retaliatory behavior result.[8] That's how the revenge system works: severe, intentional offenses go in, the desire for revenge comes out.

A psychological common denominator among the severe, intentional harms that elicit the desire for revenge is that they violate the victim's sense of honor.[9] We commonly associate the word *honor* with awards or with sexual virtue, but I'm referring here to the *Oxford English Dictionary*'s primary definition of the term: "1. High respect, esteem, or reverence, accorded to exalted worth or rank; deferential admiration or approbation. a. As felt or entertained in the mind for some person or thing."[10] Honor is a mask that we wear to say something about ourselves to other people. Historically, people have also counted on their honor to serve as a sort of shield. If I believe that you believe that I have honor, then I can have some confidence that you won't try to take advantage of me or my loved ones because you'll suspect that I'd retaliate quickly and harshly. As one anthropologist put it, honor "is almost identical with the ability to defend it."[11]

A few decades ago, sociologists predicted that honor was not long for the world.[12] However, the predictions of honor's imminent demise were too hasty. People from all walks of life continue to be preoccupied with honor. A professor worries that a lecture by an out-of-town guest will be poorly attended, dishonoring both guest and host, so she offers her students extra credit if they'll attend. An employee obsesses about how to tell his overly sensitive boss something he needs to know without making him feel stupid. Candidates for public office send battalions of attorneys to haggle over every picayune detail of their televised debates, including the order in which the candidates will be introduced, the names the moderators will use when addressing the candidates, the questions the moderators can and can't ask, the colors of shirts the candidates can wear, and even whether the candidates are allowed pen and paper.

We can't banish concerns about honor from the contemporary world, and even if we could, it wouldn't be such a good idea.

You *want* would-be burglars to think that they'd be risking their lives if they broke into your home. I *want* my students to believe me when I tell them that they'll do poorly in my courses if they don't study hard, participate in class, and turn in quality work. If they believe me, they'll be more motivated to do their best, and as a result, my job as a teacher becomes easier and more pleasant. Even the president of the United States has to think about the defense of national honor when he makes foreign policy decisions. In an interview with Tim Russert, here's how President George W. Bush justified the invasion of Iraq in the spring of 2003 (after the failure to find the much-touted and long-promised weapons of mass destruction had caused many Americans to question the U.S. presence there):

> You remember U.N. Security Council Resolution 1441 clearly stated "show us your arms and destroy them, or your programs and destroy them." And we said, "There are serious consequences if you don't" and that was a unanimous verdict. In other words, the worlds [sic] of the U.N. Security Council said we're unanimous and you're a danger. So, it wasn't just me and the United States. The world thought he was dangerous and needed to be disarmed.

> And, of course, he defied the world once again.

> *In my judgment, when the United States says there will be serious consequences, and if there isn't serious consequences, it creates adverse consequences. People look at us and say, they don't mean what they say, they are not willing to follow through* [italics mine].[13]

Honor helps to keep us out of trouble, but to enjoy the defense that honor can provide, you have to be willing to defend your honor when it's challenged. It wasn't that long ago that the defense of honor was a perfectly legitimate justification for using violence to resolve one's interpersonal disputes—even here in the West. The steadily increasing power of centralized governments in the Western world since the days of Uhtred and Thurbrand can be credited for removing the right of revenge from the hands of the aggrieved and placing it instead in the hands of objective, dispassionate legal systems.[14] Even so, when people aren't convinced that a higher authority is capable of adequately addressing an honor violation on their behalf, they'll be tempted to convert their *desire* for revenge (which no legal system can take away) into vengeful *action* (which legal systems are designed in part to prevent).[15] It's good that we live in a society in which we can use the legal system to protect our interests (even though attorneys are almost universally despised), but many of the slings and arrows of life are far beyond a legal remedy. There are (regrettably, for the betrothed, at least) no laws that prevent a bridegroom's buddy from detailing the bridegroom's previous sexual exploits at the rehearsal dinner. And there's still no legal recourse for being subjected to the mobile phone conversation across the restaurant when you had hoped for a quiet, intimate lunch.

What's more, getting your day in court doesn't mean that the legal system will come out in your favor, and effective use of the legal system is beyond the practical reach of many people in our society in the first place. For example, only in my lifetime have American women begun to receive adequate legal protection against violence from their spouses and partners, sexual harassment in the workplace, and acquaintance rape. In her important book *Wild Justice,* writer Susan Jacoby argued that until quite recently, personal revenge was just about the only form of "justice" (and, I'd add, the only vehicle for restoring their honor) that was available to many women who had been terrorized by abusive spouses and domestic partners.[16]

Concerns about honor are also acute when people live in places or subcultures in which they don't (or can't) rely on law enforcement to protect their safety and their rights. Honor concerns are prominent among inner-city gangs and outlaw motorcycle clubs, which allow membership only to "honorable" men who are willing to defend themselves and their images when necessary. If you would call the police to solve your problems, you demonstrate your lack of honor, and gangs and outlaw biker clubs will quickly show you the door.[17] People are also inclined to turn up the gain on their honor-detectors when they live in the disadvantaged inner-city neighborhoods that Elijah Anderson described so vividly in *Code of the Street.*[18]

Wherever the law or some other higher authority is incapable of reliably providing people with a legitimate means for restoring their violated honor, you'll find people with exquisitely sensitive honor detectors that are always ready to goad those people into vengeful action.[19] Tarnished honor is the "thin slice" of experience that activated the desire for revenge in Marvin John Heemeyer, in Vitaly Kaloyev, and in the sons and grandsons of Uhtred and Thurbrand, and it awakens the desire for revenge in us all.

IS THE DESIRE FOR REVENGE A HUMAN UNIVERSAL?

If the desire for revenge is an adaptation, then it should be a human universal. Believing in the universality of the desire for revenge puts me in the company of Shylock, that great poster-child for revenge from Shakespeare's *The Merchant of Venice:* "I am a Jew. Hath not a Jew eyes? hath not a Jew hands, organs, dimensions, senses, affections, passions? fed with the same food, hurt with the same weapons, subject to the same diseases, healed by the same means, warmed and cooled by the same winter and summer, as a Christian is? If you prick us, do we not bleed? if you tickle us, do we not laugh? if you poison us, do we not die? and if you wrong us, shall we not revenge? If we are like you in the rest, we will resemble you in that."[20]

Shakespeare was right to assume that there really is such a thing as a "human universal"—a trait that characterizes humans in all cultures. The universal design features of human bodies—two arms, two legs, two eyes, and so forth—are universal or species-typical because they arise from a body plan that we inherited from vertebrate forebears that went extinct hundreds of millions of years ago. Other than the stray cases that might arise from genetic abnormalities, problems in fetal development, or environmental trauma, we've all got two arms. There's no sense in sending out a bunch of anthropology graduate students to search for exceptions. Likewise, language, tool use, religion, music, jokes, and the disapproval of stingy behavior also appear to be human universals.[21] Not all human universals are adaptations, but all adaptations are universals. So to support my contention that the desire for revenge is an adaptation, it would be nice to drum up some proof that the desire for revenge (when the system is activated by the right "thin slice" of experience) is as typical of *Homo sapiens* as are two eyes, two arms, tools, and jokes. Fortunately, such evidence is easy to come by.

WESTERMARCK'S ERROR

In 1898, a Finnish social scientist named Edvard Westermarck wrote an essay on revenge that he later folded into a two-volume treatise with the austere title *The Origin and Development of the Moral Ideas*. It was an ambitious essay. Westermarck regarded revenge as a window into "the most prominent element in moral conscious- ness," and with his essay on revenge he set out "to survey what the available facts really seem to teach us regarding its essence."[22] Westermarck was an early adopter of the theory of evolution, and he was firmly convinced that revenge of the very sort that I've been talking about is an adapted feature of human nature that (recalling Richard Fletcher's turn of phrase) was shaped and refined well before *Homo* was even remotely *sapiens*. To bolster his argument, Westermarck cites example after example of pre- modern societies in which people condoned and regularly used revenge directly against their oppressors, or, in feudlike manner, against their oppressors' friends and relatives.

Westermarck was one of the first great geniuses of social science, but his comparative approach contains an unfortu- nate logical flaw: he presents his cross-cultural examples for our consideration *precisely because* they fit with his contention that revenge is a human universal. This is the same logical problem that would be inherent in an epidemiological study in which we tried to estimate the prevalence of cancer in Miami exclusively by surveying people receiving treatment in the oncology wards of the local hospitals. You can't determine true prevalence by exam- ining only those cases that you already know to have a positive diagnosis.

To exacerbate the problem, we don't know why Westermarck didn't point us to any cultures in which revenge was absent. Is it because he failed to find any, or is it because he didn't look for any, or is it because he found contradictory evidence but then swept it under the rug? There's no reason to doubt Westermarck's scientific integrity, but all the same, an absence of evidence is not evidence of absence. There may yet be cultures out there in which people never took up revenge as a problem-solving strategy. I'm sure Westermarck was doing the best he could with the evidence at his disposal, but now, more than a century after Westermarck, we can do better.

THE EVIDENCE FOR UNIVERSALITY

What we really need to do is examine a sample of diverse cultures from around the world that are selected into our analysis irrespective of whether they manifest any evidence of revenge. With that sample established, we can then see how many of the cultures in the sample actually show evidence of revenge. Two important studies have been conducted that meet this requirement perfectly.

Blood Revenge as a Human Universal

One place to look for cross-cultural evidence concerning revenge is in the Human Relations Area Files (HRAF) Probability Sample. The Probability Sample contains high-quality ethnographic material on sixty different cultures from around the world. These sixty cultures were randomly selected, and they represent each of the world's major geographic regions and language groups. The ethnographic materials are cross-indexed by hundreds of different codes. Look up the relevant three-digit codes (for example, the codes covering "blood vengeance" are codes 578, 627, 628, and 721) and you can determine what, if anything, ethnographers have had to say about the presence or absence of blood vengeance within those sixty cultures.

Four decades ago, the husband-and-wife team of Keith and Charlotte Otterbein used an earlier version of the HRAF to examine blood revenge following homicide (that is, revenge in which the family members of a homicide victim seek to take the life of the killer or one of his associates) in fifty regionally and linguistically distinct world cultures.[23] They concluded that blood revenge was "frequent" only in eight of fifty societies. In fourteen of the fifty societies, they concluded, blood revenge was "infrequent." In twenty-eight of the fifty it was "absent." Taken together, that's twenty-two hits for fifty at-bats, yielding a .440 batting average. Not too impressive if you're trying to make the case that the desire for revenge is a human universal!

But the evolutionary biologists Martin Daly and Margo Wilson (another husband-and-wife team) doubted whether this was the correct conclusion to draw from the Otterbeins' work. Daly and Wilson noticed that the Otterbeins defined revenge-infrequent societies as those in which the relatives of a homicide victim would sometimes accept compensation instead of blood revenge. They also noticed that the Otterbeins' "revenge-absent" societies included societies in which formal judicial procedures were available for punishing killers, societies in which compensation was available as an alternative to revenge, and societies in which homicide was considered to be rare in the first place. Evidently, the Otterbeins were less concerned with cataloguing whether revenge was a cross-cultural phenomenon across their sample of fifty societies and more concerned with exploring whether the fifty societies had conventions in place to provide alternatives to revenge. There would have been no need for alternatives to revenge unless the desire for revenge had been a problem in the first place.[24]

So, to ask precisely the question that interests us, Daly and Wilson determined how many of the sixty societies in the HRAF Probability Sample actually showed evidence of blood feuds, capital punishment, or the desire for blood revenge. They found that fifty-seven of the sixty cultures they examined had "some reference to blood feud or capital punishment as an institutionalized practice, or specific accounts of particular cases, or at the least, some articulate expression of the *desire* for blood revenge"[25] (italics in original). Of the sixty societies they examined, only three of them—the Cagaba society of South America, the Dogon society of West Africa, and the Thai society of Asia—lacked ethnographic evidence showing that the concept of blood revenge was well-articulated and at least occasionally practiced. That's a not-too-shabby batting average of .950 for the "universality of blood revenge" hypothesis. When you consider that ethnographic data are always at the mercy of the questions that the ethnographers choose to investigate, the rapport they've managed to establish with their informants, and the amount of time they've able to spend with them, a .950 batting average seems particularly impressive. Had more ethnographers, or different ones, written ethnographies for the Cagaba, Dogon, and Thai cultures, evidence for the presence of revenge might have been discovered in those cultures too. "What our survey suggests," Daly and Wilson summarized, "is that the inclination to blood revenge is experienced by people in all cultures, and that the act is therefore unlikely to be altogether 'absent' anywhere."[26]

Blood revenge can even run rampant in societies that lack a dedicated word for the concept of revenge. The Waorani of eastern Ecuador are horticulturalists. To subsist, they mix basic plant cultivation with hunting and gathering. There were only six hundred Waorani when anthropologists made contact fifty years ago. Homicidal vengeance used to be quite common among the Waorani, but even so, their language lacks a dedicated word for the concept of revenge. To talk about revenge, they resort to surprisingly clumsy turns of phrase (for example, "Wëwä bewitched Äwä, he died. We killed Wëwä, he died" or "They passed on spearing.").[27] But as the anthropologists who documented this linguistic curiosity observed, "One need not explicitly state something that everyone knows. The social context in which it is useful to have an abstract labeled category of 'revenge' is when one wants to make a global prohibition of vendetta. The practice or explanation of vendetta involves individual cases; its prohibition requires the recognition of a general category of forbidden behavior and motivates the creation of a label for it."[28]

Costly Punishment as a Human Universal

You'll recall from the previous chapter that one adaptive function of revenge arises from its utility for helping groups of unrelated individuals sustain cooperative norms so that they can enjoy the benefits of group cooperation. When you go out of your way to punish a group member who is behaving too selfishly, economists call it "costly punishment" or "altruistic punishment," rather than revenge, but this is semantic nitpicking: the core sentiment that drives costly punishment and the sentiment that drives blood revenge are one and the same. For this reason, costly punishment is as universal as blood revenge.

Anthropologists recently evaluated the prevalence of costly punishment in fifteen different world societies (including two groups from North America, three groups from South America, six groups from Africa, a group from Asia, and three groups from Oceania) that differed in language, climate, and economic base. The researchers had their participants play two economic games. The first was a simple ultimatum game in which participants were paired with a partner who held an endowment of money (called the "stake") that was equivalent to one day's wage in the local economy. The person holding the stake could give as much or as little of the stake to the recipient as he or she wanted. This was a "take it or leave it" sort of affair—which is why it's called the ultimatum game. If the recipient didn't like the share that had been offered, however, he or she could refuse it, and by doing so, neither player would get anything. Such a refusal would obviously involve a loss of some amount of money for the recipient (thus the "costly" in costly punishment), but it would also punish the stakeholder for being too greedy (thus the "punishment" in costly punishment). It's a simple game, but it's a truly excellent one for determining whether people place cash value on the ability to punish someone who's being stingy with them. Participants also completed a "third-party punishment" game in which they could pay a proportion of a private endowment that the researchers had given them for the privilege of punishing someone who was being stingy in an ultimatum game with a third player.

As was the case in Daly and Wilson's survey of blood revenge across cultures, the evidence for cross-cultural universality was overwhelming. In all fifteen societies people tended to punish excessively stingy behavior. As stakeholders' offers toward recipients in the ultimatum game became more slanted away from a 50-50 split, the recipients in all fifteen societies became more likely to reject those offers in exchange for the privilege of punishing the stakeholder. Likewise, people in all fifteen societies became more willing to pay for the privilege of punishing a stingy stakeholder who was playing an ultimatum game with a third party as those stakeholders' offers became stingier.

A final important result of this study is that the societies with the highest standards for fairness (that is, those with the highest likelihood of punishing lowball offers in the ultimatum game and in the third-party punishment game) also had the highest levels of generosity in a game called the dictator game. The dictator game simply involves taking a stake and giving as little or as much of it as you want to your partner—no strings attached, no right of refusal. In other words, those societies in which people are the least tolerant of unfairness are also the societies in which people tend to be the most generous. Conclusion: costly punishment may indeed be one of the dynamics that allows generosity and cooperation to thrive within large groups of unrelated individuals.[29]

The cross-cultural evidence, therefore, is convincing. Ninety-five percent of the cultures that have been examined show some evidence of blood revenge, and 100 percent of those that have been examined are stocked with people who will gladly incur a personal cost for the privilege of harming someone who has been excessively greedy. The anthropologist behind the whole "human universals" movement proposed that if 95 percent of cultures in an ethnographic sample manifested a trait, it was probably safe to conclude that the trait was in fact a human universal.[30] By this standard, it's hard to deny that the desire for vengeance (provided that the proper "thin slice" of experience has activated it) deserves membership in the catalogue of human universals. The search for the society of people who know nothing of vengeance is only marginally more likely to be successful than is the search for the society of three-armed people.

ARE WE THE ONLY VENGEFUL SPECIES?

Revenge doesn't require much brain power. All you really need upstairs is the ability to recognize other individuals, enough memory to keep track of their behavior, and an "if-then" rule that motivates you to harm those who have harmed you (perhaps by activating brain systems associated with anger).[31] It's not much more complicated than that, so there's no reason to assume that revenge could only arise in organisms like us who have advanced reasoning abilities and complex culture. On the face of things, it's very likely that revenge is within the ken of many nonhuman animals.

And because revenge really does deter aggression and promote cooperation, it would be surprising if humans *were* the only vengeful species. Aggression and cooperation are concerns to many social animals, so if revenge evolved to help humans solve problems related to aggression and cooperation, it might have evolved to help other species solve similar problems. The great Darwin himself was a believer:

> Many, and probably true, anecdotes have been published on the long-delayed and artful revenge of various animals. The accurate Rengger, and Brehm state that the American and African monkeys which they kept tame, certainly revenged themselves. Sir Andrew Smith, a zoologist whose scrupulous accuracy was known to many persons, told me the following story of which he was himself an eye-witness; at the Cape of Good Hope an officer had often plagued a certain baboon, and the animal, seeing him approaching one Sunday for parade, poured water into a hole and hastily made some thick mud, which he skillfully dashed over the officer as he passed by, to the amusement of many bystanders. For long afterwards the baboon rejoiced and triumphed whenever he saw his victim.[32]

Westermarck also spun some good yarns about animal revenge, including a story (he got from Darwin) about a camel who tears the top off the skull of a fourteen-year-old boy who had been tormenting him, and an elephant who squirts water on his provocateur—not on the animal handler who was teasing the elephant, mind you, but on the artist who ordered the handler to do so.[33] Unfortunately, observations like these from Darwin and Westermarck are vulnerable to the same bias that might have afflicted the cross-cultural anecdotes that Westermarck used to argue that revenge was a human universal: the cases Darwin and Westermarck brought to bear on the question of revenge in other species were held up as evidence precisely because they supported their contention. To know if revenge really is present in other species, we need to conduct experiments that can actually prove us wrong.

REVENGE IN OTHER PRIMATES

Primatologists Frans de Waal and Lesleigh Luttrell conducted a study to test for revenge in three species of primates: chimpanzees, rhesus macaques, and stumptailed macaques. In all three species, conflicts between two individuals are common. These conflicts often start as squabbles over food or mates, or as jousts between males to assert their dominance. It's common for a third individual to join these spats to support one of the combatants against the other. De Waal and Luttrell reasoned that if primates really do practice revenge, then when a latecomer C supports A in A's attempt to defeat B, B should be motivated to find opportunities to harm C in C's later squabbles with other combatants. De Waal and Luttrell examined this possibility by looking carefully at thousands of conflicts among individuals from three captive groups.

The chimpanzees exhibited a very recognizable pattern of revenge. If C helps A to defeat his opponent B, then B will tend to come to the aid of C's opponents in future squabbles. For rhesus and stumptailed macaques, the opposite was true: the more you intervene against them, the *less* they'll intervene against you in your later fights. Chimpanzees seemed to be out for vengeance, but the rhesus and stumptailed macaques just wanted to stay the hell away from their attackers. Why were the macaques so much more averse to seeking revenge than the chimpanzees were? Probably because the dominance hierarchies of chimpanzees are much more flexible than are the hierarchies of rhesus and stumptailed macaques. Rhesus and stumptailed macaques avoided harming their superiors; chimpanzees had no such qualms. In fact, de Waal and Luttrell found that chimpanzees of middling rank directed about 80 percent of their *contra* interventions toward higher-ranking rather than lower-ranking individuals. In contrast, middling-rank macaques directed fewer than 20 percent of their *contra* interventions against higher-ranking individuals. Chimpanzees in the middle of the hierarchy, it seems, were going out of their way to harm higher-ranking individuals, which confirms something primatologists have long suspected: chimpanzees are obsessed with power and the powerful.[34]

But the fact that de Waal and Luttrell's macaques didn't seek revenge doesn't mean that chimpanzees are the only vengeful nonhuman primates. An anthropologist named Joan Silk found that revenge (in other words, the more you gang up against me, the more I will gang up against you) was every bit as noteworthy among male bonnet macaques as it had been among de Waal and

Luttrell's chimpanzees.[35] It's possible that macaque revenge is primarily a male phenomenon. If so, de Waal and Luttrell would have had no way of discovering this fact because their groups of macaques were composed mostly of adult females. In addition, Silk's bonnet macaques were living at very low population density—more like de Waal and Luttrell's chimps and less like their macaques. Maybe high population density deters revenge among primates.[36]

There's a fourth species of macaque—the Japanese macaque—that has a method of seeking revenge that would have made an Anglo-Saxon nobleman beam with pride. Like their rhesus and stumptailed cousins, Japanese macaques have dominance hierarchies that are rigid and intimidating to subordinates, so individuals who are low on the totem pole tend not to seek revenge directly when they're victimized by more dominant individuals. Some primatologists speculated that perhaps they seek revenge by attacking the relatives of their oppressors instead of attacking their oppressors directly.[37]

To evaluate this hunch, they analyzed more than fifteen hundred aggressive encounters in a colony of Japanese macaques at the Rome Zoo. As expected, there were very few aggressive episodes in which a subordinate individual harmed a more dominant one—instead, it was the dominant individuals who beat up on the more subordinate ones. So what did the subordinate individuals do when they were attacked by a more dominant individual? They didn't retaliate directly; instead, they went after their attacker's kinfolk. If a Japanese macaque—let's call him Uhtred—has just been attacked by a particular individual whom we'll call Thurbrand, there's a 29 percent chance that Uhtred will go on to attack one of Thurbrand's younger kin within the next hour. Twenty-nine percent may not seem like very high odds of retaliation, but this represents more than an 850 percent increase in the likelihood that Uhtred will attack someone from the house of Thurbrand. Most of the time, the targets of Uhtred's redirected acts of vengeance will be youngsters who are relatively low in the social hierarchy.

(Incidentally, if Thurbrand attacks Uhtred, there's a 250 percent increase in the likelihood that one of Uhtred's relatives—perhaps his son Ealdred?—will attack one of Thurbrand's relatives—maybe his son Carl?—within the next hour. With Japanese macaques, things can easily move from simple displaced revenge to something that bears an eerie resemblance to human feuding.)

It gets even more interesting. In three-quarters of the attacks that Uhtred the Japanese macaque directs at Thurbrand's relatives, he attacks in plain sight so that Thurbrand can see exactly what he's doing. Why? Perhaps because he *wants* Thurbrand to see it. Maybe he's sending Thurbrand a message: *Don't underestimate my ability to harm you. You may be more powerful than I am, but I'm more powerful than your sons, daughters, nieces, and nephews, and I know how to get to them when there's nothing you can do about it.* When Japanese macaques take revenge (displaced though it is) they're trying to prevent themselves from being revictimized by putting on displays of their own violent potential. How very human-seeming.

Why restrict our search for animal revenge to the primate order? If revenge is such a good strategy for deterring aggression and encouraging cooperation, then it could potentially evolve in lots of species—even in species whose cognitive powers are much weaker than those of the primates—so long as those species have encountered persistent problems related to aggression and cooperation in their evolutionary histories.[38] Retaliatory behavior can even evolve to regulate interactions between members of completely different species. Brown-headed cowbirds are brood parasites. They lay their eggs in the nests of other birds and then they have the chutzpah to expect the hosts to incubate their eggs along with the hosts' own. Why don't the host birds just eject the cowbirds' eggs from their nests? Because if they do, the cowbirds come back and destroy the hosts' eggs. If the hosts let the cowbirds' eggs stay, the cowbirds leave the hosts' eggs alone. Revenge is so simple and so effective that even a bird brain can do it.[39]

FISHY REVENGE

Revenge can even evolve in fish. When a shoal of guppies or sticklebacks is looking for food and a predator fish appears on the scene—a sunfish, say—a small scouting party will leave the larger group and inch toward the predator to conduct a threat assessment. The predator inspection routine progresses in lock-step fashion: one individual in the scouting party advances a little, and then another advances a little, and so on, until they're close enough to evaluate whether the sunfish is hungry enough to give chase. If the sunfish doesn't react to the scouting party, then everybody figures that he's not hungry and that it's safe to keep foraging. If the sunfish does lunge at the scouts, however, the guppies that stayed behind know that they need to stop eating and pay attention, lest they become the sunfish's next mouthful. Predator inspection yields immensely valuable information, but the scouts face mortal danger each time they sign on for one of these reconnaissance missions. The risk of being eaten is substantially reduced in scouting parties of two or more, however. Sunfish, like people, get indecisive when there are too many items on the menu.

Predator inspection, therefore, is a dilemma of cooperation. If we cooperate by going out on a mission together, we gain precious information—advance warning about the sunfish's appetite—at a tolerable level of risk. But it's still a risk, so although we all benefit if *someone* goes on a predator-inspection mission, individually we'd benefit even more if that someone were not us. In a cooperative dilemma such as this, we should be on the lookout for a behavioral mechanism that has evolved to motivate members of scouting parties to stay committed to the task at hand.

That mechanism is revenge. In a carefully controlled laboratory experiment, a biologist discovered that if one scout begins to lag too far behind, or fails to take his turn in advancing toward the predator, the scout that is closer to the predator will suddenly swim back behind the laggard so that it's now the laggard who is closest to the predator. The retaliator won't budge again until the less intrepid scout pulls himself up by his finstraps and makes a proper advance toward the predator. After that, the retaliator joins back in, and the scouting party resumes its journey into the jaws of peril. In other words, if one of the scouts fails to hold up his end of the cooperative compact, the other retaliates. When the slacker starts pulling his weight again, he is "forgiven" and the reconnaissance mission continues.[40]

On the Turure River in Trinidad, waterfalls create natural barriers that prevent populations of guppies from interbreeding.

This has led to the evolution of two genetically distinct strains of guppies on the Turure. Above the waterfalls, the guppies have only one small predator; therefore, their risk of being eaten by a predator is fairly low. Below the waterfalls, the guppies have had to cope for countless generations with several different large predators—it's these downstream guppies whose retaliatory behavior I've just described. Because these two populations of guppies have faced very different levels of predation pressure, the researcher who discovered the presence of revenge in the downstream guppies surmised that natural selection wouldn't have had any occasion to build the same retaliatory mechanism into the behavioral repertoires of the upstream guppies. (This kind of creativity in generating scientific hypotheses only occurs when you're deeply familiar with a particular species and when you're armed with selection thinking.) To evaluate this hypothesis, he replicated his prior experiment, this time using guppies from upstream.

The data supported his hypothesis beautifully. Recall from his first experiment that the downstream guppies, which had evolved through a long history of high predation pressure, readily retaliated by swimming back if their partners lagged too far behind. When the loafers started advancing again, the retaliators began advancing again as well. This wasn't at all how the guppies from upstream (the population with low predation pressure) behaved. First of all, females from upstream didn't exhibit any retaliatory behavior at all during predator inspection (upstream females have a very low likelihood of being eaten; for males the risk is slightly higher). The males from upstream, however, did swim back when they got too far ahead of a partner who was slacking off, but unlike their downstream cousins, they didn't respond to the slacker's "contrition" by resuming their forward advance.[41]

It's probably incorrect even to think of the upstream males' tendency to swim back as a form of retaliation. More likely, it simply reflects a tendency to "school" (that is, to stay close to each other). If you swim back when you get too far out in front of your partner, but you don't start swimming forward again contingent on your partner's decision to start moving forward again, then you're not really encouraging cooperation with your swim-back behavior—you're just trying to stay with the group.

These results won't surprise you if you've been using selection thinking as you've been reading. If revenge is naturally selected because it helps animals to solve problems like the problem of maintaining cooperation during predator inspection, then there's no reason why natural selection would craft a retaliatory mechanism to maintain cooperative predator inspection in a population of guppies whose evolutionary history didn't feature cooperative predator inspection! Given the downstream guppies' persistent need for cooperative predator inspection, evolution was able to shape a retaliatory tendency out of the population's existing genetic variation. But the upstream guppies didn't *need* a mechanism like that because there wasn't an environmental pressure selecting for it. Consequently, the retaliatory trait didn't evolve in the guppies above the waterfalls of the Turure.

How long does natural selection need to craft a retaliatory mechanism for a purpose like predator inspection? Surely it must take millions of years, right? Astonishingly, if predation pressure is high enough, adaptations that help fish escape predators can evolve in fewer than forty generations.[42] It might not take much longer than that. Forty fish generations is no more than a couple of decades. Even in humans, it's an evolutionary blink of an eye.

VENGEANCE BY THE NUMBERS

It has been hundreds of millions of years since humans shared a common ancestor with fish, tens of millions of years since we shared an ancestor with the macaques, and no fewer than five million years since we shared an ancestor with chimpanzees. Just how far back do we have to go in our lineage to figure out where modern humans' propensity for revenge came from?

When you've really started using selection thinking, you realize that this is the wrong question. The fact that guppies, sticklebacks, cowbirds, macaques, chimpanzees, and humans all share a tendency to retaliate under certain circumstances doesn't necessarily mean that we all inherited this tendency from a common ancestor. Some species have faced unique environmental pressures that favored the evolution of revenge as a problem-solving strategy; others haven't. Given enough time (maybe not as much as you might be inclined to think) and enough selection pressure, simple but elegant natural selection can create vengeful fish, birds, monkeys, chimps, and people *de novo.* If revenge provides a substantial boost in fitness relative to its costs, then it could pop up in all kinds of animals. It's really just a matter of working out the math.

And of course, the animals themselves don't have to be great mathematicians for the costs and benefits of revenge to steer a species toward revenge as a problem-solving strategy. Natural selection is a compulsive accountant that fastidiously records every actor's costs and benefits, rewarding those who adopt successful strategies for solving social dilemmas and handicapping those who adopt less successful ones. Organisms that adopt behavioral strategies with low cost-benefit ratios become fitter, which is to say that they reproduce in larger numbers. Organisms that adopt strategies with high cost-benefit ratios will fail to reproduce themselves in sufficient numbers, and over time they will die off or hang on by a thread. The organisms don't have to be able to reflect upon their own existence for the evolutionary process to produce new traits: natural selection ensures that those strategies that lead to reproductive success will become more prevalent in a population of reproducing organisms.

Theoretical biologists study how natural selection results from the costs and benefits associated with particular traits, and they often do their research in the most sterile of all earthly climates—the silicon chip. They use computer programs to create simple electronic worlds in which organisms adopt strategies for interacting with their neighbors, compete for resources such as space and food, and reproduce in proportion to their success in acquiring those resources. Allowing these simulations to unfold over thousands and millions of generations inside a desktop computer that's allowed to run over the weekend can provide important insights into how natural selection produces traits. In short, theoretical biologists try to figure out what *can* evolve so that we can better understand what *has* evolved.

Theoretical biologists liken sticklebacks' and guppies' retaliatory tendencies during predator inspection to strategies for playing a game. It's a game you play with a partner in which your winnings depend on the choices you make, as well as on the choices your partner makes. Some theorists think that downstream guppies (those under high predation pressure) are using a strategy for predator inspection that has come to be called "tit-for-tat."[43] This strategy is a simple system of conditional rules. Start out by cooperating. If your partner betrays you, punish him. If your partner seems contrite after getting punished, forgive him.

As we're going to see in the next chapter, the application of game theory and computer modeling to theoretical biology has produced a surprising insight about the relationship between revenge and forgiveness. As cooperation evolves, revenge and forgiveness aren't pulling on opposite sides of the rope; they are on the same team. If you're going to be successful in cooperating, you can't be easy-going all the time or you'll quickly become everybody's doormat, and you'll pay the fitness consequences. You have to be willing to drop the hammer if your neighbor betrays you. The sons of Uhtred and Thurbrand knew this. Chimps, monkeys, fish, and birds know it too. But you can't be nasty and vindictive to all of the people all of the time, either. You have to be willing to let bygones be bygones with some of the individuals in your social world because in the long run, organisms that know how to cooperate can fare better than organisms that know only vengeance. In social dilemmas that pit the short-term gains of selfishness against the long-term gains of cooperating, evolution favors the organisms that can be vengeful when it's necessary, that can forgive when it's necessary, and that have the wisdom to know the difference.

CHAPTER FIVE

FAMILY, FRIENDSHIP, AND THE FUNCTIONS OF FORGIVENESS

The desire for revenge isn't a disease or a defect in human nature. It's authentically human, and it has always been a part of us. This fact might suggest that a dismal forecast for our species' future is in order. We're not going to get rid of humanity's desire for revenge with better social programs, better pharmaceuticals, or better psychotherapy. But there's some good news, too. Evolutionary science leads us squarely to the conclusion that forgiveness is also a built-in feature of human nature. As we'll see in the next few chapters, the capacity to forgive, like the desire for revenge, is a standard-issue human social instinct. Every neurologically intact person comes into this world outfitted with the capacity to forgive under certain circumstances.

Under certain circumstances. Those are three important words. If we want to learn how to make the world a less vengeful, more forgiving place, it's important that we figure out what those "certain circumstances" are. A good way to start is by taking a close look at the two functions for which the capacity to forgive was naturally selected—its ability to help ancestral humans get along with their genetic relatives, and its ability to help ancestral humans establish and maintain cooperative relationships with nonrelatives.

GETTING ALONG WITH OUR RELATIVES

Many animals—humans certainly *not* excepted—are known to retaliate against their blood relatives, on occasion quite harshly.[1] Yet it's relatively rare for human beings to use blood revenge against their own kin. When someone kills another person, the victim is most likely a stranger, acquaintance, or romantic partner. Only very rarely do people kill their own children, their own parents, or their own siblings.[2] True, history and literature are replete with stories of people who did kill their brothers, sisters, parents, or children in pursuit of power, wealth, or love. You can also find plenty of evidence that people have engaged in infanticide (usually in extremely dire straits) for thousands of years. But in general, people are and, as far as we can tell, always have been hesitant to seek blood revenge (and, it's probably safe to assume, other forms of revenge) against their genetic relatives unless they have an awful lot to gain if they do, or unless they have an awful lot to lose if they don't.[3]

What is it exactly that makes revenge against genetic relatives so rare? Filial bonds, gratitude, mutual dependency, brotherly love—sure, all of these help to restrain our vengeance against loved ones, but from the perspective of evolution, there's a more fundamental cause of our restraint: harsh revenge against a blood relative, insofar as it actually reduces the relative's fitness, reduces the avenger's fitness as well. Like it or not, your sister Tracy and your cousin Tommy are carrying around some of your genes (siblings share 50 percent of their genes in common; for first cousins it's 12.5 percent), so if you remove their genes from the gene pool, you're removing some of yours as well. The idea that my fitness isn't dependent simply on how many offspring *I* have (that is, how many of my genes I get into future generations through my own reproductive success), but also on how many offspring my genetic relatives have, is called *inclusive fitness*. Inclusive fitness is the real measure of how well we're actually doing in the game of achieving evolutionary immortality.

The biologist J.B.S. Haldane once quipped that although he wouldn't lay down his life for a brother, he would do so for two brothers or eight cousins. Saving the lives of two brothers is equivalent to saving half of your genes, twice. Harshly retaliating against a genetic relative, therefore, damages your inclusive fitness. Biologists often put it more subtly, perhaps asserting that the payoffs that an individual receives from retaliation are "modified by kinship."[4] But the bottom line is that if retaliating against your sister costs her two "fitness units," it's going to cost you one fitness unit right off the bat because you're one of your sister's major genetic shareholders. Therefore, a proneness to forgive our blood relatives probably evolved because people who had such a trait were able to avoid shooting themselves in the foot (or the genes?) by reducing the fitness of their blood relatives.

COOPERATING WITH NONRELATIVES

Forgiveness probably also served a second function during human evolution: encouraging cooperation among nonrelatives. As we've already seen, revenge has helped to solve that problem, but forgiveness is also part of the solution. Indeed, a big part of why we're inclined to forgive our friends, neighbors, and associates today is probably because forgiveness enabled our ancestors to develop and maintain the cooperative alliances that they needed to thrive in large groups. Rather than thinking of the relationship between revenge and forgiveness as one of disease and cure, or poison and antidote, we'd do better to think of revenge and forgiveness as a team of midwives that helped give birth to human beings' ultra-cooperativeness. It's worth taking some time to savor this idea, and we'll do so in the remainder of this chapter by breathing the rarefied air of game theory.

GAMES GUPPIES PLAY

Recall our predator-inspecting guppies from Chapter Four. Let's consider the costs and benefits of predator inspection, starting with the costs. Predator inspection requires time and energy that could otherwise be used for foraging. There's also the risk that a predator-inspecting guppy will become a sunfish's next meal. Therefore, it would be in Bob the guppy's best interests to shirk his predator-inspection duties—if only he could get somebody else do the dirty work.

However, predator inspection produces valuable information: it tells the fish whether it's safe to continue looking for food or whether they ought to clear the area to avoid getting gobbled up. Eventually, somebody's going to get eaten on the job, but the risk to any single guppy on any single mission (if it has a willing inspection partner) is fairly low. Therefore, the average payoff, in fitness terms, is higher for the individual guppies if *somebody* inspects predators than if *nobody* inspects predators. However, there is one type of fish that fares very poorly: the poor sucker who volunteers for a predator-inspection mission with a partner who plans to abandon him once they're in the thick of things. Recall that a fish is much more likely to get eaten during predator inspection when working solo than when working with a partner.

We can rank the possible outcomes in terms of their net benefits to a predator-inspecting guppy. The best outcome goes to an individual who betrays his partner once they're out on the job (high benefit in the form of information, no cost in the form of mortality risk). The second-best outcome goes to the individual who, when his turn comes, volunteers for a predator-inspection mission with a partner that will hold up his own end of the deal (high benefit in the form of information, small cost in the form of mortality risk). The third-best outcome goes to the fish if *nobody* volunteers for predator-inspection missions (no benefit, no cost), and the very worst outcome goes to the hapless fish who goes out on a mission along with a partner who shirks his responsibilities in the middle of the job (high benefit in the form of information, but very high cost in the form of mortality risk).

There's a predicament here: the self-interested course of action for a guppy on a predator-inspection mission can't be determined in a vacuum, but rather, depends on what its partner does. Figure 5.1 shows how the effect of Guppy A's strategy choices on its fitness can only be predicted if we also know what Guppy B is going to do.

FIGURE 5.4. THE PREDATOR-INSPECTING GUPPY'S DILEMMA

		Guppy B's Strategy	
		Advance	Stall or Retreat
Guppy A's Strategy	Advance	A's Outcome: Information discounted by small risk of being eaten B's Outcome: Information discounted by small risk of being eaten	A's Outcome: Information discounted by large risk of being eaten B's Outcome: Information with no risk of being eaten
	Stall or Retreat	A's Outcome: Information with no risk of being eaten B's Outcome: Information discounted by large risk of being eaten	A's Outcome: No information, no risk of being eaten B's Outcome: No information, no risk of being eaten

In the upper left corner, two guppies on a mission gain valuable information, but the value of that information is discounted by a small chance of being eaten. In the upper right corner, Guppy A advances toward the predator, but Guppy B shirks its responsibility. In this case, Guppy A gets information that is discounted steeply by a high risk of being eaten, but Guppy B gets the information for free—that is, without having to worry about being eaten. In the lower left corner, the outcomes are reversed: Guppy A, who is the free rider in this scenario, gets the information for free, whereas Guppy B has to work to get the information—a benefit that is made less valuable by the fact that it had to take a large risk to obtain it. The lower right corner depicts a situation in which neither guppy advances toward the predator. Neither gets the desired information about the sunfish's appetite, but neither gets eaten, either. When the effect of one's behavior on one's fitness depends on the behavior of somebody else, what's a guppy to do?

DILEMMAS, DILEMMAS EVERYWHERE

The predicament I've just described is a special case of a more generic problem that scientists call the "prisoner's dilemma." Here's the make-believe quandary from which the prisoner's dilemma derives its name. Two criminals are arrested on suspicion that they've committed a major crime. The police don't have enough evidence to support a conviction, so they interrogate the two criminals separately in hopes of obtaining testimony that they can use to charge one of them with the principal crime. If neither suspect betrays his accomplice, both criminals will be charged with a lesser crime, and they'll eventually get one-year sentences. If one criminal offers testimony against the other, he won't be charged with anything and the other criminal will be charged with the principal crime, which carries a three-year sentence. If they implicate each other, they'll both get two-year sentences. What's the smartest course of action in a situation like this? That's the prisoner's dilemma.

Science writer William Poundstone has called the prisoner's dilemma "one of the great ideas of the twentieth century, simple enough for anyone to grasp and of fundamental importance."[5] Because of its seemingly limitless ability to reveal surprising truths about social behavior, the political scientist Robert Axelrod has called it "the *E. coli* of the social sciences."[6] In addition to the many things the prisoner's dilemma can teach us about deception, trust, self-interest, and rational action, it also has a lot to teach us about forgiveness. In particular, it can show us how the capacity to forgive evolved to help people benefit from cooperation with non-kin.

Prisoner's dilemmas are all around us. Any time you find yourself in a situation in which the average outcome for everyone involved is highest if everyone works together, but the best *individual* outcome comes from defecting against everybody else, you're probably in a prisoner's dilemma.[7] If both prisoners stay quiet about their accomplice's guilt, their *average* outcome is the best, but they'd get the very best *individual* outcome by betraying a faithful accomplice. If both predator-inspecting guppies do what they're supposed to, their *average* outcome is better than any other average outcome, but the very best *individual* outcome is to be obtained by loafing while your partner does the inspecting.

The world's nations would have the best *average* outcome if they disavowed all aspirations for nuclear weapons, but the best *individual* outcome would result from being the only nation in the world with a nuclear bomb.

In the 1940s, a Hungarian mathematician named John von Neumann developed *game theory* to bring some mathematical rigor to these sorts of strategic dilemmas. Game theorists try to identify the courses of action that self-interested actors should pursue when they're locked into competitions, known generally as "games," with other self-interested actors whose future behavior is uncertain. The holy grail of game theory is the "Nash equilibrium," named after John Nash, a mathematician at MIT who worked out the details in the early 1950s. (Four decades later, after recovering from a long battle with severe mental illness, Nash would receive a Nobel Prize for this work, and would later be the subject of the book *A Beautiful Mind* and the film of the same title.) The Nash equilibrium occurs when both players have chosen a strategy from which neither has any rational incentive to deviate, irrespective of the other player's choices.[8]

Back to the guppies for a moment. If I'm a self-respecting guppy, I want to get the data about a sunfish's appetite with minimal risk of getting eaten in the process. My inspection partner wants exactly the same thing. The grim conclusion of game theory (a conclusion that led game theorists to recommend that the United States launch an unprovoked nuclear strike against the Soviet Union during the Cold War[9]) is that a self-interested actor competing with another self-interested actor should always defect. The Nash equilibrium for the prisoner's dilemma—the thing you should always do when your first priority is saving your own skin and you can't completely trust your partner—is to loaf during predator inspection, to rat out your accomplice, to unleash your ICBMs on your Cold War adversary. To do otherwise is to invite the misery that is the fate of patsies everywhere. Unless your opponent is extraordinarily stupid or insane, count on him to come to the same conclusion. It would be good for the fish if they engaged in predator inspection, good for criminals if they didn't betray each other, and good for the world if we refrained from nuclear first strikes, but we should expect that self-interested actors will always defect. Right?

Well, we should thank our lucky stars that U.S. presidents don't take the advice of mathematicians too seriously: in real life, fish really do inspect predators cooperatively. In real life, there often is honor among thieves. And we actually managed to avert mutually assured nuclear destruction with our Cold War enemies. Why don't these silly fish, thieves, and commanders-in-chief just do what the mathematicians recommend?

Do It Again

The reason why cooperative action in the prisoner's dilemma is more common than the early game theorists would have predicted is that in real life, we can't insulate our choices from their effects on people's behavior toward us in the future. In real life, by and large, social organisms don't roam the world at random in search of new partners with whom they can play one-shot prisoner's dilemmas. Instead, they play a much smaller set of *iterated* games—multi-round games—with a much smaller set of partners. The individual fish in a group of guppies or sticklebacks know each other, so they can reward and punish each other in the next round of a predator-inspection "game" depending on how they behaved in this round. Most of humans' prisoner's dilemmas are iterated games too. We share refrigerator space with the same co-workers day in and day out. Therefore, it's in our best interest to keep the refrigerator clean so that our co-workers will appreciate our efforts and try to reciprocate. Any single round of play is really a game within a larger game.

It was a political scientist named Robert Axelrod who worked out the math of the iterated prisoner's dilemma. Axelrod suspected that when the prisoner's dilemma is extended from a one-shot game to an iterated game, the "all-defect" strategy, which is the Nash equilibrium for the one-shot game, might not work so well. Axelrod began to explore this possibility back in the late 1970s by asking his game theory colleagues to devise strategies for playing the prisoner's dilemma that would score the most points over many rounds of play.

Fourteen entries were submitted for the tournament. The simplest strategy (called tit-for-tat, which was submitted by the Canadian game theorist Anatol Rapaport) was so simple that it only required four lines of code in the Fortran computer language. The most baroque strategy (submitted by a theorist who remained anonymous) required seventy-seven lines of Fortran code. Each of the strategies played against each of the others in five different matches. Each match was an iterated game consisting of two hundred prisoner's dilemmas. Every strategy's performance was based on the average number of points it scored in all of the matches that it played.

Axelrod found something surprising: the best performer was the humble (and concise) tit-for-tat. Tit-for-tat started the first round of each match by cooperating, and then it continued cooperating as long as its partner cooperated on the previous round. If tit-for-tat's partner defected on a given round, then tit-for-tat would defect on the next round. If the partner ever went back to cooperating, then tit-for-tat would resume cooperation as well. This is strikingly similar to the strategy that the Trinidadian guppies appeared to be using in cooperative predator inspection: start out nice, respond to cooperation with more cooperation, and respond to defections by defecting.[10] Axelrod had discovered something through computer simulation that guppies and sticklebacks had acquired through natural selection.

To make sure these results were reliable, Axelrod advertised the results of the first tournament and then solicited entries for a second tournament. Sixty-two strategies were submitted for the second tournament. Rapaport submitted tit-for-tat again. This time, the most complicated strategy was thirty times as long as tit-for-tat.

In the second tournament, all sixty-two strategies played against each other and against a strategy that chose cooperative moves and defective moves at random. Tit-for-tat won again. One of the interesting things about tit-for-tat's success in Axelrod's tournaments is that it wasn't particularly strong in any of the matches it played. Tit-for-tat performed so well over the long run not by beating its opponents into the ground, but by tying its opponents in many high-scoring matches. In fact, tit-for-tat can't beat *any opponent* because all it does is start out nice and then copy its opponent's moves. Tit-for-tat's strength comes not from the exercise of raw power but from its ability to encourage win-win behavior.

FROM ITERATED GAMES TO EVOLUTIONARY ONES

The history of game theory can be divided into two eras: Before Axelrod and After Axelrod. Before Axelrod, game theory was an effort to understand the behavior of people. After Axelrod came on the scene, game theory became a window into the behavior of all living things. Having conducted his two tournaments, Axelrod's next step was to turn the tournament into a computer simulation of "survival of the fittest." He took the sixty-two strategies submitted for the second tournament and allowed them to compete with each other, against themselves, and against a strategy that responded randomly. According to the rules that Axelrod established to simulate evolution, these sixty-three strategies existed in equal proportions at the beginning of the simulation, and at the end of each generation of competition, the strategies "reproduced" in proportion to their success in winning points during that generation. In this manner, strategies that were highly successful against their partners had a lot of offspring; those that were less successful had relatively few offspring. Axelrod thereby managed to simulate the evolutionary proposition that success breeds success.

Again, tit-for-tat came out on top. After a few hundred generations of competition and reproduction, most of the highly exploitable strategies (that is, strategies that didn't respond to defection by defecting in successive rounds) had been killed off by the nastier strategies (strategies that defected often or took advantage of cooperators). However, retaliatory strategies such as tit-for-tat could keep up with the nastier strategies by stalemating them in match after match.

After the nasty strategies had killed off all of the suckers, there was nobody left for them to pick on, so they picked on each other. As they did so, their numbers declined because their matches against each other were low-scoring matches; thus they failed to reproduce in sufficient numbers. Tit-for-tat continued to stalemate the nasty strategies, but in its competitions with itself, it could rack up high scores over and over again. As the nasty strategies suffered from low-scoring games and tit-for-tat benefited from high-scoring games when playing its twin, tit-for-tat increased its representation in the population.

Eventually, tit-for-tat became the most prolific strategy in Axelrod's computer-simulated ecology. By the end of the thousandth generation, almost 15 percent of the organisms were using tit-for-tat (recall that it constituted only 1 out of every 63 strategies at the outset), and its market share was still growing. Thus tit-for-tat appeared to be an evolutionarily stable strategy—evolution's version of the Nash equilibrium—that couldn't be overtaken by any other strategy. In Axelrod's semiconductor world, tit-for-tat seemed to be on its way to genetic immortality.[11]

WHAT MAKES TIT-FOR-TAT SO SUCCESSFUL?

Tit-for-tat has four characteristics that made it such a winner. First, tit-for-tat is a *nice* strategy: it always begins its matches by cooperating. As a result, tit-for-tat is always ready to benefit from mutual cooperation if its partner is similarly disposed. Second, tit-for-tat is a *retaliatory* strategy: if its partner defects in a given round, tit-for-tat will retaliate reflexively during the next round. By doing so, tit-for-tat prevents nasty strategies from capitalizing on its niceness. Third, tit-for-tat is a *forgiving* strategy: if tit-for-tat's partner returns to cooperation after a defection, tit-for-tat will also resume cooperation in the next round. Fourth, tit-for-tat is a *clear* strategy: it starts out nice and then repeats whatever its partner did on the previous round. In other words, it plays nice when its partners are playing nice, it's vindictive when its partners are playing nasty, and it's forgiving when its partners mend their nasty ways. That's it. Tit-for-tat doesn't overthink things. It's just the Golden Rule followed by the norm of reciprocity.

Should you retaliate when your cooperation partners harm your interests to maximize their own? Well, sometimes, yes. Tit-for-tat is a role model for this sort of eye-for-an-eye retaliation. Retaliation teaches your cooperation partners that they shouldn't try to take advantage of you and that they'd better not renege on their commitments. As we've seen in previous chapters, a propensity for tit-for-tat's style of revenge has evolved in many animal species as a method for enforcing social contracts.

But tit-for-tat also shows that if you want to be *really* successful, you can't hold on to that grudge forever. Tit-for-tat counsels us that the key to long-term success—to say nothing of genetic immortality—is a willingness to forgive partners who defect but later return to cooperation. There's no point in holding a grudge: cooperation leads to much higher payoffs than does an interminable string of defections. So if you can get back to cooperation after defection, which tit-for-tat can, then your interactions will be high-scoring interactions for you and your partner both. A willingness to forgive periodic defections—if one's partner has demonstrated a desire to return to cooperation—is indispensable for creating win-win games.

In conducting these initial studies, Axelrod intentionally omitted some of the complications of evolution, not to mention the messy wow and flutter of real social interactions. But it's possible to add some messiness back into these computer simulations, and by doing so, to make them more realistic. As it turns out, the more we tweak these "tinker-toy models"[12] of evolution so that they more closely resemble the social conditions in which ancestral humans might have evolved their ultra-cooperativeness, the more they seem to favor the evolution of strategies that are even *more* forgiving than tit-for-tat.

BRING ON DA NOISE

Most of us, I think, have had the experience of trying to say something clever, and then watching in horror as our good-natured sentiment comes out of our mouths sounding rude or insulting. Even when we really are trying to play nicely with our cooperation partners, our best intentions sometimes backfire. Organisms of all shapes and sizes occasionally make mistakes in executing their cooperative strategies.[13] Game theorists call it "noise."

Noise—the possibility that you might accidentally defect when you mean to cooperate, or that your partner might read your genuinely cooperative behavior as a defection—is a big problem for tit-for-tat. Even when the error rate is very low—say, when there's only a 1 percent chance of making an error in implementing your intentions or in reading your partner's intentions—here's what happens when tit-for-tat plays its twin. Both strategies start out nice, but eventually one of them makes a mistake. Player A wants to cooperate but instead does something that harms Player B, or else Player B misreads Player A's cooperative intentions. In either case, B will then defect against A as (what it considers to be) a justifiable act of retaliation. And because player A is also playing tit-for-tat, A will then defect on the following round in response to B's defection, and so on. Two players who started out playing the Golden Rule end up locked in an endless cycle of retaliation. Axelrod called this absurd scenario the *echo effect*. He recognized that when the echo effect is a possibility, tit-for-tat isn't forgiving enough.[14]

Martin Nowak and Karl Sigmund—a team of mathematical biologists—were among the first to investigate the evolution of cooperation in a noise-laden world. Like Axelrod before them, Nowak and Sigmund created a computer simulation of the evolutionary process. But unlike Axelrod, they allowed the organisms in this computer-simulated world to make mistakes in implementing their own rules and in interpreting the actions of others. Their simulation ran for millions of generations; every hundredth generation, they added mutant strategies to see if the mutants could invade the evolving system.

Nowak and Sigmund found, as Axelrod had, that evolution progressed in stages. Early on, the nastier strategies (those with a penchant for defecting) quickly established firm footholds in the population by winning lots of matches against nice partners (those that were a bit too keen to cooperate). However, after defeating most of the nice guys, the nasty strategies were left with nobody else to take advantage of. So they preyed upon each other. As they did so, they typically became locked into low-scoring game after low-scoring game, so eventually they too went the way of the dodo bird. The demise of the nasty strategies allowed tit-for-tat (which seemed to be an optimal compromise between strategies that are too nice and strategies that are too nasty) to increase its market share.

Tit-for-tat's days were also numbered, however. After many generations, even tit-for-tat began to struggle because of the small probability of making a mistake in implementing its intentions. Remember that even a single false move causes two players using tit-for-tat to become locked in a ridiculous cycle of negative reciprocity. This inability to overcome implementation errors was tit-for-tat's fatal flaw in Nowak and Sigmund's noisy world.

So what follows the reign of tit-for-tat? When they initially explored this question, Nowak and Sigmund crowned a strategy called "Generous tit-for-tat" as the ultimate evolutionary winner. Generous tit-for-tat, like its namesake, forgives a partner who returns from defection to cooperation, but Generous tit-for-tat has an additional feature: it grants forgiveness *unconditionally* (that is, without first requiring a subsequent round of cooperation from its partner) about one-third of the time. In other words, if you defect while playing a match with Generous, there is a one-in-three chance that Generous will turn the other cheek and continue cooperating. This tendency to forgive unconditionally keeps Generous from becoming hobbled by noise. Pleased with these results, Nowak and Sigmund wrote that after Generous appears on the scene in sufficient numbers, "Evolution then stops."[15]

But eighteen months later, they had to eat those words. More extensive simulations had subsequently convinced Nowak and Sigmund that tit-for-tat isn't the end of evolution. Instead, it merely paves the way for invasion by more unconditionally cooperative mutant strategies, which in turn paves the way for a reinvasion by mutant strategies that are more prone to defection, which takes the evolutionary process right back where it started. Undeterred, Nowak and Sigmund kept searching for an evolutionarily stable strategy. They eventually discovered that a strategy called "win-stay, lose-shift" could indeed become evolutionarily stable.[16] Win-stay, lose-shift always cooperates on the first trial. Then it follows the simple rule, "win-stay, lose-shift." That is, it repeats what it did on the previous round if it won the "temptation" payoff (the big payoff that comes from defecting while your partner cooperates) or the reward for mutual cooperation (which yields the second highest payoff), but it switches actions if it received the punishment for mutual defection (the next-to-worst payoff) or the sucker's payoff (the worst possible payoff). Win-stay, lose-shift seems to "learn" by viewing its bad outcomes as punishments and its good outcomes as reinforcers. Nowak and Sigmund gave it the nickname "Pavlov."

Pavlov forgives, but only after a mutual defection. If Pavlov and its partner both defected on the previous round, Pavlov "repents" and returns to cooperation on the next round. If Pavlov cooperated on the previous round and its partner defected, Pavlov retaliates during the next round (recall that one-third of the time, Generous tit-for-tat will forgive in this situation). Therefore, Pavlov is clearly less forgiving than Generous tit-for-tat is.

Axelrod, of course, read Nowak and Sigmund's Pavlov paper. Having spent the previous fifteen years describing the virtues of tit-for-tat and its ilk, he felt duty-bound to defend Generous tit-for-tat's sullied honor. So Axelrod and a colleague ran yet *another* simulation to see if slight changes in Nowak and Sigmund's assumptions (I'll spare you the details) led to better evolutionary performance for Generous tit-for-tat. Indeed, Generous looked like a real contender for evolutionary stability when other strategies it encountered hadn't yet adapted to noise. But when the other strategies had already been winnowed on the basis of their ability to tolerate noise, the evolutionarily stable strategy was not Generous tit-for-tat. Instead, it was a form of tit-for-tat that, if it has defected without justification, allows its partner to defect in retaliation without itself retaliating in return. Axelrod and his colleague called it "contrite tit-for-tat."[17]

Change yet another assumption about how the game is played, and you get evolutionary stability for a strategy called "firm-but-fair."[18] Firm-but-fair starts out in a cooperative frame of mind, and then it makes its next decision about how to behave based on its most recent choice and its partner's most recent choice. If those two choices were cooperative ones, firm-but-fair keeps cooperating. If its most recent choice was cooperation but its partner's most recent choice was defection, firm-but-fair retaliates. However, if firm-but-fair's partner responds to firm-but-fair's defection with a retaliation of its own, firm-but-fair returns to cooperation. Finally, if firm-but-fair most recently chose to defect, and its partner most recently chose to cooperate, firm-but-fair returns to cooperation on the next round. Thus firm-but-fair is nice, vindictive, willing to let bygones be bygones, and responsive to mercy (an alternative interpretation is that it's unwilling to exploit suckers). Firm-but-fair will take one on the chin as punishment for its own bad behavior, and it readily accepts chastened sinners back into fellowship.

The fact that a few changed assumptions lead to such dramatically different evolutionary results might not inspire much confidence that these simulations can tell us anything at all about forgiveness and evolution. However, what these studies do allow us to say is this: "all defect" isn't evolutionarily viable. Ever. And in a world with noise, even moderately forgiving tit-for-tat isn't evolutionarily viable. In fact, *all* of the strategies that have a claim to evolutionary stability forgive their partners' defections *some of the time,* and some of these strategies forgive a lot of the time. Generous tit-for-tat forgives unconditionally one-third of the time and always forgives if its partner has returned to cooperation after defecting. Pavlov forgives defection if it has defected too. Contrite tit-for-tat forgives righteous retaliation. Firm-but-fair is willing to forgive its partner if they both defected in the previous round and if a previously selfish partner ever returns to cooperating. Whatever the details of the evolution of human cooperation, it seems, the organisms that survived the evolutionary winnowing process had forgiveness in their cognitive toolkits.

EVOLUTION'S "THREE STRIKES" RULE

Still other twists on these evolutionary games deserve our attention, for they suggest that evolution may have shaped social creatures such as human beings to be hyperactively forgiving of a small circle of good friends and neighbors, but rather stingy in dispensing forgiveness to strangers and members of outgroups.

Let's start with a thought experiment. Open your address book and find the names of the eight people (other than relatives) with whom you have to cooperate most often to accomplish your daily goals (let's assume you're currently on good terms with all of these people). Now imagine that one of those eight people does something offensive or harmful to you. Perhaps your next-door neighbors go away for the weekend and leave their dog outside to bark for three days and two nights. Perhaps your office mate, with whom you work on a lot of projects, tells an embarrassing story about you at a staff meeting. Perhaps a roommate can't come up with her share of the rent for another week. Quick—how would you respond?

The odds that you'd retaliate harshly against these people are pretty slim. If your neighbors' dog barks all weekend, you're unlikely to throw eggs on their car or dump the contents of their garbage can in the street. If a co-worker tells an embarrassing story about you, you're probably not going to spend a ton of time looking for a way to embarrass him at the next one. If your room-mate is late with her share of the rent (assuming this is a first offense), you're not going to kick her out. What you'll probably do is (a) nothing, or (b) confront the offender in a construc-tive way and try to get the problem fixed. If you're really upset, you might sulk and avoid the person for a couple of days. But after that, most of us would continue on with the relationship as if nothing had happened.[19] For all intents and purposes, we'd forgive.

We tend to let these sorts of offenses go for three reasons. The first reason is trivial: we don't typically seek revenge against our cooperation partners in such situations because the harms they cause us are usually not very severe. The second reason, at this point in the chapter, should be easy to see: Axelrod and company have taught us that real-life interactions are noisy, and too-hasty retaliation in a noisy world creates unnecessary cycles of revenge and counter-revenge. One swallow doesn't make a summer, and one "defection" doesn't turn your coopera-tion partner into your enemy.

But a third reason why we avoid retaliating against our closest cooperation partners is that we're stuck with them (up to a point, anyway). If we turn these friends into enemies when they occa-sionally do things that harm us, then we'll too frequently be back out in the friendship market looking for new people to play our prisoner's dilemmas with, and good cooperation partners can be hard to find.

Granted, revenge sometimes has useful social effects. But if things get out of hand with my next-door neighbor—as any-one who has ever been involved in a dispute with a neighbor knows—home life can become astonishingly unpleasant. In the end, selling my house and moving somewhere else could become my only alternative for ending the rancor, and that's often highly impractical. If your relationship with a co-worker goes off the rails because you've decided to seek revenge, you'll have to find someone else to help you get your projects done. Even finding a new roommate involves the costs of putting an advertisement in the paper, the effort of interviewing a bunch of people, and the discomfort that comes with having to break in a new roommate. Better the devil you know than the devil you don't. For this reason, we tend to be especially forgiving of the people with whom we share our daily lives. In fact, evolutionary simulations suggest that when dealing with good friends and neighbors, we may use a sort of "three strikes (or four, or even five) and you're out" rule.

Patrick Grim, a philosophy professor who tinkers with computer simulations and game theory, was the first to figure this out. He noted that in real life, living things reside somewhere in two-dimensional space. We've all got addresses—spots on the face of the earth where we can be found working, shopping, eating, and sleeping. And we've got company—a relatively small set of friends, neighbors, and co-workers with whom we conduct most of our important day-to-day interactions. Grim wanted to capture this reality of social relations, so he tweaked the noisy prisoner's dilemma so that the organisms all resided at specific points on the surface of a two-dimensional map. Picture a 64 × 64 grid made up of 4,096 squares. If you were one of the pixilated creatures in Grim's simulation, you would occupy one of those squares, and your square would be touching the squares of the eight people with whom you can cooperate.

Grim added a second bit of realism to his simulation: at the end of each round of play, he had the organisms look around to see how their neighbors were doing, and then they all changed strategies to mirror those of their most successful neighbors. If the organism itself did better than any of its neighbors, it stuck with the strategy that it had been using. This new little wrinkle was an important one for Grim to add because many organisms—humans, nonhuman primates, and birds, for example—are good at learning new tricks from other individuals. The human mind learns new innovations as quickly as it does because it has acquired a few learning biases, or rules of thumb. One of those rules of thumb is "copy the person who does it better than you" or "copy the successful."[20] So it's reasonable to imagine our ancestors sorting out their strategies by looking around them to see who does well, and then simply copying the one neighbor who fares the best.

With these new conditions in place—giving each strategy an address (and some neighbors) and a "copy your most successful neighbor" rule—Grim found an evolutionarily stable strategy that's even more forgiving than Generous tit-for-tat. Remember Generous tit-for-tat, which unconditionally forgives about one-third of the time? In Grim's analysis, the evolutionarily stable strategy forgives unconditionally about *two-thirds* of the time. In other words, for every three unjustified slaps it received, it turned the other cheek to two of them.[21]

More than a decade after Grim published his results, two other evolutionary modelers came to a similar conclusion without even having known about Grim's earlier work. Dan Hruschka is a newly minted anthropologist (he was finishing up a post-doc at the time of this writing), and Joseph Henrich is an anthropology professor at Emory University. I won't even try to summarize the technical details of their work, but suffice it to say that they started with the assumption that social creatures have a social instinct to form "cliques"—small groups of good buddies who will prefer each other as cooperation partners over other potential partners. When you make this assumption, what evolves is a complex set of decision rules that dictate the following: "If the person who hurt you is one of your good buddies, forgive that person about 80 percent of the time. When playing against strangers, defect most of the time, unless you are short on good buddies. If you are, then take chances with strangers and start out by playing nice to see if you can turn those strangers into friends."[22]

Assuming that these modeling efforts by Grim, and now Hruschka and Henrich, really do a better job of simulating the ecological and social conditions in which humans evolved than do the models that came before (and I think they do), then it's fair to conclude that humans may have evolved to be almost promiscuously forgiving of their neighbors and good friends. The take-home message is clear: forgiveness isn't something that evolved to smooth over our relations with just anybody. Instead, it exists in large measure to help us preserve a relatively small number of geographically close neighbors or a small clique of trusted associates. According to these models, forgiveness helps us develop a social environment in which we can benefit from direct reciprocity.

ENTER GOSSIP

All the same, we do sometimes forgive people with whom we aren't friends or close relatives—even people who haven't distinguished themselves as particularly good cooperation partners. Theoretical biologists can explain this, too, but to do so, they go beyond concepts such as neighborhoods and social learning so that they can invoke other characteristic features of human society—features such as social norms, reputation, and, most surprising of all, gossip.

Before language, humans' ancestors had to rely on nonverbal means for learning about others. If you wanted to know what someone was like—whether she was aggressive, docile, selfish, timid, generous, trustworthy, forgiving, or whatever—you had to learn it for yourself, either by relating to that individual directly (that is, by learning the hard way), or by observing with your own eyes how that person treated other people. However, once language came online, new options opened up. Most important, it became possible to learn about others by talking to other people about them. There was no more need to rely on learning the hard way, no more need to rely on seeing things with your own eyes. Gossip became an option for figuring out what other people were like, and consequently, for figuring out how to interact with them. The evolutionary biologist Robin Dunbar has proposed that this evolved facility with language explains why humans' social groups exploded in size relative to the size of the social groups in which other primates live.[23]

Through the social sharing that language makes possible, people acquire reputations. These reputations have cash value: if you have a good reputation, people will be inclined to cooperate with you and treat you with respect. If you have a bad reputation, people will steer clear of you or actively work against you. Some theoretical biologists have surmised that reputation might enable cooperation to evolve in a population of self-interested individuals—even if those individuals interact with each other only once. In this evolutionary scenario, reputations are used to establish cooperation not through direct reciprocity (as when two people play an iterated prisoner's dilemma game), but through *indirect* reciprocity. Under indirect reciprocity, if you defect against me during our prisoner's dilemma, I won't retaliate against you by defecting the next time we play each other (as has been the case in all of the simulations we've been discussing until now), because there won't be a next time. Instead, I'll retaliate with my mouth: I'll tell everybody (that is, all of your future cooperation partners) what a scammer you are, which will cause them to treat you differently in the future. If you help me by cooperating during our prisoner's dilemma, I'll return the favor by telling everybody what a mensch you are.

This leads to an interesting change in how the prisoner's dilemma influences fitness. After every round of play, your fitness changes according to the usual prisoner's dilemma contingencies (if you defect against a cooperator, you earn more than if you cooperate with a cooperator, and so forth), but it also changes according to how your reputation is affected. Thus the effect of any single choice on your fitness might have more to do with how its reputational consequences influence how people treat you in the future than with its direct costs and benefits.

In this artificial world that the indirect reciprocity theorists envision, there are also complex reputational dynamics at work. You enter an interaction with a good or bad reputation, and you interact with someone who has a good or bad reputation. These social facts shape your behavior and your partner's behavior during the game, which affects not only your immediate outcome but also your reputation after the game. With a potentially new reputation in place, you might make a different choice in your next prisoner's dilemma, which would in turn influence your subsequent reputation, and so on. Through this dynamical process by which behavior affects reputation, which in turn affects behavior, ad infinitum, evolution causes norms to emerge. These norms dictate two things: the choices that people should make in their own prisoner's dilemmas, and the rules by which people's behavior influences their subsequent reputations.

In a system such as this—with all of the possible prisoner's dilemma strategies and all of the possible rules for how to respond to people with different types of reputations, a staggering number of combinations are possible—4,096 unique pairs of dynamics and strategies, to be exact. Which ones become evolutionarily stable—while also yielding high payoffs for cooperation? Two biologists at Kyushu University in Japan explored all 4,096 possibilities. As usual, they assumed that errors sometimes happen—that people can accidentally defect when they mean to cooperate, and that people can accidentally mistake someone with a "good" reputation for someone with a "bad" one, and vice versa.

The scientists found that under these conditions, only eight social norms become evolutionarily stable while providing high payoffs for cooperation. I don't have to describe each of these "leading eight" individually to convey how the entire package works. First, if you have a good reputation and you meet someone with a good reputation, you should cooperate. You'll both benefit from mutual cooperation and you'll both maintain your positive reputations. Second, if you have a good reputation and you interact with someone who defects—no matter what his or her reputation—that person is assigned a bad reputation for the next round. Defecting against a good person earns you a scarlet letter. Third, if you have a good reputation and you interact with someone with a bad reputation, you should defect. This punishes people for the selfish actions that led to their bad reputations in the first place, and you get to keep your good reputation. Fourth, if you have a bad reputation and you interact with someone who has a good reputation, you should cooperate. No matter whether your partner cooperates or defects, your good behavior will restore your good name in the next round.

Isn't that a tidy little ethical system? Good people should cooperate with other good people. People who defect against good people lose their good reputations and should be punished. If you have a good reputation and you choose to punish someone who has a bad reputation, it's credited to you as righteousness. If you have a bad reputation and you cooperate with someone who has a good reputation, expect punishment because of your bad reputation, but take heart because you can look forward to forgiveness after that. Forgiveness is an evolutionarily vital part of this ethical package because there has to be a way to restore people to good standing so that they'll be motivated to return to cooperation with all of the other cooperators in the population. If forgiveness weren't available, the average gains of cooperation would slowly decline in the population with each successive generation.

What's so striking about this set of norms is how intuitive it all seems. Those gossiping, status-conscious, computer-dwelling organisms sound just like humans! The intoxicating possibility here is that these norms seem so intuitive to us because our social instincts really *did* evolve in the way that these results suggest. Of course life is more complicated than any world we can simulate with zeroes and ones. But perhaps ethical systems such as this one, which are tough on defectors while nevertheless creating a way for bad people to be forgiven, are the inevitable outcome within populations of evolving, gossiping individuals who need each other's help but can't always use direct reciprocity to get it.[24]

FORGIVENESS IS THE BRIDESMAID; COOPERATION IS THE BRIDE

I think it's only fitting that these evolutionary simulations, with their iterations and their noise, have led to seemingly interminable cycles of scientific inquiry with no clear end in sight. Even though Bob Axelrod has been thinking about the evolution of cooperation for over a quarter of a century, he tells me that he's still not sure what to expect from natural selection. Nobody is. What you get from these models depends utterly upon your basic assumptions about how the games are played and the additional faculties with which you endow your game-playing organisms. Even so, studies with living, breathing, sentient human beings show that Pavlov and Generous tit-for-tat—two moderately forgiving strategies—are quite popular in real life, and that people fare quite well when using them or when playing with partners who do.[25] And it bears repeating that all of the strategies in the running for evolutionary stability tend to forgive at least *some of the time* and some of them forgive *a lot of the time*—especially when playing with good buddies and neighbors, and especially when reputations and gossip enter the picture.

If we distill all of these insights down to the bare essentials, we end up with a sort of recipe for the evolution of forgiveness. First, put some game-playing organisms together in the same niche. Second, let the organisms play one-shot games with lots of their neighbors, but also let them play iterated games with a more restricted set of partners who live close by. Third, make them cliquish creatures that prefer to limit their iterated endeavors to a small circle of trusted neighbors or friends. Fourth, let the organisms make occasional mistakes in implementing their intentions and in reading the intentions of others. Fifth, give them the ability to learn by observing what works for their neighbors. Sixth, give them communicative powers so they can tattle on each other and sing each other's praises. Let this blend cook for many generations, and you're likely to end up with creatures who are almost manically forgiving of their good friends and neighbors, and who are even willing to cut a break for a reformed sinner.

The evolutionary theorists who do this research, like all celebrity chefs, make cooking look easy. But is this recipe for forgiveness really any good? If so, it ought to have produced modern-day species that have a penchant for forgiving as a way of keeping their cooperative relationships intact. Predator-inspecting guppies are retaliatory, to be sure, but remember that they're also willing to forgive the repentant slacker. Are there other species that natural selection has endowed with a similar propensity to forgive? Given the evolutionary advantages that can accrue to organisms that are inclined to forgive under certain circumstances (those three words again), we should expect that many other flesh-and-blood creatures that populate our planet today—particularly those that benefit from cooperation with a long-standing group of associates—are inclined to forgive. As it turns out, such creatures aren't hard to find.

CHAPTER SIX

THE FORGIVENESS INSTINCT

"The discoverer of the role of forgiveness in the realm of human affairs was Jesus of Nazareth," wrote the political philosopher Hannah Arendt. "The fact that he made this discovery in a religious context and articulated it in a religious language is no reason to take it less seriously in a strictly secular sense."[1] In a 2003 interview, the late author Kurt Vonnegut made essentially the same observation: "Two radical ideas have been introduced into human thought. One of them is that energy and matter are pretty much the same sort of stuff. That's Einstein. The other is that revenge is a bad idea. Revenge is an enormously popular idea but, of course, Jesus came along with the radical idea of forgiveness. If you're insulted, you have to square accounts. So this invention by Jesus is as radical as Einstein's."[2]

If you buy into the disease metaphor of revenge that I introduced back in Chapter One, then Arendt's and Vonnegut's "creation story" may sound right on target to you. If revenge really is a disease, then maybe it's appropriate to imagine a time, long ago, when a revenge-weary human race was struggling under the burden of its own vengeful impulses, just waiting for some Einstein of the moral realm to arrive on the scene and come up with a solution to the problem—to "discover" or "invent" forgiveness.

However, if you find yourself buying into the evolutionary account of forgiveness that we've been exploring, then you have to take the "Arendt-Vonnegut hypothesis" with a grain of salt. According to the evolutionary perspective, forgiveness isn't an idea that Jesus or anybody else had to invent (although, as we'll see in a couple of later chapters, Jesus did have some things to say about forgiveness that were pretty innovative). The evolutionary perspective holds out the possibility that organisms that are motivated purely by self-interest can develop a penchant to forgive solely through the action of natural selection. Forgiveness enables them to promote their own inclusive fitness by avoiding a self-defeating tendency to over-harshly punish their genetic relatives, and it enables them to forge ahead with their bumbling efforts to cooperate with each other, despite the mistakes that they and their cooperation partners will inevitably make. The simplest social organisms we can imagine—creatures whose only social instincts can be summarized in a few lines of computer code—may be capable of "discovering" or "inventing" forgiveness solely through natural selection's action upon their behavioral repertoires, without any help from moral exemplars, religious leaders, political theorists, or novelists, thank you very much.

LET'S GET REAL

Theoretical biologists' research on the prisoner's dilemma certainly leaves one with the impression that natural selection could have programmed a propensity to forgive into many animal minds, including human minds, but aside from some fish playing a tit-for-tat strategy during their predator-inspection games, we haven't yet seen much scientific evidence for a "forgiveness instinct" in real, living creatures—certainly not any in human beings. Theoretical biology shows that forgiveness *might* have evolved to help organisms achieve fitness by promoting the fitness of their genetic relatives and by cooperating with nonrelatives, but did it *actually* evolve in this way? Do human beings or any other organisms really have a built-in penchant to forgive (friends and family in particular), courtesy of natural selection?

We can't go back in time to see how forgiveness evolved, but all is not lost. If natural selection acted upon ancestral humans to turn us into a species with a natural inclination to forgive our family members and cooperation partners, then we should find evidence for it by looking at how, when, where, and why humans and other social animals engage in the business of forgiveness today.

In the past three decades, animal researchers have made a profound and unexpected discovery that has revolutionized our understanding of conflict, aggression, and peacemaking: when group-living animals get into aggressive conflicts with their kin and their friends, many of these conflicts end with friendly reconciliations. This discovery has tremendous implications for understanding the human capacity for forgiveness.

A brief semantic digression into the concepts of "reconciliation" and "forgiveness" now seems inescapable.

RECONCILIATION AND FORGIVENESS

Philosophers and scientists often bend over backward to make fine-grained distinctions between the concepts of reconciliation and forgiveness, but for the purpose of trying to understand the evolutionary origins of forgiveness, I think that the laborious distinctions are mostly a tempest in a teapot. Reconciliation and forgiveness aren't conceptually *identical*, but they probably have the same evolutionary roots.

In defining forgiveness, scholars usually focus on the idea that when people forgive an offender, they come to feel less vengeful and less bitter, and they experience the return of positive motivations and good will—perhaps even love—toward the offender. Forgiveness, therefore, is a private process of getting over your ill will and negative emotions, and replacing those "negatives" with "positives" such as wishing the offender well or hoping for a new and improved relationship. Of course, these motivational and emotional changes often lead to better behavior toward the offender. If you've forgiven somebody, at a minimum you've stopped wanting revenge and you wish that person well, at least in a limited sense. You might not want to invite the person who injured you over to your place for a barbecue, but you don't crave a slow, painful death for that person, either. This is the bare-bones forgiveness of the prisoner's dilemma, with some positive feelings and intentions added into the mix.

Reconciliation, many scholars insist, is a different kettle of fish. Biologists define reconciliation in a straightforward, behavioral way: a "friendly reunion between former opponents" that "supposedly serves to return the relationship to normal levels of tolerance and cooperation."[3] Primatologists don't focus on intentions or motivations or feelings when defining reconciliation, perhaps because chimpanzees aren't very good at filling out questionnaires. Psychologists, however, who *do* consider people's feelings and intentions along with their actions, tend to define reconciliation as the restoration of a fractured relationship that happens because the victim has forgiven the offender *and* because the offender has mended his or her evil ways.[4]

So forgiveness is an internal process of getting over your ill will for an offender, experiencing a return of good will, and opening yourself up to the possibility of a renewed positive relationship with the offender. Reconciliation, in contrast, is a friendly reaching out to the person who harmed you (or the person whom you've harmed) that's supposed to fix the relationship breach. Or, if you're a psychologist, it's a relationship that's been repaired because the victim forgave and the offender repented.

I suppose this forgiveness-reconciliation distinction isn't completely useless. For one thing, it acknowledges that a friendly-seeming gesture from somebody you betrayed last month doesn't necessarily mean that all has been forgiven. Maybe I'm being nice to you in hopes of lulling you into complacency so that I can seek my revenge against you at a more opportune time. I can treat you nicely and still hate you. There's also a second reason why the forgiveness-reconciliation distinction might be useful: "forgiveness" is a morally loaded concept—"good people" are supposed to be forgiving. For this reason, it's nice to define forgiveness in such a way that people can be "forgiving" (by releasing their vengeful impulses and by wishing the offender well), even if it's ill-advised for them to resume relationships with offenders who haven't shown any remorse or any desire to change their nasty behavior (which would make reconciliation difficult and perhaps even dangerous). Defining forgiveness as something private therefore allows people to be "forgiving" without also having to be doormats.

However, reconciliation and forgiveness have much in common. Getting over your grudge and starting to feel positively again toward someone who harmed you ("forgiving") must surely be one of the most important psychological causes of reconciliation. If you had to guess why two people have had a "friendly reunion" that supposedly returned "the relationship to normal levels of tolerance and cooperation," you'd usually be right to guess that it was because the victim had forgiven the transgressor. Indeed, relationship restoration is probably the most basic social effect of forgiveness.[5] Similarly, if a fractured relationship hadn't returned to "normal levels of tolerance and cooperation," you'd suspect that one of two ingredients was missing: either the victim hadn't forgiven or the offender hadn't repented (or both).

All to say that reconciliation, at least in humans, seems to be the point of forgiveness. If natural selection really did outfit people with an ability to forgive (you can be the judge of that soon enough), it wasn't because natural selection was concerned with cheering people up or helping them to release their pent-up negative emotions (even though forgiveness often does exactly that). Instead, as we've seen, the main adaptive function of forgiveness seems to be helping individuals preserve their valuable relationships.[6] Because forgiveness so reliably precedes reconciliation in human beings, it seems safe to hazard a guess that something like forgiveness (an internal motivational and emotional change) precedes reconciliation in nonhuman animals too, if only we could measure it.

Well, we can't—not exactly, anyway. Nevertheless, by giving some close attention to post-conflict behavior in nonhuman primates and other mammals, we'll start to get a picture of something that looks an awful lot like a "forgiveness instinct."

WOLFGANG KÖHLER'S LITTLE RAP

In 1913, the gestalt psychologist Wolfgang Köhler was appointed director of the Prussian Academy of Science's primate research station, which was located on the island of Tenerife in the Canary Islands. In 1917, after several years of research at the station, he published a book on the nature of intelligence in nonhuman primates, *The Mentality of Apes*. In a lengthy postscript, Köhler goes beyond the book's primary subject matter and provides a detailed account of chimpanzees' social sensibilities. Here Köhler describes the reaction of a young chimpanzee that he had just punished with "a little rap" for repeatedly snatching food away from a weaker chimpanzee. What follows is, as far as I know, the first suggestion in the entire field of biology that nonhuman primates might possess a forgiveness instinct:

> The little creature, which I had punished for the first time, shrank back, uttered one or two heart-broken wails, as she stared at me horror-struck, while her lips were pouted more than ever. The next moment she had flung her arms round my neck, quite beside herself, and was only comforted by degrees, when I stroked her. *This need, here expressed, for forgiveness, is a phenomenon frequently to be observed in the emotional life of young chimpanzees* [italics mine]. . . . Even animals, who when they have been punished, at first boil with rage, throw one glances full of hate, and will not take a mouthful of food from a human being; when one comes again after a time will press up close . . . pressing one's fingers affectionately between their lips and making all other protests of friendship.[7]

It's a cute little anecdote, but it didn't exactly set the agenda for the next generation of research on primate social behavior. Chimpanzees that are raised around humans are different from those in the wild. For this reason, Köhler's story of a juvenile chimpanzee that wanted a hug from a caregiver after a conflict was probably interpreted by other researchers as no more than a behavioral oddity that arose from the animal's close contact with humans—if the story was noticed at all. It would be six more decades before scientists were ready to seriously consider the possibility that forgiveness and reconciliation might have a place in the social repertoire of a nonhuman animal.

THE KISS

The year 1979 was a watershed for scientific research on forgiveness. At the University of Michigan, a young associate professor named Robert Axelrod was soliciting entries for his prisoner's dilemma tournaments, and research to come from this work would soon reveal the indispensability of forgiveness for the evolution of cooperation. On another continent, a young primatologist named Frans de Waal was publishing the first scientific study of reconciliation in nonhuman animals.

Four years earlier, de Waal had begun a postdoctoral fellowship at the Arnhem Zoo in The Netherlands—one of the largest colonies of captive chimpanzees in the world. One November day in 1975, de Waal noticed a male and a female chimpanzee kissing each other. Chimpanzee kissing is not particularly rare, but what struck de Waal on this particular occasion was that only moments previously the male had attacked the female during a showy display of his physical strength and dominance. Even more unusual was the noisy ruckus that had erupted in the colony. As de Waal recounts the episode, "Suddenly the entire colony burst out hooting, and one male produced rhythmic noise on metal drums stacked up in the corner of the hall. In the midst of this pandemonium, two chimpanzees kissed and embraced."[8]

Why would two chimpanzees engage in affectionate contact just moments after one had assaulted the other? De Waal wondered if the friendly post-conflict interaction was intended to help them to undo the damage that the assault had inflicted on their relationship. Could it be that chimpanzees kiss and make up in the same way that people do?

De Waal was picking up where Köhler had left off, and he suspected he was onto something important. To verify that chimpanzee reconciliation was real, he began to gather proper scientific evidence. In 1979, de Waal and a co-worker published results from their observations of the Arnhem colony. They had discovered that friendly behaviors such as kissing, submissive vocalizing, touching, and embracing were actually quite common after chimpanzees' aggressive conflicts. In fact, they were the chimpanzees' *typical* responses to aggressive conflicts. The researchers observed 350 aggressive encounters and found that only 50, or 14 percent, of those encounters were preceded by some sort of friendly contact. However, 179, or 51 percent, of the aggressive encounters were followed by friendly contact. This was a staggering discovery: friendly contact was *even more common* after conflict than it was during conflict-free periods.[9] This finding sent a shock wave through the small community of researchers who studied primate social behavior.

The methods for measuring reconciliation have become more sophisticated since de Waal started this area of research back in 1979. Today, primatologists calculate the "Conciliatory Tendency," or CT. CT values range from 0 to 1. Values of 0 mean that the animals from a certain group aren't any friendlier toward each other after conflicts than they are during peacetime. In contrast, if the animals within the group had friendly encounters after every conflict, but never during peacetime, their CT would be 1. However, most primates do have a fair amount of friendly contact during nonconflict episodes (many primates spend hours each day grooming each other), so primate groups' CT scores rarely exceed .50.[10]

A Law of Attraction

Chimpanzees' CT estimates have ranged from a low of around .18 to highs in the .40s;[11] among chimpanzees in the wild, the estimates are toward the low end of that range.[12] These figures may look small (remember that they theoretically can go from 0 to 1), but they're bigger than zero, which means that friendly contact is *more* likely after conflict than it is during peacetime. What we ought to conclude from these figures is that chimpanzee conflicts lead most commonly to friendly contact, not interminable cycles of revenge or alienation. Wrangham and Peterson's "demonic" chimpanzees and de Waal's "good-natured" chimpanzees are one and the same. Conflict and aggression among chimpanzees (if they're from the same living group—which is a big "if") don't cause the combatants' relationships to end, and they don't cause them to become locked in interminable feuds. Instead, conflict and aggression seem to make combatants *more attractive* to each other. It seems perverse, but it's true.

Chimpanzees aren't the slightest bit unique in this respect. Other great apes, such as the bonobo and the mountain gorilla, also reconcile.[13] Several peaceable macaque species have conciliatory tendencies at least as high as those of chimpanzees. Even rhesus macaques, which are renowned for their nasty temperaments (on average, they're involved in eighteen aggressive episodes during every ten hours of observation,[14] and in my limited experience, they seem to love nothing better than throwing poo at visitors), show a tendency to reconcile after conflicts. Indeed, of the thirty or so primate species that have been studied, only a select few (for example, the ring-tailed lemur and the red-bellied tamarin) appear not to reconcile. Each reconciling species has its own signature style: chimpanzees kiss and embrace, bonobos partake of a seemingly endless variety of sexual activities, stumptailed macaques show each other their rear ends,[15] and baboons grunt at each other.[16] Most species also use heavy doses of grooming to patch things up. Humans are hardly the only primates that rely on hugs, backrubs, and make-up sex to iron out their conflicts.

It gets more interesting still, for reconciliation isn't even limited to primates. Goats, sheep, dolphins, and hyenas all tend to reconcile after conflicts (rubbing horns, flippers, and fur are common elements of these species' reconciliation gestures). Of the half-dozen or so nonprimates that have been studied, only domestic cats have failed to demonstrate a conciliatory tendency.[17] (If you own a cat, this probably comes as no surprise).

THE CONCILIATORY TENDENCY IN HUMANS

How does the conciliatory tendency of human beings compare to those of other species? Unfortunately, there isn't a single study of adult human beings that would allow us to directly compare humans and nonhumans. However, reconciliation has been studied in human children, and these studies clearly show that children as young as three or four have a strong conciliatory tendency. The CTs of young children from many countries (including Russia, the United States, and Japan) hover around a very respectable, chimpanzee-ish .40. A study of six- and seven-year-old children from the peace-loving Kalmyk (a minority ethnic group in Russia, descended from the Mongols, who practice a form of Buddhism and are known to be incredibly pacific) revealed a CT of .7, making Kalmyk children the most actively conciliatory critters of any species known on the planet today.[18]

The strategies that preschool children use for reconciling conflicts are a lot like the ones that we adults use when we've offended someone at work, angered a neighbor, or hurt our spouse's feelings. They explicitly apologize, invite each other to resume playing, offer to share the objects or goodies that they were fighting over, hug each other, and hold hands. These same basic strategies are used by children across cultures, but there's some cultural variation, too. Japanese preschoolers use apologies as their main strategy, whereas Swedish preschoolers use "invitations to play" as their main strategy,[19] and so on. But these cultural differences are trivial. What really matters is not how preschoolers' reconciliation gestures differ, but how they're all the same: little tykes from around the world seem to be working from the same basic palette of options for resuming positive relations after they've hurt each other's feelings.

This still leaves us wondering whether reconciliation, forgiveness, or both are universal among human adults. Until now, scientists have left one important stone unturned in their search for an answer.

FORGIVENESS AND RECONCILIATION: HUMAN UNIVERSALS?

In Chapter Four, I told you about Martin Daly and Margo Wilson's survey of the ethnographic data on a representative sample of sixty distinct world cultures, which showed that blood revenge following homicide is a "statistical universal." Their research showed that blood revenge has emerged as an important social phenomenon in 95 percent of the cultures they examined. This fact supports the notion that the human propensity for revenge is a product of evolution: if violent revenge were merely a "cultural artifact," rather than an intrinsic attribute of human nature, then why does it pop up in virtually every culture?

Daly and Wilson's results led me to wonder about the ethnographic data on those same sixty cultures and the story they might tell about the cross-cultural universality of forgiveness and reconciliation. After examining those ethnographic data, I discovered that the concepts of forgiveness, reconciliation, or both had been documented in fifty-six, or 93 percent, of the sixty cultures in the HRAF Probability Sample. The only four cultures in this sample whose tendencies to forgive or to reconcile have escaped anthropologists' notice are the Chukchee of the Arctic Circle, the Bororo of Brazil, and the Pawnee and Klamath Indians of North America. Across cultures, the concepts of forgiveness and reconciliation were considered appropriate in a variety of relational contexts, including spousal relations (the most common relational context in which forgiveness and reconciliation were discussed), relationships between children and their parents, relationships between warring communities, and relationships between neighbors embroiled in the mundane conflicts of daily life.

Is it possible that forgiveness and reconciliation really didn't exist among the Chukchee, Bororo, Pawnee, and Klamath? Sure, I suppose anything is possible. Or perhaps the anthropologists who studied those cultures just failed to notice the forgiveness and reconciliation that was occurring right under their noses. This second possibility is much more plausible. The evolutionary biologist David Sloan Wilson has observed that "It is actually difficult to find descriptions of forgiveness in hunter-gatherer societies, not because forgiveness is absent but because it happens so naturally that it often goes unnoticed."[20] I think Wilson may be correct, and not just about hunter-gatherers but about all cultures. Forgiveness and reconciliation may be so common and so taken for granted by anthropologists as to be regarded, quite literally, as nothing to write home about.

In either case, the 93 percent hit rate for evidence of forgiveness and reconciliation in those sixty cultures is tantalizingly close to the (somewhat arbitrary) 95 percent threshold that the anthropologist Donald Brown proposed as a standard for concluding that a behavior or psychological process is a "statistical" human universal.[21] I'm inclined to think that for subtle and often private processes such as forgiveness and reconciliation, a .930 batting average is close enough to the .950 mark that we're safe in treating these results as supportive of the idea that forgiveness and reconciliation really are standard-issue social instincts. Granted, revenge is probably a human universal, but reconciliation and forgiveness seem to be universal as well.[22]

The methods that people from these fifty-six "forgiveness-cultures" use for seeking forgiveness, granting forgiveness, and reconciling are fascinating, both for the commonalities across cultures and the diversity across cultures. Bottom-holding and horn-rubbing were found to be in short supply, but public apologies, gift exchanges, attempts to compensate injured parties, animal sacrifices, religious rituals, and third-party mediation are common elements of forgiveness and reconciliation in many cultures.

Of course, diversity abounds as well: the mystical Dogon people of Mali, for example (one of the three societies for which, you might recall, Daly and Wilson were unable to find evidence of blood revenge), have a wide variety of social mechanisms for making forgiveness happen. These include a ritual in which a contrite offender clasps the ankles of the person harmed, a ritual in which the perpetrator takes three bites from a piece of charcoal and then spits them back out in the presence of the victim, and the intervention of third parties who actively work to effect a reconciliation between feuding parties.[23] According to a Serbian tradition, the Sunday before the beginning of the Christian season of Lent was called "Forgiveness Day"—a day when young people were supposed to go around to their elders in order to mend any quarrels that had accumulated during the previous year.[24] The ethnographic evidence shows that even the Yanomamö people of Venezuela and Brazil, renowned among social scientists for their bellicosity rather than for their peacemaking prowess (thanks in large measure to the writings of the anthropologist Napoléon Chagnon[25]) have the potential to work out their violent conflicts in a conciliatory way, *under certain circumstances*.[26]

Needless to say, the proposition that forgiveness and reconciliation are human universals doesn't imply that forgiveness and reconciliation are practiced the world over in the same way, or with the same frequency—not any more than the fact that every society has a language implies that they all use Shona or Urdu or Aramaic or Esperanto. What's universal across cultures about language is that every culture has one. Likewise, although there are cultural differences in *what* people are willing to forgive, and *how* they go about doing it, it seems a fairly safe bet that human beings from every culture understand the concepts of forgiveness and reconciliation, appreciate the value of these processes, and under the right social conditions, will take the time and trouble to put them to use.

WHY *Do* GROUP-LIVING ANIMALS FORGIVE AND RECONCILE?

Biologists have introduced two hypotheses to explain why most group-living animals (humans included) have developed propensities to forgive or reconcile with each other. The first of these hypotheses, which has been championed by the UCLA anthropologist Joan Silk, is that animals reconcile in order to signal that they're sick of fighting and are ready to start treating each other nicely again.[27] According to this hypothesis, which Silk calls the "benign intent" hypothesis, the function of reconciliation is to convey to former enemies that they can drop the defensive attitude, lay down their arms, and resume lives of peace. By Silk's lights, then, reconciliation delivers two freedoms: first, it delivers a freedom from fear, second, it delivers a freedom to resume normal peaceful relations.[28]

The second hypothesis, espoused by Frans de Waal and many other primatologists, is the "valuable relationship" hypothesis: animals reconcile because it repairs important relationships that have been damaged by aggression. The very act of being nice to each other after a conflict "undoes" the relational damage that the aggression caused. By undoing this damage, the animals can preserve the relationships upon which they rely for their own fitness.[29]

If I had to pick *just one* of these two hypotheses (although, best I can tell, they're not really mutually exclusive), I think I'd go with the valuable relationship hypothesis. The idea that reconciliation gestures have the function of helping animals to restore their valuable relationships fits neatly with three independent lines of evidence. First, it squares with what the theoretical biologists have been saying about the adaptive value of forgiveness: ancestral organisms that were willing to forgive their kin ended up with better inclusive fitness than did those organisms that couldn't resist taking their pound of flesh whenever a genetic relative harmed them. And as the countless computer simulations show, organisms that were willing to forgive their cooperation partners were better at gleaning the benefits of cooperation. The evolutionary deck is stacked: natural selection leads self-interested organisms toward the acquisition of behavioral processes that allow them to forgive so that they can benefit from cooperative friendships and family relationships. This is exactly what the valuable relationship hypothesis says.

Second, the valuable relationship hypothesis fits nicely with the fact that the most conciliatory animals are also highly groupish. The great apes (excluding orangutans), lots of macaques, and many other mammals such as goats, dolphins, and hyenas are bound to their groups in important ways. They simply can't survive on their own in the wild because natural selection has made them interdependent. For example, group-living apes and monkeys assist each other in finding food, grooming, alerting each other to predators, raising young, climbing the social ladder, and hunting. Among dolphins, cooperation occurs in the context of reproduction (males work together to isolate females for sex). Goats and sheep rely on the other members of their herds for safety in numbers against predators.

Which brings us back to those nonreconciling domestic cats. Cats' only natural social groups are their birth families. Yes, a bunch of unrelated cats might look like a group because they live under a single owner's roof, eat from the same dish, scratch at the same post, and play with the same little toy mouse with the bell inside, but adult cats don't *need* other adult cats for much of anything. They're one of the few mammals whose conciliatory tendencies have been studied to date that truly are "bowling alone." And that's why they don't reconcile after conflicts.

The idea that some species became conciliatory as an adaptation to group living has received a special kind of direct support. In a head-to-head comparison of the conciliatory tendencies of two species of monkeys, de Waal and a colleague found that stumptailed macaques, whose communities are highly cohesive (probably because they have an evolutionary history marked by the need to defend themselves against external threats), are much more conciliatory than are the foul-tempered, scat-throwing rhesus macaques, whose communities are not particularly cohesive.[30]

A third bit of evidence for the valuable relationship hypothesis is this: the hypothesis implies that reconciliation will be more frequent among relatives and close allies than among nonrelatives and unrelated individuals who are not otherwise very important to each other. Research has supported this prediction very well. Primatologists found that the conciliatory tendency of a particular group of captive chimpanzees was about 60 percent among friends, but only about 20 percent among nonfriends. (How do you measure "friendship" among chimpanzees? You figure out who spends the most time socializing with whom. Friends spend a lot of time sitting in each other's presence and grooming each other. Nonfriends don't.)[31] In stumptailed macaques, the conciliatory tendency is less than 25 percent among nonfriends, but around 50 percent among friends.[32]

In perhaps the most striking demonstration of how the value of a relationship affects whether a conflict will be reconciled, a couple of scientists calculated the conciliatory tendencies of seven pairs of female long-tailed macaques before and after an experimental manipulation of relationship value. In the first phase of the experiment, the researchers simply examined how often these seven pairs of individuals reconciled. Averaging across the seven pairs, about 25 percent of their conflicts got reconciled. In phase two, the seven pairs of individuals were trained to cooperate with each other in order to get food. If one partner wanted to eat, she had to wait until the other one wanted to eat. Then they could work together to gain access to the food. No cooperation, no food. In other words, the researchers used experimental methods to turn the macaques' relationships into *valuable* relationships. After they had been trained to work together in order to obtain food, the average rate of reconciliation doubled to about 50 percent. When group-living animals are given the choice between (a) reconciling with a valuable relationship partner who has harmed them, or (b) holding on to their grudges but going hungry, they generally choose the reconciled relationship and the full belly.[33]

So we're starting to cook up a good just-so story for why group-living animals forgive and reconcile: by doing so, they can preserve valuable relationships with blood relatives and cooperation partners. This is exactly the kind of just-so story we're looking for: one with reams of scientific evidence to back it up.

ANXIOUS TO FORGIVE

After Terry the stumptailed macaque has had a fight with his buddy Joe, Terry probably doesn't start thinking, "My friendship with Joe is really important to me. And the pain I've had to suffer because of what he did to me doesn't outweigh the benefits that I'm likely to enjoy in the future by mending our friendship. Maybe I should try to patch things up with him. Maybe I ought to go grab his rear end—just to let him know that I want to be friends again." It can't be a rational thought process that motivates Terry to mend things, because stumptailed macaques don't have the capacity for rational thought. Instead, anxious tension seems to be the motivating force. Anxiety is an unpleasant feeling for humans and nonhumans alike, and we're motivated to find ways to rid ourselves of it. For the nonhuman primates, reconciliation does the job quite nicely.

We can't ask nonhuman animals to tell us whether they feel anxious, but we can infer it from their behavior. For many species, so-called self-directed behaviors such as scratching, yawning, and shaking seem to be good indicators that an individual is anxious.[34] A primatologist discovered that primates who have had recent conflicts scratch themselves furiously. He also discovered that the stronger the relationship between the two individuals prior to the conflict, the more furious the self-scratching afterwards. Finally, when the aggressive episodes are reconciled, self-scratching subsides, which suggests that reconciliation reduces anxiety.[35] Another good indicator of anxiety is increased heart rate. When rhesus macaques have a conflict, their heart rates go up; after the combatants reconcile, their heart rates go back to normal.[36]

Nonhuman primates' choices to reconcile, then, seem to be driven by their feelings. When a valuable relationship is disrupted by aggression or conflict, they get anxious, they try to patch things up, and presto! They become less anxious as a result. But we humans aren't such slaves to our emotions. Unlike apes and monkeys, we're capable of making conscious, rational decisions about whether to forgive someone who has harmed us. If somebody has injured you, it's easy to sit down and draw up a list of the costs and benefits of forgiving and a comparable list of the costs and benefits of holding a grudge. You can also reflect on abstract moral principles—principles such as justice, retribution, and care—to help you figure out what to do. After all of this soul-searching, you can then choose whether to forgive or reconcile in a thoughtful, rational way. This could be a much better model for how the human forgiveness process works, except for how incorrect it is.

Now granted, maybe there really are some people out there who could reason their way into forgiveness in such a fashion, but just because we *could* base our decisions to forgive on rationality and moral principles doesn't mean that we actually *do*. Moral choices are deeply influenced by emotion and intuition, perhaps even more strongly than they're affected by reason.[37] This is probably true of most instances of forgiveness, too: you're more likely to forgive a brother, sister, parent, or good friend because "it just felt right" or because "I missed spending time with her" or because "I felt sorry for him" than because you concluded that it was the most rational or morally defensible thing to do.

Rationality and moral reasoning do have a role to play, but it's not the role you might think. If I were to ask you after the fact why you forgave somebody or chose not to, you'd probably have a good rationale at the ready, but I'm betting that the rationale didn't cause your choice. Instead, I'd wager that your choice caused your rationale—you probably used your powers of higher-level reasoning to shore up your justification for doing whatever it was that you felt like doing in the first place. As is the case with the nonhuman primates, it's our emotions that are central, and anxiety is one of the biggies, for kids and grown-ups alike.

Everybody knows that little kids (and many adults, too) suck their thumbs and bite their nails when they're anxious. When preschoolers have had a conflict with a peer, the thumb-sucking and nail-biting increases to a fever pitch.[38] However, once the aggressor and victim have reconciled, the thumb-sucking and nail-biting cease. If the children don't reconcile, the thumb-sucking and nail-biting continue. In fact, children who have just had a conflict also experience a flood of stress hormones including cortisol (which is closely linked with fear and anxiety) and DHEA-S (which, some researchers think, might be the body's efforts to keep cortisol and its effects under control). If the conflict gets reconciled, the circulating levels of these hormones go back down to their pre-conflict levels. If the conflict doesn't end with reconciliation, the cascade of stress hormones continues.[39]

A laboratory experiment showed that similar things happen when adults recall occasions from their past when valuable relationship partners (mostly friends, romantic partners, parents, and siblings) did something to hurt them. When the researchers asked the participants to think unforgiving thoughts about their transgressors (for example, to think about their grudges or to imagine what it would be like to take revenge), the participants got anxious and tense. They had more muscle tension in their faces. In addition, their heart rates, blood pressure, and sweating all increased. These tension-related symptoms were much reduced after participants were instructed to think about their transgressors in a forgiving light.[40] In another study, researchers found that when they asked people to describe occasions when a friend or a parent had harmed them, those who reported that they had already forgiven the transgression experienced smaller increases in blood pressure than did people who hadn't forgiven. Lack of forgiveness for close, valuable relationship partners who have harmed us in the past is associated with more anxiety, tension, and physiological arousal.

Pencil-and-paper measures of anxiety and stress tell a similar story. When people report that they've forgiven a particular person who harmed them at some point in the past, they experience lower levels of self-reported stress and anxiety. In addition, the extent to which they've forgiven at one point in time predicts how much anxiety and stress they're going to be experiencing several months later.[41] These results from studies of children and adults, then, are very consistent with the sorts of conclusions that the primatologists have been drawing about the emotional factors that motivate reconciliation in nonhuman primates. Aggression and conflict lead to stress and anxiety, which motivate social animals to forgive or reconcile, which in turn alleviates their stress and anxiety.

Know forgiveness, know peace. No forgiveness, no peace.

Valuable Relations, Again

The links of forgiveness and reconciliation to anxiety are strongest when the person who hurt you is a close, valuable relationship partner. The same is true of our primate cousins. People who fail to forgive a close, important relationship partner will continue to feel anxious tension when they think about that person; when they forgive, the anxious tension disappears. In non-close, unimportant relationships, this isn't the case: forgiving someone who's not very close or important has no effect on people's levels of anxious tension. Some social psychologists demonstrated this phenomenon in several clever experiments. In one experiment, they gave people a psychological test that supposedly revealed whether they had actually forgiven "deep down" for something that a specific person had done to them in the past. Half the participants were told that the test revealed that they really had forgiven. The other half were told that the test revealed that they were still holding a grudge.

The researchers wanted to know which participants would feel upset by "learning" that they really hadn't forgiven their offenders. It turned out that if the person who harmed them was a stranger or an acquaintance, finding out that "you really haven't forgiven them after all" didn't create much anxiety. However, if the person who hurt them was a close, committed relationship partner (a good friend or a loved one, for example), then "finding out" that they really hadn't forgiven created psychological tension and negative emotion.

Conclusion: people get anxious when they haven't forgiven a valuable relationship partner precisely because the relationship is a valuable one.[42] Of course, this is exactly what the prisoner's dilemma, thirty years of primate research, and adaptationist thinking about forgiveness would lead us to expect. Improving our inclusive fitness and maintaining a stable set of cooperation partners are the *ultimate* causes of our desire to forgive and reconcile. These are the reasons why we possess tendencies to forgive and reconcile in the first place. The motivation to feel less tense and anxious is one of the *proximal* mechanisms that natural selection put in place to make sure that we actually follow through on those evolutionary mandates.

An Intellectual Bombshell Made out of Tinker-Toys and Flesh and Blood

David Sloan Wilson has called the prisoner's dilemma a "tinker-toy model" of natural selection because of the simplistic way in which it models animals' social instincts.[43] "Always resume cooperation if your partner does the same." "If your partner is a good friend, forgive him unconditionally 80 percent of the time." "If your partner is a stranger and she betrays you, let her have it." "Trash the reputations of people who attack you if you're not going to get a chance to retaliate against them directly." This sort of simplicity just seems, well, too simple.

But maybe the theoretical biologists get the last laugh here. The research on reconciliation and forgiveness in real, live, flesh-and-blood creatures shows that group-living animals seem to live by social instincts that aren't much more complicated than what the tinker-toy models suggest. Is a social rule that says, "If that guy who just stole your food is a good friend, go up to him and see if he'll let you groom him" (which is what reconciliation, interpreted through the valuable relationship hypothesis, actually looks like) really any more sophisticated than a rule that says, "Forgive your good friends unconditionally 80 percent of the time?" Maybe real life isn't always more complex than the tinker-toy version.

The idea that conflict and aggression attract animals to each other might not seem like an intellectual bombshell, but it is. Group-living mammals don't simply scatter to the four winds or beat each others' brains out after conflicts, as scientists assumed for many years. Instead, they often come together to actively undo the negative effects of conflict and aggression on their relationships. Reconciling and forgiving aren't passive enterprises. Reconciling animals are as sincere and hard-working in their efforts to make peace with each other as they are, at other times, in their efforts to make trouble for each other. Humans are also group-living animals, and by all indications we're just as prone to reconciliation and forgiveness as are the nonhuman species that have received so much attention in recent years. This gives us cause for optimism that humanity really does possess a "forgiveness instinct."

OPENING THE TOOLKIT

Natural selection seems to have outfitted us with a forgiveness instinct because it helped our ancestors preserve relationships that had biological utility. But they had to have utility, or at least the promise of utility. Natural selection most surely did *not* create a forgiveness instinct because it was useful for our ancestors to try to preserve each and every relationship—just the valuable ones. When the potential benefits of forgiveness are low and the potential costs are high, such as when a victim is figuring out whether to forgive a stranger or a sworn enemy who still seems dangerous, or of little likely value in the future, or undeserving of care and concern, we should anticipate that people will favor the alternatives to forgiveness—revenge being one of them.

Revenge and forgiveness, then, are *conditional* adaptations— they're context-sensitive. Whether we're motivated to seek revenge or to forgive depends on *who does the harming*, as well as on the advantages and disadvantages associated with both of these options. We don't weigh these considerations consciously, of course, but our brains perform the necessary computations behind the scenes. Then those brains motivate us in the direction that they think we need to go. But what, exactly, is going on behind the scenes? A journey into the human brain might be in order.

Now, you might have your doubts about whether scrutinizing a three-pound jumble of neurons can teach us anything useful about why the fathers and mothers of murder victims sometimes forgive their children's killers, or why feuds sometimes end peaceably, or why nations sometimes heal after civil wars, but this is definitely a journey worth taking. Natural selection is the ultimate cause of revenge, but people who are contemplating a single act of revenge are not thinking about their fitness. They're driven by feelings and thoughts that are generated within the brain. By studying the brain systems that come online when people are contemplating revenge, making plans for how to enact revenge, or basking in the warm glow of consummated revenge, we can better understand what a vengeful person is really trying to accomplish, and what humans might need to control those vengeful impulses. Likewise, if natural selection created human beings with a "forgiveness instinct," it did so by building a set of computational tools that crunch the numbers to figure out whom, what, where, and when we should forgive. These tools are worth trying to understand. To find them, you have to look between your ears.

CHAPTER SEVEN

THE FORGIVING BRAIN

The human brain is the most powerful information processing device in the known universe. It consists of one hundred billion neurons that are joined together by at least one hundred trillion interconnections. Thanks to recent technological breakthroughs, our scientific understanding of how the brain works is light years ahead of where it was even three decades ago. Techniques that record images of the brain's activity as people think, feel, talk, behave, and experience life have enabled scientists to examine the neurological basis of some of the most human-seeming aspects of our existence. In the past ten years, not even the most intimate of our traits—not love, language, sex, or even spirituality—has escaped neuroscientists' probing and prodding.[1] Neuroscientists have even got some important things to teach us about the neural circuitry that motivates revenge and forgiveness.

THE SEEKING SYSTEM AND THE RAGE CIRCUIT

Your brain has a system for telling you whether something out there in the world is good for you—a system that the neuroscientist Jaak Panksepp has called the "seeking system."[2] It doesn't matter what that something is: if your experience with an object, a substance, or a person in your environment has produced positive consequences for you in the past, the seeking system will create enthusiasm and a feeling of anticipation when a new opportunity to interact with that object or substance or person arises. The seeking system leads you to expect that the upcoming interaction is going to be worth your while.[3]

People who are in the midst of a satisfying and cooperative interaction with another person experience high activation in this so-called seeking system. Neuroscientists know this because a brain structure called the caudate nucleus, which receives a lot of input from the seeking system, is highly active during cooperation. The better a social interaction is progressing, the more your brain (courtesy of the caudate nucleus) seems to be saying, "This is going well for you. Keep it up."[4]

When someone harms you, though, the seeking system shuts down in an instant. Anticipating upcoming rewards is not the most important thing on your plate. You need to think about saving your hide, and, later, about ensuring that you won't be harmed by that person again. That good feeling of eager anticipation is gone, but anger, fear, psychic pain, contempt, and even disgust are there to take its place. Say you're feeling hurt because you've been excluded from a group of people whom you considered friends. This distress is generated by the same areas of the brain that create distress when we're experiencing physical pain.[5] Say, instead, that you're feeling the angry contempt of someone who has been treated with less respect than deserved. This feeling leads you to protest the unfair treatment you've received, and it seems to be driven by a part of the brain that helps create negative emotions such as disgust.[6] The most common emotional consequence of an interpersonal harm, though, is anger.[7]

Just how do the negative emotions we initially experience after being harmed—hurt, anger, and so forth—morph into the searing, focused desire for revenge that creates so many problems for our species? You might expect the involvement of the so-called rage circuit, which is found in many mammalian brains. The German physiologist and Nobel Laureate Walter Hess helped to identify the rage circuit by applying electrical stimulation to the brains of live cats. Apply electricity to certain regions of a brain structure called the hypothalamus (which is also responsible for regulating body temperature, sex drive, hunger, and thirst), and a previously docile animal is transformed into a seething, snarling, spitting rage machine with claws bared and hair erect. An animal who is receiving this sort of electrical stimulation will attack any living thing it can get its paws on. Apply electrical stimulation to the same part of human brains and people report feeling intense fury. Evidently, animals don't enjoy this electrically stimulated "sham rage" very much: when given the ability to turn off the electrical stimulation—say, by pressing a bar—they readily do so.[8]

The rage circuit leads to very quick and very focused aggressive responses to threats, so it seems reasonable to assume that it's also important for creating vengeful feelings. But as it turns out, revenge isn't primarily a product of rage: the neuroscientists tell us that it's actually a product of *desire*.

FROM VICTIM TO PREDATOR

Recall that if you use a probe to apply electrical stimulation to an animal's rage circuit, the animal will try to turn the stimulation off. If you apply electrical stimulation to another region of the hypothalamus, however, the animal seems to like it. In fact, if cats learn that they can turn on the electrical stimulation to this second hypothalamic region by pressing a bar, they go into frenzies of bar pressing, as if they believe that intense and abiding satisfaction is just one more bar-press away. They don't seem content: crazed is a more suitable description of their demeanor. When you activate this region of the hypothalamus, it turns out that you're actually stimulating nerve fibers from the seeking system that just happen to run through the hypothalamus.[9]

Now, stimulate the part of the cat's hypothalamus that produces all of that bar-pressing and then throw a mouse (even a dead one) into the cat's enclosure. What happens? Instead of blindly lashing out at the mouse in fury (which is what happens when the rage circuit is stimulated), the cat begins to quietly stalk the mouse. Panksepp calls it a "quiet-biting" attack. The rage circuit produces a cat that lashes out at the mouse as if trying to escape a predator, but the seeking system produces a cat that stalks the mouse as if craving a good meal or, at least, a good hunt. It's the seeking system that's behind this stalking behavior.

Because revenge, by definition, isn't fundamentally about stopping an attack in progress or escaping from a predator that poses an immediate threat, it's a pretty safe bet that the rage circuit isn't so important for revenge after all. It turns out that the seeking system is a much better place to begin looking for the neurological foundations of the desire for revenge.

CRAVING REVENGE

People talk about "craving" revenge. This isn't just a linguistic oddity. It's a signpost to a deeper understanding of revenge and its neural foundations. The "craving" quality of revenge was brought to light by a pioneering neuroscientist named William Shakespeare, once again speaking to us through Shylock in *The Merchant of Venice*. When Salarino encourages Shylock to drop his insistence on taking a pound of Antonio's flesh in revenge for defaulting on a big loan, Shylock reveals that his desire to be made whole is driven not just by anger, but also by hunger. For what purpose could Shylock possibly use a pound of Antonio's flesh? "To bait fish withal: if it will feed nothing else, it will feed my revenge."[10]

When you've been injured by someone, the initial response is that familiar suite of negative emotions—anger, hurt, and the rest—but after those initial negative emotions give way, the seeking system calls for a fundamental change in course. The seeking system motivates people to turn from a desire to escape pain or threat toward a search for pleasure. Recent studies show that Shylock's comparison of revenge to a hunger was more physiologically accurate than Shakespeare could have possibly imagined.

THE "TRUST GAME" STUDY

In 2004, a team of Swiss scientists used positron emission tomography (a technique that involves determining which brain areas are active during a task by measuring how much blood they consume during the task) while a group of men played a "trust game" with what they thought were a series of other sentient human beings (the participants were, in fact, playing against preprogrammed computer strategies). Economists invented the trust game to learn more about the conditions under which people are willing to trust strangers in social interactions.

The game is modeled loosely upon the relationships of an investor, someone entrusted with the investment, and the market in which the investor's money is invested. Both players start out with equal amounts of money (say, $10). At the beginning of the game, the research subject, playing the role of the investor, can choose to transfer some of his money to an anonymous player who is playing the role of the trustee. For each dollar the investor gives to the trustee, the researchers (playing the role of the market) quadruple it (as if the trustee has done a good job of managing the investor's funds). So, for example, if the investor gave all of his or her money to the trustee, the trustee would then have $50 (the trustee's own initial $10 plus $40 based on the investor's $10 investment, which grew to $40), and the investor would have zero.

Next, the trustee has the opportunity to return some of the $50 to the investor. You probably think, as most people do, that fairness would require the trustee to return $25 to the investor so that they both end up with $15 more than they started with; anything less is usually considered stinginess. But on four out of seven trials—each presumably with a different trustee—the trustees in this particular experiment didn't return any money at all. In those instances, investors reported feeling a strong desire to punish the trustees.

After each of the four betrayals, the investor was given one minute to decide whether to retaliate by taking up to $20 away from the trustee's earnings. It was during this minute that the scientists used positron emission tomography to determine what was going on in the short-changed investors' brains. By varying some of the details during the four rounds in which the computer strategy was stingy with the investor, the researchers were able to examine two different kinds of retaliation—an ability to take away up to $20 from the trustee's earnings "for free" (that is, at no cost to the investors themselves), and an ability to take money away from the trustee at a cost to the retaliator of $1 for each $2 of punishment.

In both the "free punishment" and the "costly punishment" conditions, the caudate nucleus was highly active during the moment of decision. Remember our friend the caudate? It's deeply involved in the seeking system, and it lights up when people are anticipating that they're about to receive a monetary award or a pleasant taste.[11] (You'll recall that the caudate is also highly active when people are interacting in a positive way with a cooperative stranger.) The caudate nucleus was even active in the costly punishment conditions (when the investor had to pay $1 for each $2 worth of punishment inflicted on the trustee). Moreover, the amount of activity in the caudate nucleus during the free punishment rounds was strongly related to the extent to which the investors chose to punish stingy trustees during the costly punishment rounds. This fact suggests that players who anticipated lots of satisfaction in the free punishment condition were also more willing to punish at a personal cost to them—presumably because they anticipated more pleasure to result.[12]

THE "BRAMITOL" STUDY

Some of the most striking evidence that people are actually seeking pleasure when they're seeking revenge comes from experiments by a team of social psychologists. They wanted to know whether people would retaliate against someone who had insulted them if they were led to believe that revenge wouldn't make them feel any better. The researchers convinced the research participants that they were about to take part in a study of how people form impressions of a stranger. Participants were first instructed to read an essay that either supported or refuted the idea that aggression makes people feel better. Next, they were asked to take a harmless pill that would supposedly speed up their reaction times (which, they were told, would be helpful for a later task). Next, one-half of participants were told that the pill (which went by the intriguing name Bramitol, although it was, in fact, just a vitamin B6 tablet) would also have the side effect of "freezing" their moods for about an hour. No matter how hard they tried, they wouldn't be able to change their moods after they took the Bramitol. The other half of the participants were given the same pill to speed up their reaction times, but they were told that Bramitol wouldn't have any mood-related side effects.

Next, participants were subjected to that workhorse of laboratory research on revenge: they wrote an essay that the stranger (of whom they were soon going to be asked to record their first impressions) was going to evaluate. After writing the essay, the stranger supposedly evaluated it, and then the research participants received very insulting evaluations back from the stranger (poor organization, lack of originality, weak writing style, lack of persuasiveness and clarity, and so on). The stranger also attached a handwritten note that said, "This is one of the worst essays I have read!"

Next comes the part where the Bramitol becomes crucial. The participants and the strangers with whom they were paired then competed against each other in a reaction-time test to see who was faster at pressing a button after receiving a signal. If the participant won the race, the participant got the chance to administer a loud blast of noise to the other player. How loud? That decision was left up to the participant. If the participant set the sound blast device to the highest possible setting, it was ostensibly 105 decibels (about as loud as a jackhammer operating a few meters away). On the lowest intensity, it was supposedly 60 decibels (roughly equivalent to the sound of normal conversation). Participants could also control the duration of the noise by holding their buttons down longer. These sound blasts therefore served as a nice, unobtrusive measure of participants' willingness to deliver a painful stimulus to the strangers who had previously insulted them.[13]

Results showed that the participants who believed that aggression would help them feel better (because they had read the essay that argued that this was the case) gave louder and longer sound blasts to their provokers than did those participants who read the "aggression doesn't help people feel better" essay—but only if they hadn't taken the "mood-freezing" pill. In other words, people seemed to be interested in retaliating, via the sound blast device, to the extent that they believed it would cheer them up. If they thought it wouldn't have that effect (either because they were led to believe it was generally ineffective at doing so or because the Bramitol had ostensibly frozen their moods), they

didn't bother trying to retaliate. Without the prospect of pleasure, revenge just didn't seem worth the trouble.

Planning Revenge

The prefrontal cortex sits right behind your forehead. Evolutionarily speaking, it's a rather young part of the brain, and it's
important for a variety of advanced psychological skills such as
reasoning, problem solving, and telling right from wrong. The
most important thing to know about the prefrontal cortex for
our purposes is that it helps people plan the steps for accomplishing their goals. Nature, it seems, has neatly divided the brain's
goal-planning responsibilities between the left prefrontal region
and the right prefrontal region. If you're pursuing a goal that
involves moving toward a desired object ("How do I get something I want?"), it's your left prefrontal area that's most active in
the planning process ("First, do Step 1. After that, go to Step 2.
If you fail on Step 2, try Step 2b as an alternative."). In contrast,
when you're pursuing a goal that involves staying away from
something bad ("How do I avoid something I don't want?"), your
right prefrontal cortex gets highly involved and your left prefrontal cortex goes on standby.

So guess which side of the prefrontal region is most active
when people are plotting revenge? That's right: revenge is a
left prefrontal kind of thing—a movement toward an object of
desire.

In 2001, a group of social psychologists who study the brain
brought undergraduate students into the laboratory and placed
them in a rather typical-seeming social psychology experiment.
They were asked to write an essay as a way of introducing themselves to another person with whom they were about to interact.
As in the Bramitol experiment, after writing the essay, participants read an insulting evaluation of their essays that was supposedly written by the upcoming interaction partner. Afterward,
in an ostensibly unrelated task, participants were instructed to
choose one of six substances (either sugar, apple juice, lemon
juice, salt, vinegar, or hot sauce) to mix with eleven ounces of
water. The resulting drink was going to be given to the insulting
participant as part of a "taste perception study." Like Bushman

and colleagues' sound-blast device, the opportunity to prepare a nasty drink for the insulter served as an indirect measure of aggression: if you felt like seeking revenge, you could mix up a really awful concoction for your insulter to drink during the upcoming taste perception task.

You won't be surprised to learn that the insults made people angry. They also led them to mix nastier brews for their insulting partners to drink. But what was particularly fascinating was what was going on in these avengers' brains. When they were plotting retaliation, they experienced increased activity in the left prefrontal cortex and reduced activity in the right prefrontal cortex. In fact, people who had the highest differences between left and right prefrontal activation were the ones who reported feeling angriest toward their transgressors. They were also the ones who prepared the most disgusting drinks for their insulting evaluators. So when people are planning revenge, the left prefrontal cortex seems to be egging them on.[14] Conclusion: we plan revenge using the same neural hardware we use to strive for any other outcome we really desire.

WHEN PLANS FOR REVENGE GET FRUSTRATED

What happens when those alluring revenge goals get thwarted? Apparently, it makes people feel pretty frustrated—so frustrated, in fact, that they'll try to anaesthetize their blocked goals with a stiff drink or two. Researchers at the University of Washington and the University of Wisconsin had social drinkers participate in what appeared to be a simple wine-tasting task.[15] The researchers randomly assigned these social drinkers to one of three experimental conditions that I'll describe in a moment. Before the wine tasting, all of the participants were asked to do a couple of other tasks.

First, they completed a set of difficult anagrams. In the room with the participants from two of the three groups was another "participant" (actually a stooge who was in cahoots with the researchers) who finished the anagrams in record time and then proceeded to ridicule the actual participant's intelligence, fashion sense, interpersonal manner, and overall physical appearance.

(One group was not insulted at all, and thus formed a control group). Later, participants from all three groups took part in a "learning task" in which they were supposed to use electric shock to "help" the stooge recall words from a list he had supposedly just memorized. When the stooge made a mistake, participants were supposed to provide a painful electric shock to punish the wrong answer (no shocks were actually administered, although participants apparently believed they were). In other words, participants thought they had been entrusted with equipment that could be used as a low-voltage taser weapon. However, for participants from one of the two groups of people whom the stooge had just insulted, the shock machine mysteriously malfunctioned just before the recall task began. As a result, those participants were denied the opportunity to administer painful electric shocks to their insulters.

Later, all of the participants participated in the wine-tasting task. Subjects were encouraged to drink as little or as much of each wine as they wanted to help them decide how much they liked it. What the wine-tasting task really did was provide researchers with an unobtrusive measure of participants' appetite for alcohol.

Participants who were insulted and then *denied* the opportunity to shock their insulters (because of the equipment failure) drank more alcohol than did the participants who were insulted but then given the opportunity to retaliate. Why? Perhaps because some of alcohol's most potent effects are in the prefrontal cortex—precisely where we make our plans for achieving our goals.[16] Given what we now know about the brain systems that govern the desire for revenge, it's likely that those frustrated avengers drank more alcohol because they were trying to put the left prefrontal cortex to sleep so that they could stop obsessing about their thwarted ambitions for revenge.

"EVERYBODY HERE IS HAPPY WITH THIS": THE REWARDS OF REVENGE

Pursuing a revenge goal is exciting, and having a revenge goal blocked is frustrating, but when we actually accomplish a revenge goal, it's positively exhilarating. This neurological reality was made plain on March 31, 2004, when masked gunmen in the city of Fallujah, in Iraq's Anbar Province, killed four American security contractors and desecrated their remains in the most gruesome ways anyone could envision.

The four private contractors had been escorting a convoy of three empty trucks that were going out to pick up some kitchen equipment. After the gunmen stopped the SUVs with explosive devices, they opened fire on the SUVs. They then pulled several of the wounded contractors out of their vehicles and into the street.

A crowd of three hundred men and boys rushed to the scene and joined the mob. Somebody went out and found a can of gasoline. The mob doused the contractors and their vehicles and then burned the men alive. After killing the Americans, they pounded their corpses with pipes, shovels and shoes (the latter a characteristically Arab mode of humiliation). Loose body parts were kicked and thrown about like so much street trash. Cars were used to drag two of the bodies through the streets of Fallujah. When the drivers reached a bridge on the Euphrates, the two bodies were hoisted up onto the bridge's metal frame, where they were left to hang for the rest of the day. The men from the crowd took turns having their pictures taken with the carbonized cadavers, now scarcely recognizable as the bodies of human beings.

Every photograph of this horrific spectacle that made it into the American media outlets showed that the men and boys of Fallujah were having a really good time. They didn't look angry. They looked happy. Actually, they looked ecstatic. If you photoshopped the burning cars and the charred human remains out of the pictures, you could easily think they were celebrating a wedding, or perhaps a football victory.

And from the point of view of those in the crowd that day, it really was a cause for celebration. They had dealt the Western forces a humiliating blow. They had managed to retaliate against the vastly more powerful coalition forces, which had invaded their sovereign nation and disrupted their productive lives. Recall that Fallujah was a Sunni-dominated, pro-Saddam stronghold. Under Saddam's powerful patronage system, many of Fallujah's residents had enjoyed material security and status.

So in the midst of the carnage, the men and boys of Fallujah smiled, danced, raised their hands above their heads in exultation, and chanted, "Allahu Akbar" (God is great) and "Fallujah is the graveyard of Americans!" One particularly disturbing image shows three Iraqi men beating one of the burnt bodies with their shoes. They're surrounded by a ring of maybe three dozen men who are pumping their fists in the air, clapping, dancing, and smiling. In the foreground of the picture is a boy—perhaps ten or eleven years of age—who wears that unfakeable sign of genuine joy: the Duchenne smile. The award for understatement of the day goes to the taxi driver from Fallujah who summarized the local sentiment: "Everyone here is happy with this. There is no question."[17]

The fact that the residents of Fallujah had such a fine time that March day doesn't distinguish them in the slightest from the men and boys who inhabit the rest of the world. Geronimo, the fierce Apache warrior, described his elation when he finally took revenge on the Mexican forces that had, a year before, massacred his mother, wife, and three children: "Still covered with the blood of my enemies, still holding my conquering weapon, still hot with the joy of battle, victory, and vengeance, I was surrounded by the Apache braves and made war chief of all the Apaches. Then I gave orders for scalping the slain. I could not call back my loved ones, I could not bring back the dead Apaches, but I could rejoice in this revenge."[18] Anthropologist Chris Boehm recounts an observer's description of the tribal Montenegrin people's love of revenge: "When a Montenegrin takes vengeance, then he is happy; then it seems to him that he has been born again, and as a mother's son he takes pride as though he had won a hundred duels."[19] An ambitious young Philadelphia gangster named Eddie Scarfo enjoyed revenge so much that on one occasion, after murdering someone who had insulted him, he told his associates, "If I could bring the motherfucker back to life, I'd kill him again."[20]

Clearly, these are people who find satisfaction in their work. But you don't have to be a Saddam loyalist or a gangster or a fierce Apache warrior to get satisfaction from revenge. As we might expect from the fact that the seeking system sets revenge in motion, two-thirds of people report satisfaction after they take revenge on someone who has harmed them.[21] Just as a good meal creates pleasure for a hungry person, drugs create pleasure for addicts, and a cold cup of water seems like an illicit treat when you're really thirsty,[22] seeing your perpetrators suffer for their transgressions also activates the brain's reward pathways.

In 2006, neuroscientists scanned the brains of people who had been treated either fairly or unfairly by another player in an economic game. After the game, participants witnessed their partners receiving painful electric shocks to the hand. While participants were watching the unfair players receiving shocks, they had lots of activity in the nucleus accumbens (interestingly, this effect only occurred in men). The nucleus accumbens is a central part of the brain's seeking system.[23] The more revenge the men said they desired after being treated unfairly, the greater their nucleus accumbens activity as they watched their transgressors suffer. It only makes sense that these vengeful participants were experiencing so much activity in the nucleus accumbens because the brain's seeking system was creating a satisfying, "rewarding" psychological state as they observed the suffering of the people who had treated them unfairly.

Mark Twain once wrote, "Revenge is wicked, & unchristian & in every way unbecoming. . . . (But it is powerful sweet, anyway)."[24] A twenty-first-century paraphrase might read, "Revenge pays neurochemical dividends." People who have been harmed by another person are goaded into revenge by a brain system that hands them a promissory note certifying that revenge, when it comes, will make them feel good. Upon receipt of this promissory note, the left frontal cortex goes to work to develop a plan for obtaining revenge. When avengers actually see their transgressors experiencing the pain they've planned for them, they get the pleasurable jolt that the seeking system had promised. A hard truth of human nature is that it's often pleasant to watch our enemies suffer, and it's a pleasure that we'll sometimes go to great lengths to acquire. Natural selection's logic here seems pretty easy to comprehend: by paying us back with pleasure, our brains ensure that we'll go to the trouble of seeking the social advantages that come from returning harm for harm. Injustice, modern neuroscience tells us, can make sadists of us all.

INSIDE THE FORGIVENESS INSTINCT

If the neuropsychological foundation for revenge is the desire for pleasure, then what are the neuropsychological foundations for the forgiveness instinct? It's no good to wave our arms around and insist that humans are naturally inclined to forgive if we can't point to the mental processes that enable them to actually pull it off.

A few theorists have taken stabs at neurological models of forgiveness,[25] but they've had to work without the benefit of very much hard data. However, a smattering of recent neuropsychological evidence, when paired with more standard psychological research, makes it clear that there are three psychological conditions that activate the forgiveness instinct: (1) *careworthiness* (people forgive transgressors whom they view as appropriate targets for kindness and compassion); (2) *expected value* (people forgive transgressors who, they think, might be valuable to them in the future); and (3) *safety* (people forgive transgressors whom they perceive as being unwilling and unable to harm them again).

CAREWORTHINESS

Humans are capable of experiencing deep and sincere concern for other people, but it's hard to care for every single person you come across. Caring is metabolically expensive. It consumes psychological and physical energy. And it can be personally dangerous— caring for others can literally cost you your life. Haldane's crack about his willingness to surrender his life for his eight cousins comes to mind here: the amount of care we experience for others is directly proportional to genetic relatedness. The closer the genetic relation, the more likely you'll help someone with a favor or rescue someone from a burning building. But we don't compute genetic relatedness on the spot to determine whether we should dash into that burning building. A more proximal mechanism is how close we feel toward the person in need. We care for people to whom we feel close,[26] and we feel closest to those with whom we share the most genes.[27] We also care more for the helpless and the innocent than for those who can help themselves and those who caused their own suffering.[28]

Forgiveness seems to be built on some of the same psychological scaffolding that the brain uses to generate care and concern for others.[29] This is a good news/bad news sort of thing. The good news is that we find it fairly easy to forgive our close relationship partners. The bad news is that many of the people who harm us in real life are people to whom we don't feel particularly close. Sometimes they're strangers. Other times they're people from groups that we've come to mistrust or hate.

So just how *do* you come to care for someone with whom you're not particularly close? One way is through empathic emotion. Empathy is not the warm and fuzzy emotion that it's often taken to be. It can actually feel somewhat aversive, especially when it's associated with another person's suffering. If you're feeling a lot of empathy for someone, you're likely to say that you feel "moved," "sympathetic," "compassionate," or "concerned" for that person. When you stumble into feeling empathic for someone in need, whether that person is a genetic relative or not, you'll be inclined to try and alleviate his or her suffering.[30]

One of the best ways to take all of the fun out of revenge, and promote forgiveness instead, is to make people feel empathy for the people who've harmed them. In 1997, my colleagues and I showed that when people experience empathy for a transgressor, it's difficult to maintain a vengeful attitude. Instead, forgiveness often emerges.[31] Empathy seems to promote forgiveness in relationships between co-workers, friends, romantic partners, Northern Irish Catholics and Protestants, and even perpetrators of crimes and their victims.[32] When you feel empathic toward someone, your willingness to retaliate goes way down.[33]

Neuroscience helps us understand why. In a study I described earlier in this chapter, men experienced high activity in the seeking system when they watched an unfair player receive painful shocks to the hand. However, women didn't experience the same uptick in the seeking system. Instead, when women watched an unfair player receive shocks, they experienced activity in a part of the brain that generates the distress we feel when we're in physical pain. In addition, neither men nor women experienced seeking system activation when watching a *fair* player receive painful shocks. In such instances, they also experienced activity in the brain's pain networks, and the higher their scores on a paper-and-pencil measure of "empathy," the more pain network activation they experienced. Other research shows that when people feel empathy toward someone who has harmed them, they don't experience the increased activation of the left prefrontal cortex that typically accompanies the desire for revenge.[34] You can stand by passively and watch an enemy suffer, and sometimes that feels good. However, if the suffering of your enemy evokes distress in you instead, then revenge is going to feel hollow, pointless, and cruel, and forgiving is going to seem like the thing to do instead.

A brief story illustrates this point. Steven McDonald was a New York City policeman until one day in 1986 when Shavod Jones shot him in Central Park, paralyzing him from the neck down. Strangely, McDonald found himself completely devoid of any desire for revenge: "I was angry at him, but I was also puzzled, because I found that I couldn't hate him. More often than not I felt sorry for him. I wanted him to turn his life to helping and not hurting people. I wanted him to find peace and purpose in his life. That's why I forgave him."[35]

The Central Park encounter left McDonald forever confined to a wheelchair. Life as he knew it was changed irrevocably. Still, he experienced empathy for Jones, and that empathy led to caring, and that caring made forgiveness possible. However, care on its own is rarely enough.

EXPECTED VALUE

Remember the "valuable relationship" hypothesis from the previous chapter? That's the idea that people forgive (and that non-human animals reconcile) to the extent that they perceive their relationship with the transgressor to be a valuable one. Expected value is the second psychological foundation for forgiveness.

The forgiveness epidemic that has broken out among the Acholi people of northern Uganda illustrates the importance of expected value. For two decades, rebels calling themselves the "Lord's Resistance Army" have fought to overturn the Ugandan government. To build support for their cause, they've terrorized civilians. Thousands of preteen girls have been stolen from their villages and given as wives to rebel commanders. Thousands of other children have been taken captive, brainwashed, and turned into the next generation of rebel soldiers, trained to attack and kill their own people. Villagers who have resisted the rebels have had their lips, noses, ears, hands, or breasts cut off to intimidate others into meeting the rebels' demands.

Fatigue has set in among the Acholi, many of whom have been displaced from their homes for years, so they've adopted an unorthodox strategy for peacemaking: welcoming the rebel soldiers back into their midst with offers of forgiveness. Since 2000, popular radio programs have promised the rebels amnesty if they'll simply lay down their arms and return to their communities. As time has gone on, the grassroots calls for unconditional amnesty—even for the LRA's leader Joseph Kony—have only become more insistent. One man who had been living in a camp for displaced civilians summarized how most Acholi feel about the situation: "Let [Kony] come back and live with the community because this is how reconciliation will be achieved." The International Criminal Court in The Hague has resisted requests that it drop its indictments against the LRA's leaders, but this hasn't deterred the Acholi. Indeed, the Ugandan government has officially offered amnesty to the rebels.

When rebels return home (sometimes in groups as large as eight hundred), they participate in a traditional forgiveness ritual in which they stick a bare foot into a raw egg—a symbol of innocence and new life. Next, they step over the long handle of a farming tool to symbolize their intention to return to a productive life in the community. As a final element in the ritual, they receive a figurative cleansing by brushing against the leaves of a pobo tree, "whose slippery bark catches dirty things." After the ritual, the repentant rebels must sit down with community leaders and formulate plans for confessing their sins and compensating the families that they've harmed—often by paying with livestock.

"What I'm after is peace," said one of the rebels' victims, whose nose, ears, and upper lip had been cut off more than a decade earlier. "If the people who did this to me and so many others are sorry for what they did, we can take them back." And it's not hard to understand why, especially when they repent and attempt to compensate their victims: the LRA turned children against their own villages and their own tribes, but those children continue to have value to their families and their communities, even though they were brainwashed and intimidated into doing horrible things. As a Catholic nun who works among the Acholi put it, "They are all our children . . . there is no other way."[36] As I write, the soldiers continue to return home, the peace negotiations continue to limp along, and a cease-fire agreement continues to hold firm.

The post-conflict anxiety I described in Chapter Six seems to be one of the forces that motivates people to restore valuable relationships. Concerns about losing a valuable relationship create anxiety, and that anxiety motivates us to find ways to patch things up and restore the relationship. But we've also seen in this chapter that the brain has a dedicated system for computing "value": if we expect our upcoming interactions with someone to be positive, the brain causes us to anticipate rewards.[37] This also helps us forgive valuable relationship partners.

The problem is that when somebody harms you, the harm itself drains some of the expected value from the relationship. The Acholi children who were spirited away to join the Lord's Resistance Army did horrific things to their own people, so they're now regarded as potential agents of harm. Therefore, despite the returning soldiers' implicit value to their parents, siblings, and former neighbors, the Acholi have to reevaluate their relationships with them—quite literally, they have to reassess the value they can expect to derive from the returnees in the future. It's not safe to simply assume that their future interactions will be rewarding.

But transgressions don't necessarily drain *all* of the expected value out of a relationship. Even if you harm me, I might continue to assign our relationship a high expected value if it was really valuable to me up until now, and this will dispose me to forgive you. A social psychologist at Carnegie Mellon University and his colleagues proved this point in an elegant way. They experimentally manipulated the extent to which participants focused on their romantic partners' value to them by asking half of the participants to list ways in which their lives were linked to their partners, and by asking the other half of the participants to list ways in which their lives were independent of their partners. Then, in a supposedly unrelated task, participants were asked to imagine how they would respond to twelve hypothetical acts of betrayal committed by their partners. People who had thought about the ways their lives were linked to their partners were much more forgiving of the twelve hypothetical acts than were the people who had thought about the ways that their lives were independent of their partners. The researchers went on to show that people with high levels of commitment to their relationships are much more forgiving of real-life transgressions as well.[38]

This bodes well for humans' ability to forgive people who had high expected value prior to the transgression. But what if your relationship with a transgressor had low expected value prior to the transgression (for example, if the two of you were in a long-standing conflict or didn't even know each other)? In such instances, endowing the relationship with some expected value after the fact is going to be more of an uphill climb.

An implication: if you want forgiveness from someone you've harmed, you have to overcome the fact that your victim might not be able to imagine that your relationship could have much value to him or her in the future. If you hurt your victim badly enough, he or she might view you as truly worthless. You have to change your victim's intuitions about your expected value. This is why victims around the world tend to respond positively to compensation as an overture to forgiveness.[39] Paying someone back for the harm you caused signals to the victim that your relationship has the potential to become rewarding once again. Compensation tells the victim's brain, "Remember me, friend? Even though I treated you badly, I'm back to my old, valuable self."

This can be a mixed blessing. Many people find it perplexing that battered women who manage to get away from their violent spouses often end up right back in the hellholes they spent months or years trying to escape. The problem is that despite the violence and terror that they and their children are forced to endure, battered women often perceive that their relationships with their spouses continue to have value (for example, when a husband is a woman's only source of financial support). When battered women feel tied down to an abusive partner by such constraints, they're more willing to forgive the abuse, and therefore more willing to return to the abuser.[40] A woman who forgives and later returns to an abusive domestic partner isn't out of her mind—more likely, she's at the end of her rope.

PERCEIVED SAFETY

Which takes us to the third psychological condition for forgiveness: safety. People are more inclined to forgive a transgressor whom they perceive to be unwilling or unable to harm them again in the future. It's a simple matter of trust: should you expect more pain from your transgressor in the future, or can you trust that his or her intentions toward you are basically benign? As we saw earlier, when children have conflicts, they experience increases in the stress hormones cortisol and DHEA-S; after reconciling, these hormones go back to their pre-conflict levels.[41] These hormonal changes reflect the fact that the prospect of having to endure more conflict and harm is stressful, whereas reconciliation leads to reduced uncertainty about the future of the relationship, and therefore reduced stress. With a conflict reconciled, there's less need to worry about the future, and therefore it's easier to forgive the past.

To evaluate a transgressor's safety, we try to understand why the transgressor harmed us in the first place. Did he intentionally injure you? Could she have avoided harming you in the first place? Could he have known that his actions would harm you? People more easily forgive transgressors whose behavior was unintentional, or unavoidable, or committed without awareness of its potential consequences for others. Malicious, intentional transgressions are much more difficult to forgive than are those for which one doesn't blame the transgressor.[42]

To evaluate whether an offender is safe, people are also interested in the offender's remorse and concern for the victim after the offense. Humans are better prepared to forgive a remorseful transgressor—one who seems to genuinely regret the harm she caused—than an unremorseful one. This makes good sense: the transgressor who is appalled by the consequences of her own behavior, or who is personally pained by the pain that her behavior caused another person, is advertising that she possesses psychological barriers—sympathy with the victim's suffering and a sincere desire to uphold society's moral standards—that will deter her from treating her victim in the same way a second time.[43] Research suggests that nonvoluntary behaviors such as blushing after a transgression may serve a similar function. Blushing shows that you're aware of your moral infraction and that you're eager to distance yourself from it. As a result, blushing after some moral transgressions seems to make people more forgivable.[44]

There's a paradox here: by admitting fault (either verbally or through some involuntary signal, such as blushing), offenders lock themselves into accepting a certain amount of blame, which works against forgiveness in the short run. However, when they admit fault (especially when their admission of guilt is accompanied by remorse), they're also reaffirming the validity of the social rules that they violated and they're acknowledging the harm that their behavior caused. They may also be acknowledging the psychological pain that their transgression inflicted. In the long run, affirming society's laws and acknowledging the victim's pain make the transgressor more forgivable. But the fact that admissions of guilt and expressions of remorse are such two-edged swords—sometimes getting the wrongdoer into more trouble on the way to getting him or her out of trouble later on—explains why people are often afraid to admit wrongdoing and to apologize.

To evaluate whether an offender is safe, people are also interested in whether a transgressor possesses the *desire* to harm them again as well as the *ability* to harm them again. We usually view it as a good sign when transgressors profess that they've changed their ways and that they won't repeat their offenses,[45] but vows like these usually work only when the victim already trusts the transgressor.

There's another way for a transgressor to create the intuition that he or she can't and won't hurt the victim again: making it seem physically impossible for himself or herself to do so. In many cultures, reconciliation rituals involve the surrender of weapons—perhaps because of the powerful symbolism associated with giving up one's power to harm.[46] We may therefore find it especially easy to forgive transgressors who lack both the will to re-offend and the ways to do so. Without the will or the ways, forgiveness doesn't seem like such a sucker's game.

ACTIVATING THE FORGIVENESS INSTINCT

Evolution seems to have outfitted us with a forgiveness instinct because this instinct helped our ancestors preserve relationships that had reproductive, economic, and political utility. When you care for someone who has hurt you, or you experience your relationship with that person as a valuable one, or you feel safe around that person, those brain-generated feelings are cues that prod you to forgive, and by so doing, to reestablish a relationship that may be worth trying to salvage.

The flip side is that when a transgressor doesn't seem safe, or valuable, or careworthy, people will be naturally inclined to favor the alternatives to forgiveness—revenge being chief among them. At the risk of being repetitive, I repeat: revenge and forgiveness, like all adaptations, are *conditional* adaptations. Whether we are motivated to forgive or to seek revenge depends on *who does the harming,* as well as on what happens afterward.

And ay, there's the rub. The terrible things that humanity most desperately needs to forgive—violence, homicide, genocide, war, political persecution, and disenfranchisement based on religion, nationality, or race—are typically not perpetrated by our parents, brothers, sisters, loving spouses, good friends, or neighbors—people whom we most easily experience as careworthy, valuable, and safe. Instead, they're perpetrated by strangers, enemies, and people whom we hate. The people whom we most need to forgive are the people for whom the psychological building blocks of forgiveness are naturally in short supply.

So we have a serious problem. Serious, yes, but not hopeless. Who's to say we can't create social conditions that will conjure up the psychological ingredients for forgiveness even in situations in which those ingredients are, under normal circumstances, in short supply? Maybe we didn't evolve to forgive strangers who have tried to kill us or our children, but domestic dogs didn't evolve to raise orphaned squirrels and tiger cubs, either. Remember Mademoiselle Giselle—the little papillon back in Chapter One who couldn't resist the urge to take care of an orphaned squirrel along with her own little puppies? Remember that dog from the Thailand zoo who was doing such a great job of raising a couple of little tiger cubs? The simple presence of small, defenseless, furry, four-legged creatures in need of milk was enough to activate mechanisms in these new mothers' brains that motivated them to treat the strangers as if they were their own young. Can we apply the same logic to helping people forgive? Can we evoke something natural from the human brain by creating unnatural social conditions? Perhaps. But if this approach is to stand any chance of success at all, we need to take a good, long look at those tried and true social behaviors that people use to signal careworthiness, value, and safety.

CHAPTER EIGHT

"To Promote and to Maintain Friendly Relations"
Making Forgiveness Happen

Only weeks after declaring war on Nazi Germany, and just weeks before shipping the first American troops off to Europe, Congress passed the Foreign Claims Act on January 2, 1942. Congress recognized that the nation was going to need a legal mechanism for making reparations to the foreign civilians who would inadvertently (but inevitably) be killed, injured, or made to suffer property damage as a result of U.S. military action. The Foreign Claims Act provides that legal mechanism. Currently, the law allows for compensation payments of up to $100,000. Between 2003 and 2006, the U.S. Department of Defense paid $26 million under the Foreign Claims Act to settle more than twenty-one thousand claims coming out of the wars in Afghanistan and Iraq. Most of these claims were related to automobile accidents, physical injuries and property damage incurred during detention procedures, and accidental death or property damage due to weapons fire.

Payments under the Foreign Claims Act aren't acts of penance on behalf of politicians whose consciences have begun to bother them, and they're certainly not crass attempts to put a dollar value on a human life. They're also not efforts to sidestep criminal liability: when the military learns of a crime against civilians, criminal investigations are supposed to ensue. Strictly speaking, payments under the Foreign Claims Act aren't even designed to affirm standards of moral decency (although they certainly do that, too).

So what are they for, then? The first seven words of the Foreign Claims Act explain their basic objective: "To promote and to maintain friendly relations." When the United States goes to war in a foreign land and destroys a civilian's property or injures a civilian or kills a civilian's loved ones, a settlement under the Foreign Claims Act is an attempt to quell resentment and restore a positive relationship between that civilian and the United States. In other words, it's a request for forgiveness.

Commanders on the ground in the Middle East have gotten quite good at asking for forgiveness from the civilians among whom they live and work, and they couldn't really do their jobs without it. Between 2003 and 2006, American commanders in Iraq and Afghanistan paid $31 million in *solatia* and condolence payments to civilians and their families who had been harmed or killed by American soldiers. *Solatia* is the Latin word from which we derive our word "solace." These are nominal sums that commanders pay out of their own emergency funds. The commanders often determine the appropriate amounts to pay by consulting with local tribal leaders and other experts on local customs, but they're currently in the neighborhood of $2,000 for the death of a civilian. Under extraordinary circumstances, condolence payments can go as high as $10,000.[1] Unlike compensation payments under the Foreign Claims Act, condolence and solatia payments don't result from legal proceedings. They're really just individual commanders' attempts to express sympathy; remorse; respect; and a culturally appropriate, token amount of compensation. Like settlements under the Foreign Claims Act, they're forgiveness payments, too.

The Foreign Claims Act and the Department of Defense's policies on condolence and solatia payments have been getting a brisk workout during the wars in Afghanistan and Iraq. In March 2007, for instance, Taliban insurgents ambushed a Marine Special Operations unit convoy in Nangarhar province. One marine was injured. Following the attack, the marines fled the scene. Then, some of them began to open fire at pedestrians and passing cars along the crowded street leading out of the bazaar where the ambush had occurred. They killed nineteen Afghan civilians and wounded dozens of others. The incident came under investigation by the U.S. Department of Defense, and eight marines were relieved of duty pending a criminal inquiry.

After an intensive investigation involving nongovernmental organizations and local tribal leaders, the military compiled a list of people who needed to receive solatia payments. It fell to Colonel John Nicholson of the 10th Mountain Division to meet with the victims and their families. Colonel Nicholson presented the customary payments (100,000 Afghanis, which comes out to about $2,000 per death), and he followed up with an elaborate apology and request for forgiveness: "I stand before you today, deeply, deeply ashamed and terribly sorry that Americans have killed and wounded innocent Afghan people. We are filled with grief and sadness at the death of any Afghan, but the death and wounding of innocent Afghans at the hand of Americans is a stain on our honor and on the memory of the many Americans who have died defending Afghanistan and the Afghan people. This was a terrible, terrible mistake, and my nation grieves with you for your loss and suffering. We humbly and respectfully ask for your forgiveness."[2]

Gul Agha Sherzai, the governor of Nangarhar province, was on hand to host the ceremony. As was fitting on such an occasion, he offered a stern but conciliatory rebuke to the Coalition forces, urging them to ensure that their soldiers are disciplined and well trained so that such acts are avoided in the future. Colonel Nicholson's heartfelt words of contrition also gave Sherzai the confidence he needed to reassert his faith in the Coalition forces: "The enemy will use these unfortunate events to further their cause. The tribes of Nangarhar support the Islamic Republic of Afghanistan. Just the other day a man came to a shura and told the tribal elders we should start a jihad against Coalition forces. The tribal elders told the man to leave. They told him the Taliban gives us nothing but violence and death. The Coalition and the IRoA support us with roads, education, and a brighter future."[3]

The truism has been repeated until we don't hear what it means anymore: "If you want to win a war on terror, you have to win the hearts and minds of civilians." But if you want to win their hearts and minds, you'd better be prepared to win their forgiveness, too. Colonel Nicholson put it this way: "[W]e go to great lengths to try and make it right with the people who've suffered because that is not what America stands for. They know that. They hold us to a higher standard, and they should hold us to a higher standard. And we should hold ourselves to a higher standard because we are professionals, and we can be better than that. So we work very hard to do no harm to the Afghan people and to deliver those effects that we know will achieve the buy-in by the Afghans of their own government and will help us to win this war on terror."[4]

It's easy to take the Foreign Claims Act, or the Department of Defense's policies regarding solatia payments, or Colonel Nicholson's public statements after the shooting in Nangarhar as nothing more than cynical propaganda or the turning of the wheels of a military bureaucracy. Behind the legal jargon and the official policies and the press conferences, though, an adaptationist sees a theory of human nature at work. Why are apologies, sincere demonstrations of contrition, and efforts to provide compensation so effective when you're trying "to promote and to maintain friendly relations"? An adaptationist answers, "That's how natural selection designed human nature to work."

FORGIVENESS SIGNALS

As we saw in Chapter Seven, the perception that a transgressor is safe, valuable, and worthy of care helps to elicit forgiveness and block the expression of revenge. People can cultivate these three ingredients for forgiveness by communicating to the people they have harmed with what biologists call *signals*.

Animals use a variety of behaviors to communicate information about their psychological and physiological states. As the theoretical biologists Martin Nowak and Karl Sigmund were working out the details of their evolutionary simulations of the prisoner's dilemma, they speculated that social organisms might evolve signals to help their interaction partners recognize when it was safe to switch from revenge to forgiveness.[5]

Animal researchers have discovered signals just like those that Nowak and Sigmund posited. In some species, the signals that foster forgiveness and reconciliation are pretty straightforward. Think back to the predator-inspecting guppies. If a guppy wants to signal to his predator-inspection partner that he's ready to return to cooperation after a dereliction of duty, it's simple: he falls back in line and does his turn. Think back also to the reconciliation gestures that so many group-living mammals use to mend conflict: kissing, bottom-holding, horn-rubbing, and so forth. These gestures also signal a desire to return to a positive relationship.

Other signals are useful for reconciling after the social hierarchy has been challenged. Among chimpanzees, for instance, the cardinal sin of social life is insubordination: give your superiors proper displays of deference, or else. In chimpanzees, deference is signaled by an exchange of greetings. Dominant individuals make their bodies look as large as possible; subordinate individuals bow and scrape and issue a call known as the "pant-grunt."[6] My pant-grunt to you acknowledges that I'm subordinate to you and that you needn't worry (for the time being, anyway) that I'm trying to displace you from your position in the hierarchy.

Imagine that you're the alpha male and I've decided that I'd like to go after your position on the totem pole. If I start up a fight to try and topple you from your position, there are only two possible outcomes: I'm stronger than you and I take your position, or I'm weaker than you and you end up defending your position successfully. If the former, I'm not going to let up on you until you issue a pant-grunt to me; if the latter, you're not going to show me any mercy until I've issued a pant-grunt to you. Without the signal, there can be no peace—just a protracted, stressful, dangerous struggle. There can be no "forgiveness" until the vanquished foe displays the right signals. But like magic, as soon as the signal is displayed, the fighting can end and everybody can relax.

Humans also have a repertoire of behavioral, expressive, and verbal signals for ending cycles of aggression and retaliation, fostering cooperation after conflict, and ultimately, ushering in forgiveness and reconciliation. My colleagues and I have been trying to catalogue these signals, many of which have been noted previously by other scientists.[7] I'm going to talk about three of the most common, most practical, and most effective of these signals: apologies, self-abasing displays and gestures, and compensation. That's right: the U.S. Congress and those commanders on the ground in Iraq and Afghanistan have had the right idea all along.

SIGNAL #1: APOLOGIES

Done correctly, apologies are extremely effective at discouraging revenge and encouraging forgiveness.[8] In fact, they're probably the most potent resource at our disposal for making the world a less vengeful, more forgiving place. This is the case even when the harm is very severe: in a study of victims of gross human rights violations under apartheid in South Africa, the best predictor of victims' willingness to forgive their offenders was the extent to which they perceived that their offenders were "truly sorry" for their actions.[9]

Apologies' effects differ slightly from culture to culture. For instance, the primary role of apologies in Japanese culture is to lubricate social relations so that interpersonal harmony can be restored after a transgression. In Chinese culture, apologies indicate the apologizer's willingness to submit to authority and conventional understandings of morality. In Arab consciousness, apologies are linked to the ancient motivation to curtail blood feuds. In the West, apologies assist with religious and communal notions of reconciliation, and they're also associated with acknowledging moral guilt and perhaps even legal liability.[10] If you go into a new culture taking for granted that your style of apologizing will be unquestioningly and gratefully accepted, and that it will have the effects you're looking for, you might be in for a surprise.

Even so, apologies have some core commonalities that seem to transcend culture. Linguists who are interested in the cross-cultural universals in apologies have identified five components. The first is the "Illocutionary Force Indicating Device," which is the set of words that the apologizer uses to indicate that he or she is uttering an apology (for example, in English, "I'm really sorry"). The second is the admission of responsibility (for example, "It was my fault"). These first two features, linguists tell us, appear in every effective apology in the four languages they examined (English, French, Hebrew, and German). Third, there's the explanation—the transgressor's attempt to clarify why the transgression occurred in the first place. Fourth, there's the offer of repair; and fifth, there's the promise of forbearance—a pledge not to repeat the transgression.[11] Another apology theorist has suggested a leaner list of the elements of an effective apology: (a) acknowledging the offense; (b) offering an explanation for why it occurred; (c) communicating remorse, shame, humility, and sincerity; and (d) offering reparations.[12] In general, the more of these features the transgressor offers, the more the victim views his act as forgivable.[13]

Apologies and the Alternatives

A good way to appreciate the power of a decent apology is to think of how you feel when somebody gives you a bad one. Peter Schönbach has described four basic forms of "accounts" that people can use in efforts to "account for" their bad behavior: refusals, justifications, excuses, and apologies (which Schönbach calls "concessions").[14] In a *refusal,* the transgressor denies responsibility for a harmful action or denies that her action was to blame for the negative outcome. In an *excuse,* the transgressor tries to reduce her responsibility by citing mitigating circumstances. *Justifications* are slightly more satisfying than refusals and excuses because they at least acknowledge one's responsibility for a transgression. However, justifications don't go far enough because they attempt to give the offensive behavior a more positive spin (for example, "The ends justify the means").

Justifications and excuses are better than nothing at extinguishing the desire for revenge[15] and (I suspect) helping people forgive, but a *concession* is what people really want out of a decent apology. In a concession, the transgressor "accepts both the responsibility and the undesirability of the situation; one admits partial or full guilt, expresses regret, and offers compensation."[16]

The American political scene is a candy store for writers who want to illustrate how these attempts to account for one's misbehavior can go desperately, miserably, painfully wrong. In January 1998, President Bill Clinton issued a textbook "refusal" when he wagged his finger at the American people and denied vehemently that he had had "sexual relations with that woman, Miss Lewinsky . . ."[17] Months later, with his back to the wall because of a certain blue dress that had surfaced as evidence against his protestations of innocence, Clinton finally offered a partial concession by admitting that he "did have a relationship with Miss Lewinsky that was not appropriate. In fact, it was wrong. It constituted a critical lapse in judgment for which I am solely and completely responsible." Better late than never.

Even then, however, Clinton couldn't resist the opportunity to criticize the independent counsel who had caused him so much grief: "I intend to reclaim my family life for my family. It's nobody's business but ours. Even presidents have private lives. It is time to stop the pursuit of personal destruction and the prying into private lives and get on with our national life."[18] This table-turning maneuver weakened Clinton's concession by making it seem like an excuse or a justification (as if Clinton were really trying to say, "I wouldn't have to be admitting to all of this if that Special Prosecutor hadn't been so mean to me.")

Still, in the months to come, Clinton would offer incrementally better concessions for his misdeeds. By September 4, he could finally say, "I made a big mistake. It is indefensible and I am sorry. . . . I can't disagree with anyone else who wants to be critical of what I have already acknowledged is indefensible. There's nothing that he [Sen. Joseph Lieberman] or anyone else could say in a personally critical way that I don't imagine I would disagree with since I have already said it myself, to myself, and I'm very sorry about it, but there's nothing else I can say." But by September 9, he had found more to say: "I also let you down and I let my family down and I let this country down. But I'm trying to make it right. And I'm determined never to let anything like that happen again. And I'm determined to redeem the trust. . . . So I ask you for your understanding, for your forgiveness on this journey we're on. I hope this will be a time of reconciliation and healing." And the day before the Senate's December 12 vote on the articles of impeachment, Clinton would say, "What I want the American people to know, what I want the Congress to know, is that I am profoundly sorry for all I have done wrong in words and deeds. . . . I never should have misled the country, the Congress, my friends and my family. Quite simply, I gave into my shame. . . ."[19]

One wonders whether Clinton might have saved himself months of political pain—and further shame—if he had made a better concession early on in the process, costly and humiliating though it would have been.

The inability to use apologies effectively is a bipartisan disorder. Consider Senator Trent Lott's efforts to extricate himself from blame, and to save his political hide, after comments he made on December 5, 2002, at a Washington celebration in honor of Strom Thurmond's one hundredth birthday: "I want to say this about my state [Lott is a lifelong Mississippian]: When Strom Thurmond ran for president, we voted for him. We're proud of it. And if the rest of the country had followed our lead, we wouldn't have had all these problems over all these years, either."[20]

The problem with Lott's effusive praise for Thurmond is that Thurmond ran on a segregationist platform during his 1948 presidential bid. Some would say it was the *only* plank in Thurmond's platform. This didn't leave Lott looking too good.

The Lott-Thurmond story took a few days to grow legs in the media, but several days afterward, Lott was forced to explain himself. His first account for his behavior was the weakest of all—a two-line refusal issued by his spokesman: "Senator Lott's remarks were intended to pay tribute to a remarkable man who led a remarkable life. To read anything more into these comments is wrong."[21]

But Senator' Lott's feeble refusal to acknowledge the offensiveness of his comments got him nowhere. By Monday, December 10, facing outrage from fellow Republicans and Democrats, he was forced to issue a better, but still rather flaccid, denial: "A poor choice of words conveyed to some the impression that I embraced the discarded policies of the past. Nothing could be further from the truth, and I apologize to anyone who was offended by my statement."

Lott tried again on Tuesday, December 11: "It was certainly not intended to endorse his segregationist policies that he might have been advocating or was advocating 54 years ago. But obviously, I am sorry for my words, they were poorly chosen and insensitive and I regret the way it has been interpreted. This was a mistake of the head, not of the heart because I don't accept those policies of the past at all."[22] But this account didn't take care of Lott's problems either. In fact, by first denying that he had done anything wrong, and then claiming that his mistake came down to a poor choice of words that were *improperly interpreted,* and then failing to acknowledge that people had *indeed* been offended by his statement (instead, Lott used the universally ill-advised "I apologize to anyone who was offended" line), he managed to make himself look even worse.

Lott's problems were resolved only after Lott, under pressure from his colleagues in the Senate and President George W. Bush, made a formal statement from his hometown of Pascagoula, Mississippi, on Friday, December 13: "I have asked and am asking for people's forbearance and forgiveness as I continue to learn from my own mistakes and as I continue to grow as both a person and a leader. . . . I apologize for reopening old wounds and hurting so many Americans. I take full responsibility for my remarks and only hope that people will find in their heart to forgive me for this grievous mistake. Not only have I seen the destruction wrought by the racist and immoral policies of the past, I will do everything in my power to ensure that we never go back to that kind of society again."[23]

A week later, Lott resigned from his position as Senate Majority Leader (which he hadn't even officially assumed yet). His original mistakes and his failure to account for them early and fully cost him a great deal of political status, but after many false starts, he finally managed to apologize with enough apparent humility and genuine regret to save his political life.

Eventually, Clinton and Lott got their apologies right, and things gradually became better for both of them. Lott was even elected Minority Whip after the 2006 mid-term elections.

THE BENEFITS OF APOLOGIZING

Good apologies, according to Aaron Lazare, meet several needs. They help to restore a victim's self-respect and dignity. They provide assurance that the victim and the transgressor share the same moral values. They reassure victims that the transgressions they suffered weren't their fault. They reassure victims that their transgressors are safe (despite their deplorable behavior). They make the transgressors suffer. They also hold out the possibility that a victim might get some reparation for the harm he or she suffered.[24]

Lazare's list of the benefits of apologies is right on the mark. By restoring a victim's self-respect and dignity, a good apology undoes the damage to a victim's honor that the transgression created in the first place. Restored honor brings with it safety from future predation, and therefore it's a key to quelling the desire for revenge. By providing assurance that the victim and the transgressor share moral values, the apology provides a perception of safety: it helps a victim to feel that the transgressor has internal inhibitions that would prevent him or her from repeating the same offense a second time. Affirming jointly shared moral values also makes victims feel closer and more similar to their transgressors, thereby making those transgressors seem more valuable and careworthy.

Finally, by making a transgressor suffer the humiliation of admitting his or her moral shortcomings, an apology satisfies people's deep desire to see their transgressors suffer. People who felt that Clinton had lied to them (or had dishonored the presidency), and people who felt that Lott really was a racist, got some satisfaction from seeing them squirm on national television. As we saw in Chapter Seven, the desire for vengeance runs right through the brain's "seeking system," and the suffering that a good apology entails might be enough to slake the brain's craving for revenge. Also, by making transgressors suffer, apologies may cause victims to feel empathy for their transgressors, which also deters revenge and promotes forgiveness by generating feelings of care.[25]

Although apologies seem to be what victims most desire from their offenders,[26] they're effective in preventing revenge and promoting forgiveness only up to a point. At the end of the day, they're just talk, and the gulf between words and actions can be vast. Perhaps, for example, I'm asking you to forgive me *not* because I've actually experienced an internal change that renders me careworthy, safe, and valuable, but because I want to avoid a severe punishment or because I want you to let your guard down so that I can take advantage of you again.

This isn't as big a problem as it seems, though, because apologies are only one signal at our disposal for making forgiveness happen. Modern humans and our ancestors have been forgiving and reconciling for millions of years; we've only developed the physiological capacity for spoken language in the past half-million years.[27] In fact, anthropological evidence gathered from the anthropologist's best friend—the Human Relations Area Files—suggests that people don't even begin to use apologies until their societies develop a high level of hierarchical structure. In the most elementary societal forms, which were highly egalitarian, people probably didn't use apologies at all.[28] Fortunately, apologies didn't have to do all of the work in the past, and they don't have to today, either. We have at least two other good signals at our disposal for making forgiveness happen.

SIGNAL #2: SELF-ABASING DISPLAYS AND GESTURES

Charles Darwin wasn't so sure what to make of the blush. He doubted that it served any particular social function. Maybe, he surmised, it arises purely from humans' ability to imagine themselves from other people's points of view.[29] But Darwin may have been wrong to think that blushing lacked a special social function, especially because it's so often precipitated by breaches of etiquette or more serious transgressions. Mark Twain may have gotten to the heart of the matter of blushing when he wrote, "Man is the only animal that blushes. Or needs to."[30]

The social psychologist Dacher Keltner and his colleagues adhere to the Mark Twain school of thought when it comes to blushing. They've proposed that blushes and similar expressive behaviors (such as gazing downward or trying to suppress a smile) are good clues that someone is experiencing embarrassment (an emotion that arises from breaches of culture-specific social conventions, such as those related to how one should eat, dress, and address others) or shame (an emotion that arises from more serious moral infractions that reveal one's character defects). Facial expressions of shame and embarrassment seem to make people more forgivable. For example, if you know that someone looks ashamed after he or she does something wrong, you feel more sympathy for him or her. Keltner and colleagues also found that people recommended lighter sentences for hypothetical criminal defendants who supposedly experienced embarrassment or shame than for defendants who supposedly experienced neutral emotion or contempt.[31] These facial and vocal expressions of shame and embarrassment (which we might call *self-abasing gestures*), when added to verbal apologies, can add the weight of sincerity to otherwise cheap-seeming talk, thereby making offenders more forgivable.

People can also use their entire bodies for self-abasing signals to make forgiveness happen. In some cultures, self-abasing gestures involve actual manipulations of one's physical stature (bowing, crawling, or kneeling) so that an offender seems smaller and weaker than he or she actually is. Self-abasement can also be accomplished by voluntarily submitting oneself to punishment (or mild retaliation). In comparison to the offender who engages in such self-abasing acts, the victim of the transgression seems strong, powerful, and independent. For this reason, a certain amount of self-abasement on the part of an offender can help a victim recover the social status that he or she might otherwise try to reclaim by seeking revenge, thereby making revenge moot.

Rolf Kuschel, a social psychologist at the University of Copenhagen, has studied these gestures extensively. He has concluded that in many premodern cultures, self-abasing rituals often involve four behaviors: (a) exposing vulnerable body parts; (b) lowering your body relative to the body of the person you're trying to appease; (c) touching unclean things (for example, the feet or genitals of the person you're trying to appease); and (d) allowing someone else to touch your head or hair.[32] The information that such signals are intended to symbolize is obvious: I'm weak, you're strong. I'm defiled, you're pure. I'm dishonorable, you're honorable. Aren't these the very sorts of messages people often are trying to send when they seek revenge? It's no wonder, then, that these self-abasing gestures are an important part of the suite of signals at humans' disposal for ending quarrels and promoting forgiveness.

In Chris Boehm's book *Blood Revenge,* in which he analyzes the traditional practices of feuding and peacemaking in tribal Montenegro, he has a great example of the effectiveness of self-abasing gestures. He retells Rovinskii's century-old anthropological account of how two clans made peace following a long feud in which both clans had suffered many deaths. Ultimately, the feud was settled when a member of the clan that originally began the feud engaged in a self-abasing ritual. There are two principal characters: Bojković, whose clan began the feud by committing the first killing, and Zec, whose father was the feud's first fatality:

> At the ceremony, the two clans stayed away from each other "like two hostile regiments." Rovinskii describes the ceremony in detail: "A short moment of silence falls, and then a group of people steps out from the other side. The son of the murderer, in a single undergarment, barefoot and without a cap, creeps on all fours. And on his neck hangs a long gun on a strap (it is always a long gun, for a greater effect, even if the murder was just by pistol). . . . Seeing this, Zec hastily runs ahead in order to shorten this severe, humiliating scene. He runs to Bojković in order to raise him up more quickly, but at that very moment Bojković kisses him on the feet, the chest and the shoulder. Taking the gun off Bojković's neck, Zec addresses him with the following words: 'First a brother, then a blood enemy, then a brother forever. Is this the rifle which took the life of my father?' And not waiting for a reply, he hands the gun back to Bojković, expressing by this the full forgiveness of the past, and they both kiss each other, embracing each other like brothers."[33]

Bojković appears before the crowd in the most humiliated, dishonorable, self-abased state possible. He's in his underwear, crawling along the ground like an animal, or an infant, or a wounded man. He's also wearing a rifle around his neck to represent the weapon that was used to ignite the feud. There is no mistaking the point of this ritual: it's intended to symbolize the actor's smallness, weakness, and dependence, the strength and stature of the opposing side, and the actor's desire to put the feud behind him.

It's hard to imagine anyone in the contemporary world engaging in a ritual that's quite as exaggerated as this one was, but its efficacy as a signal for communicating the desire for forgiveness and peace is undeniable. Zec is overwhelmed with empathic distress and rushes to the humiliated Bojković to end the ritual as quickly as possible. Zec's clan's honor has been restored: Bojković's clan has been made to look weak, dependent, and dishonorable (but smart, too, because they knew when it was time to make the feuding stop). Zec's clan has been made to look large, strong, and honorable in contrast. The forgiveness that emerges is automatic and heartfelt. There's no point in making anyone's suffering drag out any further.

Signal #3: Compensation

As good as they are, apologies and self-abasing gestures aren't always enough to make forgiveness happen. In March 2004, Todd Bertuzzi, a right wing for the Vancouver Canucks, skated up behind Steve Moore from the Colorado Avalanche and sucker-punched him in the side of the head (presumably in retaliation for Moore's attack on a Canucks player several weeks before). Moore fell head-first onto the ice, and the much larger Bertuzzi fell on top of him. Moore received serious and probably career-ending injuries (including a concussion and three broken neck bones).

Although the attack on Moore was callow, brutal, and obviously intentional, it's hard to imagine that Bertuzzi actually meant to end Moore's career. And two days later, Bertuzzi offered a public apology that seemed heartfelt—one that met at least some of Lazare's criteria for effective apologies. It acknowledged Bertuzzi's offense and the extent of the damage done, and it communicated remorse, shame, humility, and sincerity.[34]

In the ensuing months, Bertuzzi would receive some fairly stiff punishments. Through a plea-bargaining deal, he pled guilty to an assault charge in criminal court and received a one-year probation. He lost nearly $1 million in pay and endorsements, and he was suspended for twenty games (the fourth-longest suspension in NHL history). He also had to do eighty hours of community service. So Bertuzzi had to accept some suffering because of his behavior, even though it didn't come anywhere close to matching the damage he had inflicted on Moore.

Still, Moore refused to forgive Bertuzzi, even though Bertuzzi made more than ten attempts in the ensuing months to apologize to Moore directly. Bertuzzi's efforts to get Moore to forgive him likely failed because they lacked two ingredients. First, Bertuzzi never really offered a proper explanation for his behavior, which weakened his apology. On the contrary, he refused to take responsibility for his actions: "If I could [explain why I attacked Moore] I wouldn't be here," he said in a prepared statement to the press more than a year after the incident. "Trust me, I've been off for a long time and had a lot of sleepless nights trying to think of things but you know what? It happened."

Second, and perhaps more important, Bertuzzi hasn't provided any compensation to Moore for the harm he caused him. Moore filed a civil suit against Bertuzzi and the Canucks in 2006, seeking $19.5 million for the loss of pay and endorsements that he might have accrued over the rest of his career, as well as for aggravated and punitive damages.[35] That case is still working its way through Canada's courts. Why did Moore decide to sue? "It's something where I don't really have a choice. . . . That was my rookie season, and I haven't had any income since then. It's a situation very few people in the game have had to deal with. Maybe nobody. It's not something I want to do. I have no choice."

Moore still hasn't responded to Bertuzzi's attempts to apologize. Bertuzzi puts it in perspective like this: "You have to respect people's decisions on things, and some people forgive a lot easier than others and you just got to deal with it and move forward." That's true, but what might have happened if Bertuzzi had made a more convincing apology and a creative gesture that indicated a willingness to partially compensate Moore for his lost income, his bodily injuries, and his ruined career? The whole affair might have had a very different ending.

Compensation is a tried-and-true mechanism for fostering forgiveness.[36] Compensation undoes some of the damage that the transgression created, and it forces the transgressor to experience some pain at the same time. In addition, when you compensate a victim for the pain you caused him or her—when you make the victim "whole," as attorneys like to say—the victim will be less preoccupied with thoughts about the damage he or she suffered in the past, and he or she can perhaps begin to think of you as someone who has the potential to be valuable in the future. Steve Moore is suing Bertuzzi and the Canucks, at least in part, because he could use the money. If he wins the civil suit, he might be in a better position to give up some of his resentment.

The importance of compensation for quenching the desire for revenge and encouraging forgiveness can't be overstated. In their landmark cross-cultural work on blood revenge, Martin Daly and Margo Wilson noted that many of the premodern cultures they studied had developed compensation strategies for quelling revenge. The acceptance of "blood money" is a common alternative to killing a murderer or one of his kin in retaliation for homicide,[37] and compensation and gift-exchange are common elements of reconciliation and forgiveness rituals in many cultures.[38]

People use compensation all the time as a way of making themselves more forgivable in the eyes of people whom they've harmed. Compensation used to be a key component of criminal law as well. However, as the governments of Western Europe assumed more and more responsibility for social control, offenders became responsible to *the state,* rather than to their victims, for their crimes. As a result, compensation fell to the wayside. This was a perverse turn of events because it ignored people's intuitive moral sensibilities: people want to be compensated directly by their offenders. This unfortunate cultural change undermined one of the most effective strategies at humans' disposal for settling serious grievances.[39]

Compensation is extremely effective—so effective, in fact, that it can provide "satisfaction" even when a victim's losses aren't covered completely. Often, people will give up their desire for revenge, and forgive instead, in response to compensation that's much less than the losses they've incurred. Solatia and condolence payments are pathetically small in comparison to the harms that they're intended to help remedy, but even so, their effectiveness in quelling resentment and promoting forgiveness is undeniable.

In one experiment that illustrates this point, researchers had participants play a prisoner's-dilemma-style game in which they believed that they were interacting with another person (they were actually playing against a preprogrammed computer strategy). After a few rounds of cooperative play, the computer strategy (which I'll call the transgressor) began to defect, undoing the history of cooperation that had emerged over the previous rounds. This usually led to a few rounds of mutual defection in which players hurt themselves and their partners.

After a while, the transgressor sent an apologetic message and then offered an interesting form of compensation: inviting the victim to recoup some losses by choosing the "Defect" option while the transgressor simultaneously chooses the "Cooperate" option (this allowed the human to collect the "temptation payoff," which is the best payoff the prisoner's dilemma has to offer). There were actually three compensation conditions. In the low-compensation condition, the transgressor let the victim collect the temptation payoff on the next round of play. In the high-compensation condition, the transgressor let the victim collect the temptation payoff on the next two rounds of play. In an "open" compensation condition, the transgressor asked the victim, "What can I do to get you to cooperate again?" The victim then indicated the number of rounds (between 0 and 5) in which he or she wanted to collect the temptation payoff before he or she would be willing to return to cooperation.

Surprisingly, the low- and high-compensation conditions were equally effective at coaxing betrayed players back into a cooperative frame of mind. Participants who received an apology but no compensation offer returned to cooperative play, on average, during only 2 of the next 5 rounds. People who received an apology plus the low-compensation offer cooperated during 3.5 of the next 5 rounds. People who received an apology plus the high-compensation offer cooperated on 3.3 of the next 5 rounds.

What's more, the small and large compensation offers worked just as well as an open offer of compensation. When people were asked outright how much compensation they would need to return to cooperation (choosing from 0 to 5 trials on which they would get a maximum payoff with their partner getting nothing), they didn't request enough to cover their losses. The average was 2.3—only slightly more than what they'd lost because of the aggressor's initial defections, and nowhere near what they'd lost through the aggressor's initial defections plus the losses due to the string of mutual defections that ensued (during which neither player benefited).[40]

The conclusion to draw from this study is that people are more willing to accept partial compensation than you might think—especially if the offenders seem sorry for their actions as well. This principle holds in the real world as well as in the social psychologist's laboratory. Crime victims say that they'd be willing to accept even small amounts of financial reparation for their material losses *provided that it's the transgressor who provides the reparation.*[41] This is because compensation can be paid not just with cash, but also with currencies such as suffering and sympathy.

Justice Restored

Apologize. Act like someone who's truly sorry. Try to undo the damage you've caused. Good advice for helping children resolve their playground disputes, but is it advice that can help grown-ups mend their conflicts too? Without question. We've already seen how indispensable signals such as apologies and solatia payments have become for helping Coalition forces maintain goodwill with the citizens of Iraq and Afghanistan. The restorative justice movement also applies these ideas to obtain positive outcomes for the victims of crime and the offenders alike.

In conventional Western criminal justice systems, crime victims' contributions to the criminal proceedings are usually limited to reporting the crime, giving an interview to prosecutors, perhaps testifying in court, and giving a victim impact statement during the sentencing hearing. Once prosecution and sentencing begin, victims quickly become peripheral. As a result, many victims feel estranged from the criminal justice process. The idea that crimes hurt human beings, and that the criminal justice system is supposed to help victims be made whole again, is strangely absent from the process. The criminologist Heather Strang depicts the situation like this:

> Imagine a criminal justice system in a democratic state which has evolved over hundreds of years. Imagine those accused of crime in that state acknowledging their legal guilt despite a deep-seated sense of grievance, while advocates on their behalf minimize

culpability on grounds their clients scarcely recognize. Imagine the victims of crime in that state having no chance to explain the consequences of the crime, their views seen as irrelevant and even dangerously distracting in the pursuit of justice. Imagine further a criminal justice system in which the guilty parties, having distanced themselves entirely from the consequences of their actions, are punished by the only means available—financial penalty, community service, or loss of liberty—all of them characterized by unconnectedness to the crime, and meaningless to victims except in terms of their desire for revenge. Is this the best we can do?[42]

The sorry state of the criminal justice system that Strang is decrying slowly began to improve in the late 1970s, thanks largely to grassroots activism and the writings of a few academics. By the mid-1990s an international "restorative justice" movement was in full blossom. Restorative justice can be viewed "as a particular method for dealing with crime that brings together an offender, his or her victims, and their respective families and friends to discuss the aftermath of an incident, and the steps that can be taken to repair the harm an offender has done." As a philosophical approach to crime, restorative justice embraces the following values: that offenders should be accountable to victims, that the effects of a harm should be undone, that offenders should be reintegrated into their communities when possible, and that dialogue between victims and their offenders should be respectful. Many communities around the world have adopted restorative justice practices for dealing with crime, and more than fifteen hundred restorative justice programs exist in North America and Europe. Some of them operate in lieu of formal sentencing, some operate alongside formal adjudication of crimes, and some programs are completely independent of the standard criminal justice setting.[43]

A centerpiece of restorative justice is the victim-offender conference, in which the people who are affected by a crime and their supporters (sometimes as many as one hundred people pack into a single room) get the opportunity to speak with the offender and his or her supporters. Professionals, such as community police officers, often preside over these meetings. Participation is completely voluntary for victims and offenders alike. Conferences usually are devoted to giving offenders an opportunity to explain their behavior, offer an apology, and work with their victims to identify a way to repair the damage they've done. In addition, they provide victims with an chance to gain perspective on why they were victimized, to ask questions of the offender, and to describe how the crime affected them.[44] Conferences typically last two hours or so, but for serious crimes, they have been known to last as long as eight hours.

Restorative justice conferences are extremely effective at reducing the desire for revenge and fostering forgiveness. Crime victims who participate in conferences with offenders who have robbed, burglarized, or assaulted them are 23 (!) times more likely than typical crime victims to feel that they've received a sincere apology from their offenders, 4 times *less* likely to experience a lingering desire for revenge, and 2.6 times more likely to report that they've forgiven their offenders (although the effects of these conferences on forgiveness seem to be more pronounced in some settings than in others).[45] In addition, victims who participate become less angry toward their offenders, less afraid of them, and more sympathetic toward them. Roughly 90 percent of participants are pleased with the outcome and say that they'd participate again in such a process.[46]

Strang and her colleagues surmise that victim-offender conferences obtain such positive outcomes because they give people the chance to reprocess the traumatic experiences and to talk to their offenders in a safe, nonthreatening way—a process that has been shown to reduce the symptoms of post-traumatic stress disorder. They also point to the empathy for the transgressor that often results, the positive emotional benefits of ritual participation, the debasement of the transgressor that comes with an apology, and the elevation of the victim that comes from the offender's acknowledgment that he or she violated the victim's rights.[47]

But it seems to me that they're as effective as they are because they promote the exchange of the signals I've been describing. Offenders who participate in restorative justice conferences have admitted their guilt. They usually offer sincere apologies and explanations for their behavior and, one imagines, nonverbal signals of shame and self-abasement. The conferences put offenders in a submissive position and require them to experience emotional suffering. And last but not least, the conferences are supposed to end with a plan for the offender to pay reparations to the victim. Although the restorative justice movement was created without reference to the principles of evolutionary psychology, no evolutionary psychologist could do much to improve upon this combination of ingredients for making forgiveness happen.

The Risks of Appeasement

As the success of restorative justice shows, the person with the greatest ability to help you forgive might not be you, but instead, the person who harmed you. This fact opens up important possibilities for making the world a more forgiving place. It's also a problem, of course, because many offenders have little appetite for taking the steps that would help their victims forgive.

From a perpetrator's point of view, signals such as apologies and compensation have three potential drawbacks. First, accepting blame for an offense you committed involves accepting *pain*—in the form of punishment, social disapproval, or other sanctions. With a $19.5 million lawsuit hanging over his head, it's not surprising that Todd Bertuzzi has been so cagey about acknowledging his culpability for hurting Steve Moore, and perhaps it's not so surprising that he hasn't gone out of his way to make a voluntary offer of compensation. Apologies also involve a loss of status and honor: the offender takes a one-down position and offers the victim some status instead. As we've seen, people are highly averse to losses of status and honor. In fact, losses of social status lead to a cascade of physiological consequences in many species, including increases in stress-related hormones, increased blood pressure, increased levels of LDLs (the "bad" cholesterol), and increased risk for cardiovascular disease.[48] Who wants to sign up for all that? As Bill Clinton's and Trent Lott's bungled efforts to apologize show, the temptation to hide from the truth of your misdeeds is often irresistible when lost status is the price of acknowledging your guilt.

Second, offenders sometimes worry that apologizing or acknowledging guilt might make it easier for a victim to feel justified in retaliating. People live to regret their decisions to appease their victims when those victims end up pursuing revenge anyway,[49] so the longer a perpetrator refuses to accept blame, he or she might think, the longer he or she can delay revenge.

Third, people don't want to apologize and acknowledge guilt when they really, truly believe that their causes are pure and their actions were just. Saddam Hussein never was contrite about Iraq's invasion of Kuwait in 1990—perhaps because he really did believe in the legitimacy of his claim that Kuwait is Iraq's nineteenth province.[50] Why offer a sincere apology if you don't think you did anything wrong? Many perpetrators' reticence to engage in signals that would foster forgiveness is aggravated by the fact that offenders tend to see their hurtful acts as more justifiable, less hurtful, and less immoral than their victims do.[51] As a result, offenders and victims often fail to see eye-to-eye about the gravity of a transgression. What's more, in most of the world's thorniest social problems involving violence and revenge, people often see themselves as both victims and perpetrators, which can make forgiveness-enhancing signals seem even more unattractive.

Most people have experienced the power of apologies, self-abasing rituals, and compensation. They know that these signals can quench the desire for revenge and can activate the forgiveness instinct, particularly in relationships with family members and close friends. In such relational contexts, the exchange of such signals often happens naturally and effectively without scientists and social reformers having to get involved. But to make forgiveness happen among strangers and non-kin—particularly after blood has been shed—people have always relied on formal rituals, formal institutions, and other formal social innovations. To wit: solatia and condolence payments work, especially when combined with sincere apologies and when presented in an appropriately solemn and dignity-enhancing way. If they didn't have their intended effect—to win people's hearts and minds by winning their forgiveness—the commanders in Afghanistan and Iraq wouldn't be wasting their time with them.

The restorative justice movement is another great example of an institution that brings out people's best selves in the aftermath of conflict and violence. Humans were able to appease and to forgive long before the contemporary restorative justice movement, but restorative justice works because it enables people to use their evolved moral intuitions to address the pain of crime in the mega-societies in which most of us live. Without the institution, people would have a harder time putting their natural inclinations to work so that they could help themselves forgive and be forgiven.

So if you set out to build "the forgiving society"—a society in which forgiveness flourishes and revenge is ever more infrequent, what sorts of conditions and institutions would you need to put in place? And what kind of society would you end up with?

CHAPTER NINE

FROM NEURONS TO NATIONS

Forgiveness takes place inside individual human minds. The kind of mind that can forgive is a mind that has come to perceive an offender as someone who is careworthy, valuable, and safe. A mind that has had its vengeful impulses satisfied (at least a little) by knowing that an offender has been punished or otherwise made to suffer may also be ready to forgive. People who want to be forgiven try to create these psychological conditions by apologizing, engaging in self-abasing displays, and trying to compensate their victims.

These principles for sating the desire for revenge and for activating the forgiveness instinct, which are so effective at the individual level, are scalable. We can use them not only to help individual victims forgive their transgressors but also to change the world. Groups can be helped to forgive other groups, communities can be helped to forgive other communities, factions can be helped to forgive other factions, and nations can even be helped to forgive other nations. The leaders or legitimate representatives of groups, communities, factions, and nations can offer apologies on behalf of their people to groups with whom they've been in conflict. They can also offer gestures that express remorse and empathy for the suffering of another group, and they can provide compensation to groups of people whom they've harmed—just as individuals can. When they engage in such gestures, it is often to great effect.[1]

In fact, these familiar signals—apology, self-abasement, and compensation—are regularly used on the world stage to soothe resentments and foster forgiveness. Pope John Paul II apologized to Jewish people everywhere for Christendom's participation in centuries of injustice against them. Japanese leaders have offered dozens of public apologies over the years for the war atrocities they committed against China, Korea, and their other Asian neighbors. The United States has made attempts to offer apologies and a token amount of monetary compensation to Japanese-Americans who were incarcerated and stripped of their property during World War II. And when Iraq's Prime Minister Nouri al-Maliki unveiled a twenty-four-point plan for trying to piece Iraq back together in June 2006, it was loaded down with revenge-quelling, forgiveness-promoting pro-posals such as (a) compensating people who had been harmed by terrorism, military operations, and sectarian violence; (b) compensating former government employees who had lost their jobs after Saddam was deposed; and (c) amnesty for "resistance" fighters so long as they hadn't been involved in terrorism, war crimes, or crimes against humanity.[2]

The devil's in the details, of course. Nothing even close to Maliki's plan for reconciliation was widely accepted afterward.[3] Just because the principles for activating the forgiveness instinct are simple doesn't mean that putting them to work in the midst of a complex intergroup conflict is easy. It never is. To make matters even more complicated, you'll always have cynics on the receiving ends of such forgiveness-promoting gestures who doubt their sincerity (and the course of human events often vindicates them for their cynicism). But when these complications can be surmounted, actions designed to quell revenge and foster forgiveness at the intergroup level have tremendous power to start honest and effective conversations about conflicts and injustices of the past, and to help people make the transition to a peaceful future. For instance, many people doubted the sincerity of the Irish Republic Army's 2002 apology for the deaths of noncombatants during the war in Northern Ireland, but the political capital that the IRA's leaders had to spend on such a risky move made it self-evident that the IRA truly were hoping fervently that the Ireland of the future might be less bloody than the Ireland of the previous century, and that they were willing to go to great lengths to make it so.[4]

STRONG STATES CAN CONTROL REVENGE

Beyond encouraging groups locked in conflict to engage in the behaviors that quell the desire for revenge and facilitate forgiveness, we also need to think about the sorts of macro-social conditions that are effective at controlling revenge in the first place. First off, the states that are most effective at controlling vengeance are those that are effective at enforcing the law, protecting their citizens from harm, and punishing violators. As we've seen, natural selection designed the desire for revenge so that people would be motivated to protect themselves from harm, defend their honor, and punish cheaters. When a state is effective in carrying out such functions, people are more willing to give up the burden of executing those self-protective functions for themselves.

In his 1939 book *The Civilizing Process*, the German sociologist Norbert Elias proposed that one of the factors that led to the centuries-long decline in Western Europe's rates of lethal violence—a process that began in the late Middle Ages—was the emergence of strong states that developed into "monopolies of force." When there's a true monopoly of force, the state and only the state has the legitimate power to punish people for harming other people. Nowadays, we're so accustomed to this macro-social reality that we scarcely recognize just what a momentous change it was for Western civilization. As Elias wrote, "When a monopoly of force is formed, pacified social spaces are created which are normally free from acts of violence."[5] In other words, when the state sucks up all of the legitimate power to harm and kill, revenge-motivated violence within the state plummets.

As the governments of Western Europe became better and better at monopolizing force, people eventually (and reluctantly, I suspect) acquiesced to the bargain put before them. The state promised to protect them from their neighbors, but in turn they had to promise to let the state settle things for them in lieu of taking the law into their own hands. What followed were twentyfold to fortyfold reductions in the homicide rates in England, The Netherlands, Belgium, Germany, Switzerland, Italy, and the Scandinavian countries. The Cambridge University criminologist Manuel Eisner has confirmed with historical data that homicide rates in Europe plummeted from 1350 until about 1975.[6] Remove people's legitimate ability to take revenge, and assure them that you'll look out for their rights through less vengeful means, and life consequently becomes much safer for everybody.[7]

Conversely, when the state's monopoly of force is disrupted, people are placed back in the position of having to take up the duty of self-protection for themselves, and life becomes more vengeful and more dangerous once again. As I write, the world is watching a natural experiment into what happens to revenge when a monopoly of force is disrupted. Before the March 2003 invasion of Iraq, there was approximately one violent Iraqi death per ten thousand residents per year. In the forty months between March 2003 and June 2006, this figure had soared to as high as seventy-two per ten thousand per year.[8] Extrapolating from these results, some epidemiologists estimate that as many as six hundred thousand Iraqis died violent deaths between the beginning of the invasion and June 2006. However, less than a third of those six hundred thousand deaths were attributable to the actions of Coalition forces. Of the remaining two-thirds, untold thousands (maybe hundreds of thousands) were due to revenge-fueled sectarian violence at the hands of militias representing the Kurdish-Shia and Arab-Sunni factions.

Saddam Hussein's ruling government, composed as it was largely of Sunni Arabs, did much to exacerbate the Sunni-Shi'ite rift. At the same time, the oppressive state and the strong military force also did a lot to keep revenge-motivated sectarian violence under control. When the United States and its allies toppled the Iraqi government and disbanded the Iraqi army in 2003, they did away with the monopoly of force that was keeping those ethnic and sectarian hostilities in check. In the power vacuum left behind, people began to rely on ancient tribal identities to protect themselves and their loved ones from kidnapping, torture, mutilation, and death—and to avenge themselves of the same. "This fighting, killing Sunnis and Shias, this is deep in the history of these tribes," an Iraqi observer told one reporter. "They call it revenge. This is in the history of the country, in the blood of the people."[9] Actually, revenge is in the history and the blood of peoples everywhere, but strong states can control it like no other institution can.

As I sit here writing these words, it's hard to predict how the cycles of sectarian violence and revenge in Iraq are going to end. The bodies just keep turning up in ditches and garbage dumps, riddled with broken bones, holes from drills and bullets, and acid burns. "If we could stop the cyclical nature of this in Baghdad, we could really change the dynamics here," said Major General William B. Caldwell, who was the main spokesman for the U.S. forces in Iraq.[10] No one disagrees that Saddam Hussein's regime was one of the truly awful ones in recent decades, and that his Baathist government was a nightmare for most Iraqis, but the revenge-motivated sectarian violence should come as no surprise because we did away with the only social institutions that were capable of containing it.

In this light, it's useful to go back to Western Europe for a moment to consider why homicide rates have been rising during the past thirty years, after a centuries-long trajectory of decline. Much of the increased violence that we're seeing in these already-strong European states is linked to the expansion of organized crime.[11] Increased trade and freer movement across Europe's borders have been a boon for many legitimate European economic interests, but the liberalized borders have also enabled organized crime syndicates to traffic drugs, launder money, smuggle people, and engage in many other sorts of illegal commercial activity more freely, too.

Because people involved in organized crime are by definition unable to call the police when a business partner double-crosses them or when they're trying to prevent another group of criminals from encroaching on their monopoly, and because they can't use legitimate sanctions to discipline their own members, they use revenge to get the job done. More organized crime in Europe means more vengeance in Europe, and more vengeance in Europe means more dead people in Europe. Unless European leaders and their constituents can develop an appetite for more policing (which is expensive) or even more drastic social changes, they might just have to live with the revenge that thrives in what Elias would call the "unpacified social space" of European organized crime. At the end of the day, European organized crime and Iraqi sectarian violence are more similar than different: the same social force—or rather, the absence of the same social force—is what enables them to thrive.

FORGIVENESS MAY REQUIRE A STRONG DOSE OF TRUTH

But endless war, motivated by sectarian hatred and the desire for revenge, doesn't have to be the end of the story in Iraq, or anywhere else. A day will likely come, as it usually does, when Iraqis grow too tired to continue fighting. We now understand better than ever what will be required to make forgiveness and reconciliation happen when that day finally does arrive. William Long and Peter Brecke, social scientists at Georgia Tech University, systematically analyzed the interactions between warring factions in ten recent civil wars, including three that ended with the reemergence of conflict (Colombia, North Yemen, and Chad) and seven that ended with a lasting peace (Argentina, Uruguay, Chile, El Salvador, Mozambique, South Africa, and Honduras). They concluded that the civil wars that end in forgiveness, reconciliation, or both are characterized by four processes.[12]

First, the countries that achieved lasting peace succeeded in redefining the affected people's identities. How do you redefine people's identities after a civil war? By helping them return to the lives they led before they were drawn into the conflict. Plans must be implemented to reconstruct people's homes and the infrastructures of their towns. Soldiers must be given help so they can resume their former lives as farmers and bank tellers. The role of the military must be redefined from that of an enforcer of government policy to that of a protector of the nation and all of its people.

Second, nations that successfully reconcile after civil war implement countless small actions (I'd call them signals) designed to announce and memorialize warring parties' desires to establish new, better relations with each other.

Third, they orchestrate a process of public truth telling through which the warring factions can reach consensus about how to understand the injustices they've suffered and the harms they've perpetrated upon each other. The truth and reconciliation commissions that have been used in South Africa, Cambodia, and elsewhere exemplify what Long and Brecke have in mind here.[13]

Fourth, they're able to enact a "justice short of revenge" in which "retributive justice [can] neither be ignored nor fully achieved."[14] Full retributive justice simply isn't a realistic goal in these situations because you have to be careful not to disturb the nascent, fragile peace, and overharsh retributive justice might provoke the factions that are still able to wield military power. Moreover, if the judicial system has been torn to shreds, there may be no legitimate body left to carry out retributive justice in a principled way. In addition, the legal authorities themselves are often complicit in the human rights abuses that occur during civil wars, making them unsuitable as arbiters of retributive justice when the war comes to a close. And sometimes, full retributive justice is impractical because combatants remain firmly convinced that their actions, however awful, were justifiable acts of war.

Nevertheless, in every case of successful reconciliation that Long and Brecke studied, partial justice was provided through a combination of three ingredients: (a) legal consequences for some perpetrators and losses to their moral standing and reputations, (b) amnesty for other perpetrators, and (c) reparations to some victims. Echoing my earlier point about people's surprising willingness to accept partial rather than full compensation for their losses, Long and Brecke write, "Disturbing as it may be, people appear to be able to tolerate a substantial amount of injustice by amnesty in the name of social peace."[15] We must remember that in many circumstances, people really, truly don't need an eye for an eye to give up their desire for retaliation: sometimes, half an eye, or even just a sincere apology, some public shaming, a credible pledge not to repeat the behavior, and a meaningful attempt at compensation will suffice. Justice short of revenge is a price that most people are willing to pay for peace.

RECONCILIATION BETWEEN STATES

The world's most pernicious problems with revenge, however, don't unfold between individuals or even between groups within a single nation. They take place between nations. The human race hasn't yet found a foolproof way to control the tendency for nations to wage war against each other, and these wars are often motivated or aggravated by the desire for revenge that national leaders can stoke so easily through persuasive speeches and subtle references to transgressions and humiliations suffered in the past.[16]

By acting as the world's policeman, the United Nations was *supposed* to be the strong supranational government that could prevent warfare between nations. However, the UN's ability to stop nations from attacking each other has been hamstrung by the fact that any member of the UN Security Council (which includes the most militarily powerful nations in the world) can veto any proposed UN military action that it views as a threat to itself or one of its allies. By design, it seems, the UN Security Council has no teeth. Until the UN becomes strong enough to stop violence between nations before it gets out of hand, or until some stronger form of supranational governance comes along, violence between nations, spawned and nurtured by feelings of vengefulness, will likely continue to be a fact of life.[17]

But even here there is room for some hope. As is the case with conflicts within nations, Long and Brecke tell us that reconciliation, if not forgiveness per se, can occur *between nations* as well. The forces that promote reconciliation between nations are surprisingly different from those that promote reconciliation after civil war. The basic hurdle to be surmounted in reconciling two nations that have been at war isn't the need to reestablish a coherent group (as is the case when trying to achieve reconciliation after a civil war) but rather the warring nations' need to be convinced that their enemy is genuinely interested in peace. Nations can demonstrate their commitment to peace most persuasively, Long and Brecke argue, by a sort of negotiated bargaining in which the leaders of the two nations exchange public "signals" that communicate their commitment to improved relations.

To be effective, Long and Brecke write, these signals should be perceived as novel (that is, something beyond the usual posturing on the international stage), freely given, and costly to the giver (as when leaders risk a loss of esteem in the eyes of their electorate in order to issue a public apology, or when a nation reduces its military capabilities in the interests of jumpstarting a deescalation process). Signals can be as simple and tentative as a speech that advertises that one nation's leaders want the war to end, and they can be as concrete and extensive as demilitarization, troop withdrawal, or an invitation to begin formal peace negotiations.[18]

In the exchange of these sorts of costly signals, it's useful for the group that's commonly viewed as militarily or economically more powerful to begin the process.[19] There are two reasons why this is the case. First, the more powerful nation has more resources to contribute to a cooperative future. Second, when the stronger nation makes conciliatory overtures toward its enemy, it has to lower its guard (at least symbolically), and this causes the less powerful nation to become temporarily less anxious about the power differential, and therefore more likely to reciprocate with peaceful gestures of its own. It's asking too much of an economically or militarily weaker nation to initiate the exchange of conciliatory gestures because when the weaker nation does so, the power differential between the two enemies seems to widen.

However, the power differential also makes it complicated for the more powerful nation to instigate a process of reconciliation. The more powerful nation is usually holding more of the cards already, so it has more to lose from addressing the injustices of the past and upsetting the status quo.[20] Because the requirements for effective reconciliation and forgiveness put high-power groups in such a bind, our expectations for forgiveness and reconciliation in the international sphere— particularly for forgiveness—should probably not be very high. Long and Brecke found that successfully resolved conflicts between nations very rarely contain the ingredients such as public truth-telling and limited justice that are so effective in healing civil wars: "It appears that a natural affinity does not yet extend to all nations . . . at least not enough to allow forgiveness to operate."[21]

In the short term, peacemakers should probably focus instead, as Long and Brecke suggest, on obtaining peace through the exchange of credible signals. After relations between two warring nations have become normalized, it's often possible to revisit the past in order to foster forgiveness, but that revisiting process might not occur for decades (as in the case of Japan's reluctant willingness to own up to its World War II atrocities) or perhaps even centuries (as in the case of the Roman Catholic Church's acknowledgment of its anti-Jewish sentiment and behavior).[22] Once this formal revisiting of the past takes place, official acts of apology and forgiveness may merely draw attention to the already-positive relations between the entities, rather than doing anything special to improve those relations.

Long and Brecke's findings regarding the meager prospects for forgiveness between nations are sobering, but we shouldn't give up so easily on the idea of forgiveness between nations after war: human nature has other tricks up its sleeve that we're only now learning to use. When we figure out how to use them, we'll be closer to figuring out how to make forgiveness happen on a truly global scale.

THE NONZERO EXPANDING CIRCLE

When we're harmed by strangers and long-standing enemies, we tend to favor revenge as a problem-solving strategy. When we're harmed by friends, cooperation partners, and family members, we tend to favor forgiveness. The psychological mechanism that sorts our social worlds into "friends and neighbors" versus "strangers and enemies" is innate, powerful, and automatic.[23] However, as Darwin acknowledged more than a century ago, the march of civilization brings with it a gradual shift of more and more of the people on the planet into our "friends and neighbors" piles, leaving fewer and fewer of them in our "strangers and enemies" piles:

As man advances in civilization, and small tribes are united into larger communities, the simplest reason would tell each individual that he ought to extend his social instincts and sympathies to all the members of the same nation, though personally unknown to him. This point being once reached, there is only an artificial barrier to prevent his sympathies extending to men of all nations and races. If, indeed, such men are separated from him by great differences in appearance or habits, experience unfortunately shews us how long it is, before we look at them as our fellow-creatures.[24]

One of the most formidable obstacles to making the world a more forgiving place, then, is figuring out how to turn groups we regard as enemies or strangers into groups we consider potential friends. As Darwin observed, the ability to make friends with members of other social groups—"outgroups," as social psychologists like to call them—is well within our innate social capabilities. But Darwin, ever the realist, also recognized that our ability to pull this off is easily confounded by wedges such as skin color, language, religion, culture, and ideology.

The science writer Robert Wright has taken Darwin's insight in an interesting direction that can lend some intellectual heft to our efforts to solve this how-do-we-turn-enemies-into-friends problem. The thesis of Wright's book *Nonzero* is that human society has developed to its current level of complexity (complexity, in the sense in which I'm using the word, is a good thing) because humans are endowed with a tendency to move people from the strangers and enemies pile into the friends and neighbors pile as soon as the perceived incentives for doing so outweigh the perceived risks. Wright argues convincingly that from humans' earliest existence in small kinship-based bands, to tribes, to chiefdoms, to states, to the mega-states of the modern era, cultural progress has occurred and human welfare has (generally) improved because our minds are prepared to spot the central lesson of the iterated prisoner's dilemma when it pops up in our daily lives: over the long run, cooperation pays better than competition.[25] As a result, we're ready to play ever-more-sophisticated "nonzero-sum" games with ever larger collectives of people that are ever further flung out around the globe.

Thus, according to Wright, when the perceived payoff is sufficiently compelling, people will readily cooperate not only with people from other families or tribes but also with people who are culturally different from them in every conceivable way. This inclination to cooperate explains why so many otherwise intelligent and wary people are taken in by simple con games such as the notorious "Nigerian bank scams" that use e-mails to trick unwitting dupes into cooperating in supposedly nonzero-sum (and undoubtedly illegal) games with shady bank officials whom they've never met: "Give me your bank account number in the US and help me launder the money sitting in this derelict account, and I'll share millions in proceeds with you."

Because humans are such compulsive cooperators, we're often willing to put aside our differences with each other (and groups of people are able to put aside their differences with other groups of people) when the incentives for cooperation are so high that they swamp our countervailing tendencies to seek revenge. If Wright is correct (and I think he is), then it follows that people will become more motivated to put their histories of bloody conflict behind them and try to forgive their former enemies when the benefits of cooperation are undeniably superior to the unforgiving, zero-sum status quo.

The Princeton philosopher Peter Singer has taken Darwin's insight in a different but equally useful direction. In *The Expanding Circle,* Singer describes how a few social instincts (he uses the examples of reciprocal altruism and kin altruism), combined with the increasingly sophisticated moral reasoning that seems to be seeping ever more deeply into human discourse as the centuries march on, are allowing human societies to gradually expand the scope of their moral concern.[26] (If you're dubious about this claim of moral progress, think about the advancement of women's rights, civil rights, children's rights, patients' rights, gay and lesbian rights, disability rights, labor rights, prisoners' rights, and even animal rights over the past two millennia).

Coincident with Norbert Elias's "civilizing process," which has led to ever greater state control over revenge, and the cooperation-based ratcheting of cultural progress that Wright describes in *Nonzero,* Singer notes that we are incorporating ever wider swaths of humanity into our circles of moral regard as civilization advances. The "simplest reason" really does show that it's fatuous to hold one human life to be less worthy of care and dignity than another just because that life happens to hold a passport from a different country than you do. In Singer's formulation, the moral universe can be an infinitely expanding one. If we use our reasoning powers wisely, there's no theoretical upper bound on the number of individuals, or the kinds of individuals, that we can consider worthy of our moral concern, and therefore, our forgiveness.

The problem with this optimistic vision for the future that Wright and Singer have sketched out is the one that Darwin identified a century ago: our tendency toward ingroup favoritism is innate, pervasive, and stubborn. Ingroup favoritism is probably driven by our deep history of relying on small, tight-knit groups of kin and well-known neighbors to survive and thrive.[27] We spontaneously trust ingroup members, and spontaneously distrust outgroup members. We give ingroup members the benefit of the doubt when they do wrong, but we don't extend the same courtesy to outgroup members. Consequently, we more readily forgive ingroup members than outgroup members.[28] If you ask people to forgive another group of people at the perceived expense of their own group, you'll only make things worse. But research has shown that strong incentives for cooperation, and some of the cognitive effects that flow out of effective cooperation, are powerful enough to overcome our hostilities toward outgroups. The Robbers Cave Study is a good example of these processes at work.

THE ROBBERS CAVE STUDY

It's the summer of 1954, and twenty-two twelve-year-old boys have just arrived at Robbers Cave State Park in Oklahoma for three weeks of summer fun. Without the boys' knowledge, a social psychologist named Muzafer Sherif and his colleagues have already divided the boys into two random groups of eleven boys each. For the first week of camp, the two groups will live in separate locations and perform their camp activities in complete isolation from each other—in fact, they won't even know that they're sharing the camp with another group of boys. During this first week of ingroup bonding, the boys are encouraged to develop distinctive names for their groups. One group calls themselves the Rattlers and the other group calls themselves the Eagles. They also create a set of rituals and emblems (T-shirts, flags, and mottos) to make their groups distinctive. All the while, Sherif is posing as the janitor for the camp so he can observe the boys' behavior surreptitiously.[29]

After the week of ingroup bonding, the researchers arrange for the two groups to meet each other. The two groups are automatically suspicious and slightly hostile toward each other, and the researchers fan these flames by arranging for them to compete in a week-long tournament consisting of a series of win-lose activities such as tugs-of-war, baseball games, tent-pitching contests, and treasure hunts. The competition is intense, and things quickly get nasty. The boys from the two groups begin to exchange insults, raid each others' cabins, and steal and destroy each others' personal property. Next, as if on cue, come the retaliatory raids and flag-burnings. Fights are breaking out during meal times. The boys begin carrying around baseball bats and socks filled with rocks, should the need for weapons arise.

Clearly, the Eagles and the Rattlers are not happy campers.

At the end of tournament week, the Eagles are declared the winners. They're festooned with medals, trophies, and prizes. The Rattlers, dejected, go away empty-handed. At the tournament's conclusion, the two groups are more cliquish than ever and they despise each other more than ever. Efforts to heal the Rattler-Eagle rift with communal meals and movie nights do little more than provide them with new opportunities to hurl food and insults at each other.

It's at this point in the project that Sherif and his colleagues bring out their secret weapon. They begin to stage a variety of small emergencies around camp that can be solved only if the Eagles and the Rattlers work together. These projects, which Sherif and company call "superordinate goals," include (a) locating the break in the system of pipes that brings drinking water into camp; (b) raising the money needed to rent a film they all want to watch; and (c) figuring out how to start a stalled truck with the tug-of-war rope so that a camp leader can fetch the groceries needed to prepare lunch. After several days of tackling and accomplishing this spate of superordinate goals, the intense animosities that had developed between the Rattlers and the Eagles are being put aside. During the last few days of camp, the Rattlers and Eagles start letting their guards down—perhaps even becoming friends. As time passes, the boys are intermingling so freely that it looks like their distinct group identities have ceased to matter very much. On the last day of camp, the Eagles and the Rattlers go home, together, crowded into the front of a single bus, singing "Oklahoma" in unison.

Three Good Things Cooperation Can Do

The Robbers Cave study is so cute that it's been a staple of social psychology textbooks for decades, but as famous as it is, I don't think we've even begun to take full advantage of the two lessons it can teach us for making the world a more forgiving place. The first of these lessons is that it takes little more than a flag, a few T-shirts, and some intense intergroup competition over valued resources to create fierce intergroup hostility. We can't lose sight of that. But the second lesson is that intergroup hostility can be undone by engaging hostile groups in activities in which they have to rely on each other to accomplish mutually valued goals. Here, the principle of "valuable relationships," which is so important for forgiveness between individuals, also surfaces as an important factor for encouraging forgiveness between *groups* as well.

Cooperation helps groups make the transition from conflict to forgiveness by promoting three different social-psychological phenomena: decategorization, recategorization, and mutual intergroup differentiation. These three mechanisms aren't mutually exclusive. In the process of moving toward intergroup forgiveness, we might use decategorization at times, only to switch to recategorization, only to switch later to mutual intergroup differentiation, and so on. Let's take a closer look at all three.

Decategorization

First, cooperation causes individuals from the other group to become decategorized: you stop thinking about them primarily in terms of their group membership. When you're trying to work with someone to solve a collective problem, it doesn't matter whether he or she is a Rattler or an Eagle. What matters is only whether he or she possesses the attributes that will make your cooperative dilemma easier to solve.

Decategorization is great in theory, but you have to walk a tightrope to pull it off in the real world. If you work too fervently to make people's group, ethnic, or religious identities less salient, they get worried that you're trying to strip from them an essential and invaluable part of their identities or their cultures in the service of peacemaking.[30] This can make people retreat back into their galvanized group identities, which short-circuits forgiveness and reconciliation.

One might also wonder, as Darwin did, whether people's allegiances to their political parties, nationalities, ethnic groups, religions, and so forth are so strong that efforts to decategorize are destined to fail—especially when group boundaries are demarcated by physical features such as skin color or behavioral features such as language and religious practice. With strong, tangible markers of coalitional alliances in place, won't the human cognitive apparatus have an especially hard time "undoing" its ingroup biases?

Maybe not. Take race as an example. Race is a social category that seems to be a huge impediment to people's efforts to get along, but it turns out to be surprisingly easy to get people to ignore it. The evolutionary psychologist Robert Kurzban and his colleagues argued that it's evolutionarily implausible that the human mind would possess an evolved mechanism for encoding race because "race" wasn't a part of the social landscapes in which our brains evolved. Instead, they argued, we care about race today, and split people into categories based on perceived race, only because race has been a faultline for intergroup conflict over the past several centuries. Kurzban and colleagues surmised that when it's really important to know whether someone is an Eagle or a Rattler, and when race is quite irrelevant to making that sort of judgment effectively, people don't pay attention to other people's race at all. They went on to conduct some clever experiments that showed just that. When the researchers provided participants with other, more reliable visual indicators of people's coalitional allegiances (for example, by having members of one mixed-race group wear yellow shirts while the members of the other mixed-race group wore gray shirts), the research participants suddenly became race-blind: they stopped lumping people together mentally on the basis of their racial features.[31] These results suggest that visual markers of group membership are only valuable to the extent that they really do help us figure out which "teams" people are on.

Implication: if we help people create new coalitions across the traditional faultlines of race, ethnicity, religion, and ideology so that those old faultlines are no longer useful as indicators of people's current coalitions, the old faultlines will cease to be faultlines at all. When that happens, forgiving this or that group for what they did to "us" in the past might be something we can make happen with less effort than you might think.

Cross-group friendships are another powerful tool for decategorization. People who have more friendly contact in their daily lives (in the form of friendships, work relationships, or family relationships) with members of groups with whom their group has been in conflict are more forgiving of harms from the past. For example, Northern Irish Catholics who have lots of contact with Protestants in their daily lives have more forgiving attitudes toward Protestants for "the Troubles" in Northern Ireland, and vice versa.[32] Even though you can't pick people's friends for them, the fact that cross-group friendships lead to intergroup forgiveness certainly suggests that if we can create societies in which such friendships are easier for people to form, intergroup forgiveness will be made easier, too.

RECATEGORIZATION

Cooperation leads to a second cognitive effect, which social psychologists call *recategorization*. At Robbers Cave, the campers came to recognize that in addition to their identities as Eagles or Rattlers, they were also members of a more inclusive group because they all had a set of collective problems that they had to work together to solve. If what's salient about our relationship is that I'm a Rattler and you're an Eagle, then our relationship is likely to be a troubled one. Why? Because my instinctual tendency to break my social world into categories of "us" and "them" tells me that being friendly with you puts me at risk of being disloyal to my own group. However, if what's most salient is that we're both members of a larger group—an undifferentiated bunch of boys who need to put their heads together to solve some problems—then I'll be more inclined to put our history of intergroup conflict behind us. Increasing the salience of the group to which we both belong, rather than the groups that make us different, can help us forgive each other.

Recategorization is an example of what the evolutionary scientists Peter Richerson, Robert Boyd, and Joe Henrich call a "tribal work-around."[33] By defining members of an outgroup as part of a superordinate ingroup to which we also belong— perhaps defined as a group of people who all use the same language, or who practice the same religion, or who reside in the same geographic region, or who are members of the same species (or, in the case of the Eagles and Rattlers, the superordinate group of twelve-year-olds who want to have a good time at Robbers Cave State Park during the summer of '54)—we can activate the ancient concerns for kith and kin and apply them to much larger groups, just as Darwin proposed. Lawrence Keeley, an expert in the anthropology of war, was really talking about recategorization as a mechanism for making forgiveness and reconciliation happen when he recommended that "we should strive to create the largest social, economic, and political units possible, ideally one encompassing the whole world, rather than allowing those we do have to fragment into mutually hostile ethnic or tribal enclaves."[34]

Here's recategorization in action. Some social psychologists were interested in what happens to people's willingness to forgive historical intergroup transgressions when they altered the social context that was used to "frame" the transgressions. When the researchers described the Holocaust to a group of Jewish participants as an incident in which Germans committed atrocities against Jews, participants said they were much less willing to forgive than when the researchers described the Holocaust as an incident in which a group of human beings committed atrocities against another group of human beings. Similarly, when the researchers asked Native Canadians to check some boxes on a piece of paper to indicate their ethnic identity *before* describing how they felt about the poor treatment of Natives in Canadian history, their attitudes were much less forgiving than were the attitudes of participants who hadn't been asked previously to identify their ethnic identity.[35] Thinking about the harms our little groups have suffered at the hands of other little groups makes us less forgiving; thinking about the harms that some of the members of our Big Group have done to other members of our Big Group makes us more forgiving.

MUTUAL INTERGROUP DIFFERENTIATION

Cooperation can also encourage a third cognitive effect that social psychologists call *mutual intergroup differentiation.* At Robbers Cave, both groups of boys eventually came to appreciate that the other group had unique strengths and assets *as a group per se,* and that mutual success was to be obtained by capitalizing upon the strengths of both groups.[36]

As two distinct groups, they accomplished things they couldn't have accomplished on their own. This discovery helped them to make peace.

SOWING SEEDS OF PEACE

Simply forcing Iraq's Sunnis and Shias or Northern Ireland's Catholics and Protestants or Rwanda's Tutsis and Hutus to brush up against each other more frequently doesn't do much to make things better, and sometimes it makes things a lot worse. If you want one group of people to forgive another group of people, you have to encourage the *right* kinds of contact.

Seeds of Peace is an innovative program that's trying to encourage the right kinds of contact. The late journalist John Wallach started this organization in 1993 in an effort to contribute to peace in the Middle East by getting to the next generation of leaders while they're still teenagers. Seeds of Peace does its work through summer camps, but unlike the kids at Robbers Cave, who had to be sundered into competitive, hostile groups before they were willing to hurl mashed potatoes at each other, the kids who attend Seeds of Peace camps come from nations that have been hurling bullets and bombs at each other for years or decades.

The kids who get the privilege of attending a Seeds of Peace camp are selected by the education ministries in their home countries on the basis of their leadership potential. The camp revolves around helping the teens develop lasting relationships with, and respect for, young people from the other side of the conflict. Seeds of Peace camps contain heavy doses of the same silliness and Kum Ba Yah good feeling you'd experience at any other summer camp in the United States, but there's a lot of serious talk and respectful listening, too. The entire agenda is infused with opportunities for campers to develop durable friendships with people from the other side, appreciation and respect for the concerns that keep the conflict going, and firm conviction that a peaceful and respectful coexistence is possible.

The Seeds of Peace philosophy is simple: if the young people who attend a Seeds of Peace camp build up a storehouse of new positive experiences with members of the outgroup while they're in the sheltered camp environment, they can use those experiences as a sort of psychological scaffolding to help them undo the pernicious ingroup-outgroup effects I've been talking about. As a result, it is hoped, they'll go on to become effective ambassadors for forgiveness and reconciliation when they return home.

In the summer of 1993, the fledgling program brought forty-six Israeli, Palestinian, and Egyptian teenagers together at a camp in the woods of Maine. Tamer Nagy is a young Egyptian man who was part of that first camp: "[Y]ou come [to the camp] to share your story, and find that things are a lot more complex than you had thought." Describing how the camps are run, he says, "It always began with very intensive discussions, with crying and yelling, but eventually, you run out of things to argue about and you start listening to what the other side has to say."

In recent years, Seeds of Peace has hosted nearly four hundred campers each summer. Most sessions still focus on the Middle East, although camps have also been run with students from conflict areas in Asia, Europe, and even the United States. It's too soon to tell what the long-term effects of the program will be. That first group of Arab and Israeli campers have only recently entered the workforce. Nevertheless, Nagy is optimistic that a new future awaits Israelis and Arabs when these young people assume positions of influence: "Despite everything happening in the Middle East, we have managed to communicate with one another. . . . and the conversation will continue until the day of our generation arrives."[37]

CHAPTER TEN

DIVINE FORGIVENESS AND RIGHTEOUS REVENGE

The Amish are at the top of every anthropologist's list of the world's peaceful societies, but they're no strangers to violence. Like the other Anabaptist sects that took root in Switzerland, France, and Germany, the Amish faced a horrific religious persecution during the seventeenth century. The Swiss government was particularly brutal toward the "non-conformists": with a blessing from the official state church, the Swiss set up a secret police force of "Anabaptist hunters" to hunt them down and arrest them. The Anabaptists were stripped of their property, tortured, and deported. Some were burned at the stake, and some were sold into slavery—all because they refused to conform to the state religion, swear an oath of loyalty to the state, or serve in the military. But despite the persecution they faced, the Anabaptists refused to take up arms against their tormentors. Violence, even in self-defense, simply wasn't in their toolbox. Standing on their principles eventually drove them out of Europe, and into America.[1]

This violent history, and the Anabaptists' peaceful response to it, has etched an indelible ethic of forgiveness into Amish culture and identity. So in a sense, the Amish had had four hundred years to prepare their response to what happened on October 2, 2006. That Monday morning, a gunman entered a one-room Amish schoolhouse in Nickel Mines, Pennsylvania, and took ten young Amish schoolgirls as hostages (all of the adults and all of the boys in the classroom were sent away). The police quickly arrived on the scene, but before they could disarm the man, he shot and killed five of the girls, wounded the remaining five, and then killed himself.

Within hours of the Nickel Mines shooting, people from the Amish community in Lancaster County were assuring the reporters who flocked to the scene that the Amish would find it in their hearts to forgive the killer. Indeed, within days, they were reaching out to the killer's family with expressions of love and concern. Donald Kraybill, one of the leading experts on the Amish, explained their reflexively forgiving response to the senseless slaughter in the simplest of terms: "Retaliation and revenge are not part of their vocabulary."[2] The Amish people model their lives on the life and teachings of Jesus, as most Christians claim to do, but something enables the Amish to practice what they preach in a way that most people—self-professed Christians included—would find unfathomable.

"We're really strongly taught to forgive like Jesus did," one Amish woman told a reporter. "We forgive the way Christ forgives us."[3] Kraybill writes, "The Amish take the life and teachings of Jesus seriously. Without formal creeds, their simple (but not simplistic) faith accents living in the way of Jesus rather than comprehending the complexities of religious doctrine. Their model is the suffering Jesus, who carried his cross without complaint. And who, hanging on the cross, extended forgiveness to his tormentors. . . . And that is why words of forgiveness were sent to the killer's family before the blood had dried on the schoolhouse floor."[4]

The Amish aren't the only people whose religion seems to motivate them to forgive. Chante Mallard, whom I introduced back at the beginning of this book, hit Gregory Biggs with her car in the wee hours of October 26, 2001. She didn't call 911 or even try to help Gregory, despite her training as a nurse's aide. Instead, she drove home, put her car back in the garage, and left Gregory trapped in the car's windshield to die a lonely, gruesome, terrifying death. Later, she and two friends dumped his body in a nearby park.

When Gregory's only son Brandon learned how Mallard had allowed his father to die, he quickly resolved to move past hatred and resentment. "Yes, it was a process. But it was a quick process. I knew I had to extend forgiveness immediately." Biggs accepted an apology from Mallard during the trial. In return, he offered his forgiveness to her. "I wanted her to know that I had forgiven her and that I hoped she would accept the forgiveness of Jesus Christ. That was really in my heart. That was what I wanted her and her family to know, that no matter how great the crime was or how great the sin was, that God is still able to forgive and that we offer our forgiveness to their family."[5]

The link between religion and forgiveness is even deeper than these stories suggest. Many of the world's paragons of forgiveness—Martin Luther King Jr., the Dalai Lama, Archbishop Desmond Tutu—have been religious leaders. Religious texts from many world religions, including Judaism, Christianity, Islam, Hinduism, and Buddhism, command (or at least commend) forgiveness.[6] According to the 1998 General Social Survey, over 80 percent of American adults feel that their religious beliefs frequently offer them help in forgiving others.[7] Many other studies have shown that religious people report themselves to be more forgiving than do people who aren't so religious.[8]

One such study was a survey of 826 former political prisoners from the Czech Republic. Following its transition from a repressive Communist regime to a democracy, the Czech Republic established a broad range of social policies to provide compensation, justice, and belated apologies to the political victims of the oppressive post–World War II Communist era. The study showed that those former prisoners who were actively involved in a church were substantially more likely to report that they had forgiven the people who had harmed them—even after statistically controlling for the amount of harm they had suffered, how much reparation they had received, and how much their perpetrators had been punished.[9]

But religion can also spawn vengeance. It has motivated and sustained some of the most stubborn and vengeful conflicts the world has ever known. Islamists can still muster feelings of humiliation and rage over the Crusades. The rancor between the Sunni and Shi'ite Muslim sects is almost as old as Islam itself. Religious differences have pulled at the seams of Ireland's social fabric for centuries. Christian bitterness toward Jews for the death of Jesus (which, as we'll see, is a misplaced bitterness at that) has smoldered for two millennia. In other words, religion seems to be just as good at helping people keep their grudges alive as it is at inspiring them to forgive.

For instance, a 2004 survey found that Americans with strong conservative Christian beliefs were nearly three times more likely to believe that Muslim Americans should be forced to register with the federal government so that their whereabouts can be monitored, 50 percent more likely to believe that Islam encourages violence more than other religions do, and 50 percent more likely to think that the United States should be able to detain terrorists indefinitely. What's interesting here is not that Americans want to be tough on terrorists, but that strong Christian beliefs motivate people to be tough not only on terrorists but also on the millions of American Muslims who've done absolutely nothing wrong.[10]

The harder you dig to understand the connections of religion to forgiveness and revenge, the bigger the contradictions seem. Take Islam as another example. Muhammad and his early followers valued Islam so much in part because it provided an *alternative to revenge*—not a justification for it. The Arabic root *s-l-m*, from which we derive the word "Islam," is also the root for *salam*, meaning "peace,"[11] which is why President George W. Bush's post-9/11 proclamation that "Islam is a religion of peace" was doubly meaningful.

But did you know that among Allah's ninety-nine names is not only "the all-forgiving" and "the pardoner" but also "the avenger"? In Osama bin Laden's famous "Letter to America," which was published on the Internet in 2002 and later by England's *Observer* newspaper, he directly cites Islam for condoning, if not inspiring, Al Qaeda's attacks against the United States: "Allah, the almighty, legislated the permission and the option to take revenge. Thus, if we are attacked, then we have the right to attack back. Whoever has destroyed our villages and towns, then we have the right to destroy their villages and towns. Whoever has stolen our wealth, then we have the right to destroy their economy. And whoever has killed our civilians, then we have the right to kill theirs."[12]

Don't fool yourself by thinking that such beliefs are held only by the lunatic fringe. This is wholesome, mainstream stuff in many Muslim nations at this time in history. A 2005 survey by the Pew Global Attitudes project revealed that about one-quarter of Turkish Muslims, one-third of Indonesian Muslims, and more than one-half of Jordanian and Lebanese Muslims believe that violence against civilians on their own soil is justifiable (at least on occasion) to defend Islam.[13]

What in the world is going on with religion, forgiveness, and revenge? Why are so many religious Americans, with their religion of turning the other cheek and the long-suffering Jesus, so gung-ho about allowing their government to track other loyal Americans who just happen to belong to a distrusted religious group? Why are so many devout Muslims, with their religion of peace and God the "all-forgiving," so willing to resort to violence against civilians to defend their religion? Are religious people just hypocrites? Is religion part of the solution to the world's problems with revenge, or does it make them worse? Maybe it's both. To get closer to a decent answer, let's back up for a moment and explore a more fundamental question.

WHAT'S RELIGION FOR?

Everyone seems to have a different answer to this question.

Religious people, of course, believe that religions (their own religion, at least) draw people closer to God, or equip people to negotiate a world that's populated by powerful supernatural forces, or encourage people to be good. Traditional social scientists, in contrast, believe that religions exist because they enable the elite to control the masses, or because they provide people with consolation and hope in the face of setbacks, or because they can assuage people's fear of death.

But evolutionary scientists take a different tack. They're perfectly willing to acknowledge that religions often are useful for control and comfort and so forth, but most of them doubt that religion could have evolved *because of these effects*. They tend to think of these effects as by-products of religion rather than the *functions* of religion—that is, they're not the things religion does that caused it to evolve in the first place.[14]

Instead, most evolutionary scientists believe that religion itself is a by-product of more basic mental processes—for example, an innate tendency to assume that other people have minds or spirits that animate their actions, and our innate tendency to believe that objects in motion were set into motion by some sort of force. Once evolution put those basic mental building blocks in place, by-product theorists argue, it wasn't long before people began to believe that people possess souls that outlive their physical bodies and that the world is full of spirits that can create volcanoes, lightning, and disease. If the by-product theorists are right, then primitive religion emerged as a natural outcome of the mind's basic cognitive architecture rather than because of anything special that religion does *for* people.

Once primitive religion came online, though, it seems plausible that it was eventually promoted from its status as a humble by-product of more basic mental processes to the more exalted status of *secondary adaptation*. Secondary adaptations are traits whose genes are refined and conserved by natural selection on the basis of adaptive properties they acquire *after* they've already appeared on the scene for other reasons. Feathers make for a good analogy here. The earliest feathers probably weren't designed for flight, but rather, for temperature regulation. Over time, the natural selection of feathers on the basis of their heat-trapping properties caused them to take on a shape that, purely by coincidence, gave small prehistoric reptiles a bit of lift (picture the modern-day chicken getting just enough lift to get over a short fence or into the crotch of a tree). This newly acquired flying ability would have yielded a formidable selective advantage as flying animals got better and better at catching food and evading predators. Thus a trait that arose for one purpose (temperature regulation) was later modified on the basis of another property (flight).[15]

Perhaps humans' religious inclinations are like birds' feathers—something that evolved to serve a function that had nothing to do with the reason it came into being in the first place. If so, what kind of "flying" has religion assisted humans in accomplishing? The answer almost surely has something to do with living in large groups.[16] The evolutionary biologist David Sloan Wilson has suggested that religions can be understood by thinking of them as "adaptive groups" whose function is to help their membership flourish in specific ecological and social settings. To fulfill this function, they encourage beliefs and behaviors that promote the group's fitness amidst a population of other groups. If a religion can't create beliefs and behaviors that assist with this goal, the group fails.[17]

CHRISTIANITY'S UNEASY RELATIONSHIP WITH FORGIVENESS AND REVENGE

A simple-minded hypothesis can guide us for the next while (we'll have time for some nuance a bit later). If revenge toward a certain outgroup, under certain conditions, at a certain phase in a particular religious group's life course improves its fitness, then religious doctrine and historical precedent will be invoked out of the religion's texts and traditions to justify vengeful behavior. Likewise, if forgiveness toward a certain group of people works better for that particular religious group at that point in time, doctrinal and historical support will be marshaled to justify that stance, too. In other words, don't be surprised to find that successful religions—especially the world's mega-religions such as Christianity and Islam, which have been wildly successful across a wide variety of environments—can promote a seemingly infinite variety of beliefs and practices regarding revenge and forgiveness. This is because the religions that have stood the test of time are long-lived precisely *because* they've been flexible enough to respond effectively to the wide variety of social contingencies that they've faced during their cultural evolution. To see these ideas in action, Professor Wilson points us to the four gospels of the Christian Bible, which chronicle Jesus' ministry and Christianity's gestation period.[18]

You can't help but be moved by Jesus' preoccupation with extending forgiveness to people who lived on the fringes of respectable Jewish society. Take tax collectors, for instance. Judean tax collectors in Jesus' day were private contractors for the Romans. Tax collectors were renowned for their greed and dishonesty, were despised for "collaborating" with a foreign occupier, and most Jews scorned them. But Jesus seems to like them. He even invites the tax collector Matthew to become one of his twelve disciples.

In other passages, Jesus offers comfort and forgiveness to a woman who has been caught in adultery (John 8) and to a "sinful woman" (maybe a prostitute) who washes his feet with her tears (Luke 7). In yet another passage (Matthew 9), Jesus heals a man with paralysis and declares that the man's sins are forgiven, and in John 9 he restores sight to a man with congenital blindness (people with such infirmities were second-class citizens). In John 4, he befriends and offers consolation and salvation to a Samaritan woman (ordinary Jews thought of Samaritans as halfbreeds). Even on the cross, according to Luke 23, Jesus promises a place in heaven to one of the common criminals being crucified alongside him. There's no mistaking the message: Jesus has a soft spot for crooks, collaborators, whores, outcasts, and misfits. No bit of scripture captures Jesus' forgiving attitude toward those on society's margins more colorfully than does his retort to some of his critics in Luke 5:31–32: "It is not the healthy who need a doctor, but the sick."[19]

Jesus' eagerness to forgive those who lived at the margins of Jewish society stands in abrupt contrast to the horrors that he forecasts for those who embrace his message but fail to live according to his teachings. In Mark 14, Jesus warns of the harsh punishment that awaits Judas the betrayer, and in Matthew 24 and 25, he offers cautionary tales about unfaithful servants who are "thrown into the darkness" or "cut to pieces."

If you look at all of this from an adaptationist point of view, it's not too hard to figure out what's going on. Put yourself in Jesus' sandals for a minute. You're trying to build a new religious movement, and you need to attract new converts and keep the converts you've already won. Extending forgiveness and acceptance to the sorts of people who are getting a raw deal under the current religious system is an excellent tool for growing your flock. Also, threats of harsh punishment in the afterlife will help to raise some serious barriers to getting out. Jesus' policies on forgiveness seem tailor-made for building this new religious movement.

There's a third group of people that the gospel writers address in relation to the new Christian movement: the Jewish establishment. During the first few decades after the death of Jesus, Christianity was an offshoot of Judaism, both religiously and ethnically. However, as the first century came to a close, a profound demographic shift had turned Christianity into a *bona fide* gentile religion. As a result, the debate about Christianity's status in relation to mainstream Judaism was transformed from an "intramural spat" (to quote the religion scholar John Fitzgerald) between two factions of the same faith into a bitter rivalry between two ethnically distinct religions. Professor Wilson notes that the survival of the Jesus movement in those latter decades therefore depended critically upon creating ideological distance from, and animosity toward, the Jewish establishment.

Remember that the gospels were written many decades after Jesus died. Before that, the stories of Jesus were passed down by word of mouth. The long lag time between the actual events of Jesus' life and the writing-down of those events gave plenty of leeway for the sort of historical tweaking that would help generate ill will for the Jews when the need arose toward the end of the first century. One way the gospel writers seem to take advantage of this leeway is by pointing the finger at the Jewish community for Jesus' death. According to the gospel of Matthew, Jesus is arrested and then brought to trial by the Jewish leadership for the crime of blasphemy, where the chief priests elicit false testimony against him, convict him, and then beat him up. Next, they take Jesus to the palace of the Roman leader of Judea, Pontius Pilate. There, a baying crowd urges a reluctant Pilate to crucify Jesus. Finding no good reason to put Jesus to death, Pilate hesitates, but to appease the angry crowd he eventually gives in to their demands.

Historical documents outside of Christian scripture from the same era cast doubt on the accuracy of this impotent depiction of Pontius Pilate. The writer Philo of Alexandria describes Pilate as an extraordinarily cruel ruler. The Jewish historian Josephus describes Pilate as a governor who was unsympathetic to Jews' complaints about violations of their religious consciences—and as one who wasn't at all squeamish about using some degree of violence to quell Jewish discontent. According to Philo and Josephus (who, it's worth mentioning, may have had axes of their own to grind[20]), then, Pilate doesn't seem like the type of guy who would have capitulated to Jewish pressure to execute another Jew unless Pilate himself had also wanted Jesus dead. It seems unlikely that Pilate would have agreed to squander Rome's resources (including the considerable outlay of manpower required to conduct an execution, maintain crowd control, and then guard Jesus' tomb for several days thereafter) to put to death a man who had done absolutely nothing wrong under Roman law—unless he had his own reasons for wanting to execute Jesus. Nevertheless, the author of the gospel of Matthew clearly shows where he wants to lay the blame for Jesus' crucifixion:

> "What shall I do, then, with Jesus who is called Christ?" Pilate asked. They all answered, "Crucify him!" Why? What crime has he committed?" asked Pilate. But they shouted all the louder, "Crucify him!" When Pilate saw that he was getting nowhere, but that instead an uproar was starting, he took water and washed his hands in front of the crowd. "I am innocent of this man's blood," he said. "It is your responsibility!" All the people answered, "Let his blood be on us and on our children!" (Matthew 27: 22–25).

There is another reason to question the veracity of the gospel account: the gospel of Matthew suggests that Jesus' show trial took place before the Sanhedrin (which was traditionally a group of some seventy Jewish judges). But Matthew also tells us that Jesus' trial took place on the Passover. Now, the idea that the entire Sanhedrin could have been assembled on a Passover night simply strains credulity. Another gem from John Fitzgerald: "Getting the Sanhedrin together on Passover would have been about as easy as assembling the United States Congress on Christmas Eve." Therefore the gospel writers' assignment of blame to Jewish leaders and their mob, and their move to free Pilate and the Roman government from moral culpability for Jesus' death (in Luke 23:34, Jesus even prays for his Roman crucifiers, asking God to forgive them because "they do not know what they are doing"), looks even more like a frame-up job.

One can only wonder in horror at just how much revenge-motivated violence has been perpetrated against Jews "and their children" during the past two thousand years under the trumped-up justification that the "killers of Christ" had it coming. Wilson puts it a bit more politely, and a bit more biologically: "[I]t is entirely possible that the New Testament has predisposed Christians to hate Jews long, long after it ceased to be adaptive."[21]

For the next nineteen centuries, the Christian church's policies on forgiveness would go on to change as its own fortunes changed. In the fourth century, Christianity gained official political support under the Emperor Constantine. Thanks to the theological influence of Augustine during the centuries that followed, the church also acquired political power and untold wealth. Eventually, Christianity became the recognized religion of the empire. Forgiveness was no longer a tool for attracting Christians, or even for retaining Christians: *as far as Christendom was concerned, the whole civilized world was Christian.*

So times changed for the once-tiny Jesus movement, and the role of forgiveness in public life for Christendom changed too. As Donald Shriver notes, forgiveness became a matter of individual conscience, but not the watchword for Christianity's relations with "the world" that one might have expected on the basis of Jesus' teachings about turning the other cheek, forgiving seventy times seven, and so on.[22] The church's policies regarding the role of forgiveness in public life changed to fit with the church's meteoric rise to the top of the religious food chain, and with its own ambitions to acquire and hold on to worldly power.

Even so, Jesus' words haven't lost their power to motivate forgiveness, especially when individuals or small groups lacking real political power face injustice, persecution, or heartbreaking violence. How many of the early Christian martyrs drew comfort from Jesus' words, "Father forgive them, for they know not what they are doing" as they allowed themselves to be imprisoned, humiliated, and torn apart by wild animals for Rome's amusement? How many of the thousands of Anabaptists who were murdered or chased out of Europe recited those same words? How many of the civil rights workers of the American South, and how many of the victims of apartheid in South Africa, who faced beatings, snarling dogs, imprisonment, and even death, fell to the ground with those words on their lips?

FORGIVENESS SAVES THE WAORANI

A different example of how religious teachings about forgiveness and revenge can interface with a group's needs comes from fieldwork on the Waorani people of eastern Ecuador.[23] You may remember the Waorani from Chapter Four because I mentioned them as an example of an extremely vengeful society that nevertheless lacked an actual word for the concept of "revenge." Anthropologists first made contact with the Waorani in 1958, when they numbered about six hundred. In short order, the Waorani became renowned in anthropological circles for their ferocity and for the ease with which their interactions with each other could spiral into blood feuding. In fact, by the time the anthropologists caught up with the Waorani, revenge was starting to tear this tiny culture apart. Homicide was the leading cause of death among adults, and the blood feuds were so rampant that entire family groups were being wiped out. Not surprisingly, the young men and women were also having difficulty finding mates and establishing the next generation.

The Waorani knew that their way of life was disappearing before their eyes, but all they could do was stand by and watch it happen. Even the old rituals for signaling value, safety, and careworthiness (such as exchanges of gifts like meat, blowguns, and hammocks, and friendly visits between people from different villages) had stopped working. Then, in an evolutionary nanosecond, the cycles of revenge were stopped in their tracks, and Waorani culture was transformed. Something important had happened.

That something was the introduction of Christianity by Western missionaries. When the missionaries had arrived back in 1956, they hadn't exactly received a warm welcome. Several Waorani warriors had attacked with spears and killed five of the missionary men during a raid at Palm Beach. This encounter set the stage for all that was to come, because the Waorani warriors couldn't understand why the missionaries had refused to use their guns to defend themselves (one warrior was in fact killed by a bullet during the Palm Beach raid, but people seem to agree that that single bullet had been fired into the air in hopes of scaring off the attackers). The fact that the remaining missionaries refused to retaliate after the raid (even though one of them lost a brother and another, a husband) only added to the Waorani's fascination with them. Instead of trying to wreak vengeance on the Waorani, the missionaries wanted to "save" them.

The Waorani began to conclude that it was the missionaries' religion, with all its talk of Jesus and love and forgiveness, that made them different. Perhaps this strange religion could help the Waorani solve their own problems with revenge.

The warriors who killed the five missionaries would be among the earliest adopters of the missionaries' new religion. Then, seeing that Christianity was powerful enough to cause even their fiercest warriors to surrender their grudges, many other Waorani eventually followed suit. By 1973, about five hundred Waorani had converted to the Christian faith. They settled into a new community of converts, where they were able to reunite with their loved ones, enjoy protection from old vendettas, and benefit from access to the trade goods that were being imported from the modern world. Of all the benefits that their new way of life afforded them, though, the most appealing were the Christian injunction against revenge and its message of forgiveness. The missionaries encouraged the converts to demonstrate the sincerity of their conversions by surrendering their vendettas (a common mantra of the new converts was "On behalf of Jesus, do not spear.").[24] As one convert explained,

> Before the kowodë [missionaries] came and taught us about God we lived spearing. Back and forth, back and forth we speared, they died. We tried to stop killing. We would say, "that's enough, leave off spearing." Then someone would kill and we would return to killing back and forth. After hearing and believing in God, Kemö and I told them not to spear on our behalf, no matter how we died. And we ceased killing others back and forth. Just a few years ago when some Waorani men killed my sister, I refused to spear on her behalf. Had I not believed, they would all be dead now.[25]

For the Waorani, adoption of Christianity seems to have operated as an honest, costly signal of their commitment to lives of forgiveness. The fact that the missionaries didn't use violence to defend themselves or to retaliate lent validity to their Christian beliefs, so when Waorani warriors became converts as well, they also made commitments to abandon their old grudges. Their conversions, too, then came to be viewed as "honest signals" of their commitment to a more forgiving way of life. The late adopters eventually followed suit, recognizing that if they too accepted Christianity, they might also enjoy the protection and social stability that the Christian way of life could offer, as well as the freedom to forgive. From within this haven of safety, they could rebuild their families and their culture.

By and large, it worked. Today, there are about two thousand Waorani. Their population has more than tripled since the arrival of Christianity half a century ago. In other ways, the past five decades have not been kind to the Waorani. Environmental degradation, pollution, and hostility from the modern world threaten from all sides. However, it's not exaggerating things to conclude that religion, by encouraging forgiveness and discouraging revenge, brought the Waorani back from the brink.[26]

There are some interesting chicken-and-egg questions to consider here. On one hand, we can think of the introduction of Christianity as the chicken that hatched the forgiving way of life that the Waorani adopted. It was their commitment to Christianity that inspired them to restrain their vengeful impulses and embrace forgiveness. On the other hand, the fact that those first missionaries, and their earliest converts, were so forgiving in the face of violence was what made Christianity so attractive in the first place. Indeed, it's hard to imagine that a Christianity that taught that God was aggressive and vengeful, and that his followers must show their devotion by doing likewise, would have been very attractive to the Waorani because they already had all the revenge they needed—and more—without having to go to the trouble of converting to a strange new religion. Forgiveness led to religious conversions, which led to more forgiveness, which led to more conversions. So was it Christianity that made the Waorani so forgiving, or was it forgiveness that made the Waorani turn to Christianity?

Religion as a Vengeance Engine

There's a passage in the nineteenth and twentieth chapters of the book of Judges in the Hebrew Bible that's as graphically violent as any Tarantino film. It tells the story of a man and his concubine (a second-favorite wife, more or less, which under normal circumstances wasn't as bad as you might think, but read on) from the Israelite tribe of Levi. On a journey back home from Bethlehem, they stop for the night in the Benjamite town of Gibeah. During the night, some of the "wicked men of the city" knock on the host's door and demand that the host "Bring out the man who came to your house so that we can have sex with him." The host refuses, but he offers this alternative: "Look, here is my virgin daughter, and his concubine. I will bring them out to you now, and you can use them and do to them whatever you wish." The Levite guest hands his concubine over to the wicked men, and they rape and assault her through the night. Then they let her go. She crawls back to the house where she and her husband have been staying, and she dies on the doorstep. (What happened to the host's daughter, or for that matter, what the Levite guest is doing to occupy his time while the wicked men are raping and murdering his wife, are anyone's guess.)

The next morning, the Levite takes his concubine's body with him back to his homeland, where he proceeds to cut it up into twelve pieces. As a variation on the standard practice of cutting up an ox and sending the pieces to various constituencies to raise an army during a crisis, he sends one piece to each of Israel's twelve tribes as way of shocking them into action against Gibeah. Outraged, representatives from the tribes assemble to decide on a course of action. They respond with one voice: "None of us will go home. No, not one of us will return to his house. But now this is what we'll do to Gibeah: We'll go up against it as the lot directs. We'll take ten men out of every hundred from all the tribes of Israel, and a hundred from a thousand, and a thousand from ten thousand, to get provisions for the army. Then, when the army arrives at Gibeah in Benjamin, it can give them what they deserve for all this vileness done in Israel."

Before attacking, the tribes of Israel implore the Benjamites to hand over the offenders peacefully, but the Benjamites refuse.

Therefore, Israel amasses an army of four hundred thousand swordsmen. After two days of intense fighting, during which Israel suffers tens of thousands of casualties, the Israelites pray for guidance on whether they should continue their assault. God answers: "Go, for tomorrow I will give them into your hands." Israel proceeds to slaughter all but a few hundred of the remaining Benjamite soldiers, who flee to the desert. The Israelite army then moves into the towns of Benjamin and levels them all, butchering every man, woman, child, and animal they come across.

What happens to someone who reads this passage today? Brad Bushman and his colleagues expected that it would make people more aggressive, especially if they happen to be devoutly religious. So these researchers created several variations of the story and ran a little experiment. Half of the participants who read the story were told that it was from the Bible, and half were told that it was taken from an ancient scroll. These two halves of the participants were further divided. One half within each of the two groups read a version of the story in which God explicitly condoned the retaliatory attack; for the other half, God didn't register an opinion.

After reading the story, the research participants were asked to participate in a standard laboratory procedure for eliciting aggression. They played twenty-five rounds of a competitive reaction time game with a partner. During each round, the players received a signal. The first player to press a button after hearing the signal delivered a blast of noise into the headphones that the other player was wearing. Before each round, players could adjust the sound volume on their sound-blasting apparatus, with options ranging from 0 (no noise) to 105 decibels (imagine the sound of a jackhammer or a chainsaw from a couple of meters away).

Bushman and his co-workers wanted to know whether believing that the story was from the Bible, or believing that the passage contained God's endorsement of the violence, would cause participants to choose higher sound-blast levels in the seemingly unrelated reaction time test. In a first study, the researchers studied a group of undergrads from Brigham Young University (what with BYU being a Mormon school, kids who go there tend to be pretty devout). They found that the students who believed the passage was from the Bible gave about 40 percent more high-intensity sound blasts (that is, sound blasts that were set to 9 or 10 on the machine) than did students who had been told that the passage was from an ancient scroll. Likewise, participants who read the passage in which God endorsed the retaliation gave about 40 percent more high-intensity sound blasts than did the people who hadn't read that God had endorsed the attack.

In a second study, Bushman and his colleagues tested the same hypothesis with a group of students from a secular university in the Netherlands (only about one-half of whom said they believed in God). The students who read the passage in which God endorsed the retaliation gave 77 percent more high-intensity sound blasts than did those who read the passage in which God didn't endorse the retaliation. Moreover, people who said that they believed in God and in the Bible gave more high-intensity shocks, and—here the results are even more disturbing—it was the Bible-believing, God-fearing students whose aggression levels were most pumped up by believing that God had sanctioned the attack.[27]

The "Book of Judges" study is not the first to suggest that religious practice and ideology can motivate revenge. In another study, researchers had participants answer a series of questions about their religious lives (for example, how frequently they went to religious services, the number of religious activities in which they participated, and how frequently they donated money to their religious congregations), and a self-report measure of their overt attitudes toward vengeance. They also obtained a behavioral measure of revenge by having participants complete a competitive reaction time task like the one that Bushman and his colleagues used (except that in this study, participants delivered shocks instead of noise blasts). The researchers wanted to know how much shock participants would administer to their competitors after they had endured a string of increasingly provocative shocks themselves (which culminated in the competitor's attempt to deliver the maximum-intensity shock that the machine could deliver).

For about the bizillionth time, the researchers replicated the well-established finding that religiously devout people espouse less favorable attitudes toward vengeance than do less religious people. Religious people will often tell you that they disapprove of revenge in theory. Yet the participants' actual behavior betrayed their true feelings about revenge. People who reported that they made frequent financial donations to their churches (a frequently used, though by no means perfect, indicator of devoutness) administered higher levels of shock to their provokers than did the infrequent donors.[28] This association between frequent donation and more severe retaliatory shock held up even after statistically controlling for age, gender, and the other measures of religious behavior.

These two studies illustrate some tangible ways in which religious ideology, transmitted through scripture or through commitment to a particular community of faith, can promote revenge. But of course, the link between religion and revenge is no more inexorable than is the link between religion and forgiveness. The history of Christianity, which I've already described, shows as much. Islam's history does too.

ISLAM'S UNEASY RELATIONSHIP WITH REVENGE AND FORGIVENESS

Islam, like Christianity, has had an uneasy relationship with forgiveness and revenge. Scholars take pains to point out that the Arabian Peninsula was a chaotic, vengeance-ridden mess before Islam came along.[29] Life in Arabia gradually became less vengeful as Islam showed that it was able to provide Arabs with a common group identity that took priority over their clan-based identities. But just as the rule of law in Western Europe relied on threats of deadly force to contain homicidal blood revenge, Islam's civilizing influence was also backed up by force.

This amalgam of the desire for peace and the willingness to use violence when required characterized Muhammad himself. In two short decades, Muhammad metamorphosed from a virtuous merchant to a gentle prophet who long-sufferingly faced the abuse of the rich Meccan rulers to a battle-scarred leader of a mighty Islamic army. Tradition has it that after decisively routing the Meccans and overseeing their mass conversion to Islam in 630, Muhammad was quick to forgive them (although even this seemed to be contingent upon their conversion to Islam).[30]

The Qur'an, too, presents an interesting blend of forgiveness and revenge. Sociologist Mark Juergensmeyer points out in *Terror in the Mind of God* that the Qur'an has explicit prescriptions against killing and that it's particularly queasy about killing civilians.[31] Moreover, mainstream Qur'anic thought through the centuries has embraced religious pluralism and has held that freedom of religious expression is a god-given right for all people.[32] Nevertheless, as with Christianity, there's enough flexibility in Islam's texts to allow Muslim leaders to formulate all sorts of behavioral responses—including vengeful ones—to the social circumstances that might arise. To wit: during the past century, radical Islamist scholars and political leaders have succeeded in reviving a seven-hundred-year-old brand of Muslim theology that emphasizes scriptural literalism, intolerance for the other traditions, and the legitimacy of jihad against Jews and Christians. By embracing this fundamentalist form of Islam, they've managed to stir up a seemingly bottomless pit of hatred against the modern world.

In particular, these radical interpreters of Islam have managed to stretch the Qur'an's definition of "justifiable violence" to include not only the defense of one's physical safety or the freedom to practice Islam, but also, the defense of one's dignity and one's material well-being, and even the advance of Islam itself.[33] Sheikh Omar Abdul-Rahman, who was convicted for his role in inciting the 1993 bombing of the World Trade Center, was once asked in a television interview to explain why, "wherever you go, people end up dead." Presumably he thought he was speaking for all Muslims when he replied, "We can never call for violence. We call for love, forgiveness, and tolerance. But if we are aggressed against, if our land is usurped, we must call for hitting the attacker and the aggressor to put an end to aggression."[34] Islam, like Christianity, has enough flexibility and diversity to justify both revenge and forgiveness.

RELIGIONS ARE LIVING SYSTEMS

In diagnosing the role of religion in encouraging forgiveness and revenge, we're quickly moving toward a rather unsexy conclusion: successful religions, especially the world's mega-religions, whose adherents number in the millions and billions, can be whatever they need to be in order to survive and thrive in the conditions they've customarily encountered throughout their development. The proof of this is the fact that they *are* successful. This means that the same religions that can promote messages of nonviolent resistance, forgiveness of enemies, and brotherly love are also able to promote righteous retaliation, a thirst for the blood of one's enemies, and the exaltation of revenge to a solemn religious duty. There's no contradiction here: religions can do what needs to be done because they've historically been flexible enough to do what *needed* to be done.

The only religions that have had long-term viability while maintaining a rigid pro-forgiveness, nonviolent stance are those that have lacked natural "predators," or that have been willing to migrate to new habitats when competition from other groups became too fierce, or that obtained protection from host cultures that were willing to defend the pacifists with their own capacity for violent force. This describes the Amish to a tee. In fact, the great American theologian Reinhold Niebuhr famously criticized the Mennonites (another group of Anabaptists) before World War II by claiming that their form of Christian pacifism was "a parasite on the sins of the rest of us, who maintain government and relative social peace and relative social justice."[35] If anybody's army decided to head up to Lancaster County, Pennsylvania, to try and exterminate the Old Order Amish who have made a home for themselves there, they'd have to get through the United States National Guard first.

But maybe Neibuhr was being too harsh (not to mention offensive) by comparing the Anabaptists to parasites. Unpleasant thought, but perhaps the Amish really would stand by passively and allow themselves to be wiped out if a bloodthirsty horde rushed in to destroy them. After all, when the religious pressure for behavioral conformity is strong enough, people will endure all kinds of ordeals that are decidedly *not* adaptive—think of castration, vows of celibacy and poverty, and handling poisonous snakes (yes, some Appalachians who handle rattlesnakes, water moccasins, and copperheads do get bitten, and they've got the withered hands, missing fingers, and memories of dead relatives to prove it). Just because the Amish have never been put in the position where they *had* to choose between violent self-defense and extinction doesn't mean that they wouldn't stick by their beliefs in unconditional forgiveness to the bitter end. They might.

By the way, did you notice how even the master theologian Niebuhr gets seduced by the power of biological language like parasitism for thinking about the relations among religious groups? Maybe David Sloan Wilson is right to suggest that religious groups (like all groups) really are "alive" in a way that's distinct from simply saying that the group's members are alive (just as it makes sense to say that David Sloan Wilson is alive in a way that's distinct from saying that the cells that make up his body are alive). If Wilson is right, then maybe we can squeeze a bit more mileage from the drab-seeming conclusion that successful religions can promote both forgiveness and revenge because they've already survived countless social crises that required them to do both.

Let's push the metaphor of religious groups as living systems a little closer toward absurdity to see what it buys us. Think of a religious group as a big nervous system, and the individual members as neurons. Instead of using chemical and electrical signals to communicate, the neurons communicate among themselves with doctrine and social pressure. This giant nervous system is sensitive to its surroundings, so when it detects conditions that would require it to respond with forgiveness, the neurons secrete doctrine and social pressure that ultimately give rise to forgiveness. Likewise, when it detects external conditions to which it thinks it should respond with revenge, the neurons secrete doctrine and social pressure that motivate vengeful behavior.

This little flight of fancy leads to the following message for the world's reformers: if you want religious groups around the world (as organism-like things unto themselves) to be forces for forgiveness, you need to create the conditions that will cause them to perceive that forgiveness is in their best interests. When you do, they'll emphasize the doctrine and traditions that favor forgiveness. If those religious groups perceive instead that revenge is the behavioral option that will work best for them, then that's what you'll get from them. In the end, religion will be a force for forgiveness in the world when, and only when, there's a perceived payoff to those groups themselves. The challenge for harnessing religion's power to motivate forgiveness is to create the kind of sociopolitical world in which religious groups can't help *but* perceive that forgiveness is in their best interests. In figuring out how to make these kinds of sociopolitical realities happen, we'd be fools not to try to work with the reformers within those traditions who can offer help and guidance.

Religion is here for the foreseeable future, and religious groups are going to keep doing exactly what they please, largely shaped by their perceptions of their self-interest. We can either ignore religion's power to shape forgiveness and revenge to our own peril, or else we can try to understand that power and work with it. We shouldn't let misplaced optimism cause us to expect anything more, but we shouldn't let unwarranted pessimism cause us to strive for anything less.

CHAPTER ELEVEN

HOMO IGNOSCENS

Carolus Linnaeus, the Swedish botanist, was the Adam of the scientific age. He set out not only to name the animals (and the plants, and the minerals) but also to devise a system of rules for naming and classifying them. His system has been in use, with modifications, ever since. In the Linnaean system, every species gets two Latin names. The first name identifies the genus to which the species belongs. The second is an epithet that's supposed to describe what makes the species distinctive. Linnaeus named our species *Homo sapiens: Homo* for man, *sapiens* for "the knower" or "the wise."[1] You have to admit that this is pretty good, for no species has managed to know more about the world, and about itself, than *Homo sapiens* has.

Occasionally, though, a social scientist comes along who can't resist the urge to try out a different epithet. There's *Homo faber*—"Man the maker," *Homo ludens*—"Man the player," and *Homo economicus,* and even *Homo religiosus.* And the list goes on. So I suppose it's inevitable, if a bit cheeky, that I might propose yet one more. How about *Homo ignoscens*—"Man the forgiver"? It's not such a big stretch. The capacity to forgive is a built-in feature of human nature. We're prone to forgive our family members, our friends, and the people with whom we're engaged in cooperative ventures. The forgiveness instinct arises when we experience an offender as safe, valuable, and worthy of our care.

People are willing to forgive when offenders offer appropriate signals, such as apologies, self-abasing gestures, and offers of compensation. When we design societies so that people's rights are protected, so that they experience justice, and so that they have incentives for cooperating (rather than competing) with their former enemies, then forgiveness arises as a natural consequence of how our minds evolved to operate.

Being a "forgiving" species doesn't make us terribly distinctive, however. The epithet *ignoscens* could be used to describe many of our primate relatives (and vertebrates more generally) nearly as well as it describes us. But as "Man the knower," we gain a forgiveness advantage over the other animals, for we can talk about forgiveness, record extraordinary acts of forgiveness for posterity, study forgiveness in the laboratory and in the field, and change the world to make it a more forgiving, less vengeful place. Our status as "Man the knower" puts us in a position to become the most forgiving of species.

The most serious problem with using the name *Homo ignoscens* as a depiction of human nature, though, is that it's a portrait taken from our good side. We *are* a forgiving species, but we're also a vengeful one. As the ugly realities of world events often remind us, *Homo ultor*—man the avenger—is no less apt a name than *Homo ignoscens* is. Unfortunately, there's no reason to think that the desire for revenge is on its way out of the evolved psychological apparatus that characterizes our species.

This is a problem, for the future of humanity may very well rest on our ability to control revenge and promote forgiveness. As the bad people of the world get angrier, more organized, and better funded, we really do have to worry about what the desire for revenge might be capable of doing to our world as this century unfolds. But I'm optimistic, because our species has three other characteristics that can enable us to stack the deck in favor of the world becoming a more forgiving place.

WE'RE CONTEXT-SENSITIVE CREATURES

Every living thing must adjust its behavior in response to changes in the environment. Context-sensitivity is a hallmark of life itself. Among humans, natural selection has raised context-sensitivity to unprecedented heights. Few species have managed to thrive under as many different environmental conditions as *Homo sapiens* has. We can live in some of the harshest climates on the planet (from deserts to the arctic tundra), and for many of those we can't inhabit on a long-term basis (the ocean depths, for instance), we can travel on temporary visas. Almost anywhere people go, they figure out how to feed themselves, clothe themselves, and find shelter.

Our flexibility in adjusting to dramatically different environmental contingencies is a direct result of the extraordinary temperature fluctuations that the earth has endured over the past 800,000 years. Until quite recently, it wasn't uncommon for average temperatures to swing ten degrees within a single century. (A small and perhaps worthwhile digression: the past 11,500 years have been a period of unprecedented stability in the earth's surface temperature, and we've benefited greatly from that stability, which is why climate scientists hector us not to take it for granted.) To adapt to these quick temperature changes, ancestral humans had to evolve a high degree of behavioral flexibility, and they did. Their brains got bigger, and with increasing brain size, their ability to learn from direct experience and to use tools got better, too.[2]

If you're able to learn to do new things through direct contact with the environment, and if you're able to fashion new tools to help you do those new things, then you can be a very flexible creature indeed. You're ready to learn the lessons that life has to teach you about how to thrive in your environment, and you're able to build the gadgets that can help you. As two scientists recently put it, "Humans are the virtuosos of cultural diversity. We fish, hunt, shepherd, forage and cultivate. We practice polygyny, polyandry and monogamy, pay bride-prices and dowries, and have patrilineal and matrilineal wealth inheritance. We construct or inhabit all manner of shelters, speak about 7,000 different languages and eat everything from seeds to whales."[3] These different approaches to life's challenges are the outworking of evolutionarily crafted mental mechanisms that enable humans to adapt to new surroundings through direct experience with the world, rather than exclusively through genetic programming.

Our adaptations for revenge and forgiveness are context-sensitive, too. They're solutions to problems that humans persistently encountered during evolution, and people still encounter many of those problems today. When people live in places where crime and disorder are high, where policing is poor, where governments are weak, and where life is dangerous, they will tend to use revenge as a problem-solving strategy because its ability to punish aggressors, its ability to deter would-be aggressors, and its ability to discourage cheaters made it adaptive in our ancestral environment. Likewise, in places where people are highly dependent on complex networks of cooperative relationships, where policing is reliable, where the system of justice is fair and trustworthy, and where social institutions are up to the task of helping offenders to depict themselves as careworthy, valuable, and safe, they will respond with higher rates of forgiveness because when such conditions were present in our ancestral environment, forgiveness was adaptive.

The lesson for social reformers is clear: if you can identify the factors that sustain revenge or prevent forgiveness in the settings in which you have the ability to implement change, and if you can implement those changes without creating unintended undesirable consequences (which one can never take for granted when thinking about social change), you may be in a position to make your corner of the world a more forgiving place.

WE'RE CULTURAL CREATURES

There's another reason why our species has coped so well with new contingencies: we have an evolved mechanism for quickly adjusting our behavior so that it responds more faithfully to the challenges our environments set before us. That mechanism is culture. By "culture" I mean "information capable of affecting individuals' behavior that they acquire from other members of their species through teaching, imitation, and other forms of social transmission."[4] I'm talking here not about art and music, but about more prosaic forms of culture, such as the know-how for getting the tannins out of acorns so you can eat them, knowledge about where to find clean drinking water, or the skill needed to make a projectile point out of a flake of obsidian.

Culture enables us to modify our behavior to better suit our environment more quickly than natural selection, acting on our genes, ever could, and more adroitly than if we had to find a solution to every new problem on our own. Our capacity for culture enables us to do something that relatively few species can do: learn from other individuals by sitting back and watching their successes and failures. By watching others to see what works for them—how to catch fish, how treat an infection, how to make good counterfeit twenties, or how to make a good dry barbecue rub—we can tackle a much wider range of problems than we'd have the time and brains to figure out all on our own.

There are two good scientific reasons to consider the human capacity for culture if you want to make the world a less vengeful, more forgiving place. The first is that cultural changes can produce changes in revenge and forgiveness even when we can't change the social and environmental contingencies directly. This is because culture's function, as far as forgiveness and revenge are concerned, is to help people to learn rules about when it's appropriate to forgive and when it's appropriate to seek revenge without always having to learn those rules through the school of hard knocks.

Because we are cultural learners, we can learn valuable lessons about where and when to seek revenge, and about where and when to forgive, simply by observing our parents, siblings, friends, associates, teachers, and mentors. We also learn culturally by paying attention to formal vehicles for transmitting culture such as religious teachings, myths, traditions, the arts, advertisements, items in the news, and so forth. The "code of the street" that governs social behavior in many inner-city U.S. cities, and the culture of honor that governs behavior in many traditional herding societies, for example, are big bundles of revenge-promoting cultural information. Likewise, the Amish are fed a steady diet of pro-forgiveness religious teachings and other cultural inputs that make them into the superforgivers they are. Most of us are in between the two extremes, raised on a diet of mixed cultural inputs, some of which promote revenge and others of which encourage forgiveness.

We're not the only species whose habits regarding revenge and forgiveness are influenced by cultural learning. In one study, juvenile rhesus macaques were co-housed for five months with juvenile stumptailed macaques, who by nature are much more conciliatory than rhesus macaques tend to be. Over the five months of co-housing, the rhesus macaques took on the conciliatory traits of their more conciliatory stumptailed roommates. In fact, even after the rhesus macaques were separated from the stumptails, they went on to manifest three times as much reconciliation behavior as rhesus macaques ordinarily do.[5] Here's a case of monkey see, monkey do—simple imitation (that is to say, cultural learning). Stumptailed macaques are heavier than rhesus macaques, and in this study the stumptails were older than the rhesus macaques, too, which might have made them particularly good models for cultural learning (especially if cultural learning is governed by innate learning rules such as "copy the big guy," or "copy the older guy").[6]

Parents also are important cultural influences upon nonhuman primates' conciliatory styles. Brown capuchin monkeys that have secure relationships with their mothers go on to have more relaxed conciliatory styles than do capuchins that have insecure relationships with their mothers.[7] Other researchers found that rhesus monkeys that had been weaned and separated from their mothers early in life, and then reared in relative isolation, lacked even the weak conciliatory tendencies that are typically seen in rhesus macaques.[8] When early caregiving experiences are disrupted, something happens to impede the development of the conciliatory styles that are characteristic of these species.

At first glance, this troika of studies on monkeys might seem to throw cold water on my whole evolutionary story about revenge and forgiveness. By showing how easily the readiness to reconcile can be modified by social or cultural factors, don't these findings contradict the idea that the desire for revenge and the capacity to forgive are biologically based adaptations that were created through natural selection?

Not at all. What these findings show is even more interesting: that species-typical adaptations develop in response to environmental (and, in these examples, cultural) inputs. Change an organism's cultural experience, and the development of its adaptations can change, too. Separate infant monkeys from their mothers, and they'll grow up to be less conciliatory than is species-typical. Raise them among individuals from a more conciliatory species, and they'll become more conciliatory than is species-typical. To say that culture influences the development of psychological adaptations is no more controversial than saying that a cultural tradition that calls for compressing infants' skulls with a flat board (which was a rather common practice around the world for thousands of years) will change the shape of those skulls as they develop.[9] In both cases, culture causes an adaptation (one skeletal, one behavioral) to take on a different "shape" than it would under different cultural influences.

So if you want to create cultural changes that will help your world develop into a more forgiving place, where should you start? I'm not the expert on the spheres of life in which you have influence, so that's your problem to tackle. But as you try to put such changes into place, you can take heart that cultural changes are already afoot, on a more macro scale, that are also conspiring to make the world a more forgiving place.

To see these macro-level cultural changes for yourself, you can consult the electronic databases that document the spread of scientific and cultural knowledge. There's a database that tracks scientific publications in my field of psychology. In 1976, this database informs us, psychological knowledge about forgiveness was virtually nil. Only one article was published in 1976 that had anything to do with forgiveness, and at that time, you could have summarized everything that psychologists knew about forgiveness in the right margin of this page. But the scientists who came afterward began to build upon that tiny sliver of knowledge. In 1986, ten articles related to forgiveness were published. A decade later, in 1996, nineteen new articles were published. Over the next decade, the cultural floodgates really opened: in 2006 alone, over one hundred new scientific articles concerning forgiveness appeared in psychological journals. The sheer amount of scientific knowledge on forgiveness—which, as a type of "information capable of affecting individuals' behavior that they acquire from other members of their species," is a type of culture—has been growing at an astonishing rate. We know more than ever about how to make the world a more forgiving place.

Here's another macro-level cultural change that has been making the world a more forgiving place. Few people knew very much about the idea of a "truth and reconciliation commission" before the early to mid-1990s, when El Salvador and South Africa put commissions in place to investigate human rights abuses during civil war (in the case of El Salvador) and apartheid (in the case of South Africa). Since then, the "truth and reconciliation commission" idea has been disseminated worldwide through newspapers, television programs, and other information outlets. This cultural information has been digested by millions of members of a species of cultural learners, and many of these cultural learners have created copies of that cultural information by establishing truth and reconciliation commissions within their own nations—often to great effect. The United States Institute of Peace documents more than twenty nations that have tried out the truth and reconciliation commission idea following their civil wars.[10] This is cultural learning at its finest, and at a truly global scale.

The same could be said of the idea of "restorative justice." Nobody ever talked about restorative justice in the popular media until the 1990s, but coverage of the topic has grown substantially since then. Not long ago, restorative justice simply didn't exist as a formal cultural practice, but as I mentioned in Chapter Eight, there are now more than fifteen hundred community-based restorative justice programs in North America and Europe. The "idea" that reconciliation can be an effective way of healing a nation after a civil war isn't El Salvador's or South Africa's idea anymore, and the idea that "restorative justice" can do something to make the world a more peaceful and forgiving place doesn't belong exclusively to a bunch of academics anymore. Because we're a species of cultural learners, these ideas now belong to all of us.

There's a second reason to keep in mind that humans are cultural creatures: culture is such a powerful influence on what we learn to do, and what we teach others to do, that it can cause a behavior to come unhinged from the environmental contingencies that made the behavior useful in an earlier era. Culture can maintain behaviors among a cultural group even after the environmental factors that made such behaviors adaptive have dissipated. It's useful to be prone to revenge when you live in a hostile and unstable social environment, and cultural forces that would encourage you to develop into a vengeful person would clearly be advantageous in such an environment, but what happens when the environment becomes safer and revenge therefore becomes less necessary? Cultural forces can continue to keep the behavior going for no other reason than because "that's the way we've always done things." We can get stuck in cultural eddies that sustain behaviors that have become unproductive, or even positively maladaptive.[11]

Recall those undergraduate men from the University of Michigan, described in Chapter Three, who were in an experiment in which they were bumped and insulted by another student. Half of the men had been raised in the American South, which was originally settled by people from herding cultures; and half had been raised in the North, which was settled originally by people from farming cultures. Although these students were attending one of the nation's finest universities, no doubt in preparation for careers in business, science, law, communication, art, and public service (professions in which raising livestock and growing crops would play a fairly small role), the Southern men manifested the "herder's response" when provoked: psychologically, physiologically, and behaviorally, they got ready for violent action. They started behaving as if they had herds that they needed to defend by making themselves look fierce and fearless, even though it had probably been centuries since their ancestors had made a living in a herding economy. This pre-retaliatory behavior, which had become unhinged from the environmental contingencies in which it would have been adaptive, was being maintained instead by cultural forces.[12]

A study of students at the University of Pennsylvania and at University of California-Berkeley illustrates a similar phenomenon. Jewish participants tended to believe that some offenses are unforgivable, whereas Protestant participants tended to think that all offenses are theoretically forgivable. What ecological factor might have caused this religious difference in students' attitudes about forgiveness? There probably wasn't one, unless you count culture as an ecological factor. Jewish theology teaches that some offenses are unforgivable (some offenses are too severe to forgive, some can't be forgiven because only victims have the right to forgive, and some can't be forgiven because forgiveness is contingent upon the transgressor's repentance). Protestant theology, in contrast, teaches that all offenses are forgivable (except for the "unforgivable sin," a topic about which the Christian scriptures are surprisingly laconic). Of course, the horrors of the

Holocaust might have also influenced the Jewish students' attitudes, too, but even the effects of the Holocaust on the Jewish students were culturally mediated through family stories, film depictions, and other cultural devices. They didn't experience the Holocaust directly.[13]

So culture matters, just like environmental and social contingencies matter. You can make the world a more forgiving place by changing the real social and physical environments in which people live, or if you can get a big enough lever on the cultural forces that promote (and maintain) revenge and forgiveness, you can also make the world a more forgiving place by changing culture.

WE'RE COOPERATIVE CREATURES

One of the most provocative proposals in evolutionary biology in recent years (to my mind, anyway) is evolutionary biologist Martin Nowak's claim that cooperation is essential not only for the evolution of social relations, but also for the evolution of life itself. He went on to assert that "natural cooperation" should be added alongside mutation and selection as a fundamental principle of evolution.[14] Nowak writes, "Genes cooperate in genomes. Chromosomes cooperate in eukaryotic cells. Cells cooperate in multicellular organisms. There are many examples of cooperation among animals. Humans are the champions of cooperation: from hunter-gatherer societies to nation-states, cooperation is the decisive organizing principle of human society."[15] Even coming as it does from one of the world's foremost experts on evolution and cooperation, it's a pretty gutsy claim, but Nowak might just be right. To create biological specialization and complexity from simple parts, cooperation seems to be just as essential as mutation and natural selection are.

It's even possible that the first strands of RNA that began to replicate in the primordial soup required cooperative relationships with "helper molecules" to keep their own replication processes going.[16] Without the first replicating RNA, there would have been no DNA and no genes. Had genes not begun cooperating to their mutual benefit, there'd be no bacteria. Had bacteria not begun cooperating to their mutual benefit, there'd be no eukaryotic cells. Had the eukaryotic cells not established cooperative pacts with each other to form multicellular organisms, there'd be no us. And had we not stumbled upon the benefits that come from living in small groups, society would never have formed. The role of cooperation in the evolution of life has a fractal beauty, with communities of simple units eventually merging into new and more complex life forms, which themselves combine into more complex life forms.[17] This process of generating complexity from simple parts can be seen at every scale at which life unfolds—from the molecular to the macrosocial.

Does mother nature have more complexity in store for *Homo sapiens*? It just might (that is, if global terrorism, nuclear Armageddon, ecosystem collapse, or some other catastrophe doesn't intervene first). If the history of life on this planet is any guide to what might come next, then the next transition for human evolution will probably involve yet more cooperation. We're already organized into very large groups called nation-states, so perhaps the next evolutionary transition will result in a lasting bond of cooperation among the world's nation-states—an organism-like entity made up of organism-like groups of organisms.

The success of such a super-superorganism would rest largely upon whether the emergent complex system is resilient enough to tolerate the constituent nations' occasional efforts to defect in the service of feathering their own nests. Within complex biological systems, the lower-level units remain committed to their self-interest, so conflict and attempts at rebellion are inevitable. From cancer cells, which begin as rogue cells that escape detection by the body's sophisticated systems of policing so that they can replicate unfettered, to the members of Congress from the fifty United States who vie for limited federal dollars that they can take back to their home states, to the nations that make up the United Nations security council, conflict and competition among the lower-level units must be actively managed.[18] If a complex biological system is to stand the test of time, incentives must be in place to sustain cooperation, and checks and balances must be in place to limit selfishness. In addition, the system must be resilient enough to avoid breaking apart at the first signs of rebellion from the lower-level units.

In other words, complex social systems need to be forgiving systems if they are to evolve (think tit-for-tat, Generous tit-for-tat, and so on). But as I've described time and again, the benefits of cooperation themselves can also create an incentive for the lower-level units to forgive each other (remember the valuable-relationships hypothesis). So cooperation can give rise to forgiveness, but forgiveness can give rise to cooperation, too. Start wherever you like: make the world a more forgiving place and see cooperation flourish, or, if you prefer, make the world a more cooperative place and watch forgiveness flourish. From the long view of evolutionary history, conditions seem quite favorable for more forgiveness, more cooperation, and more complexity.

Sound flaky? Keep in mind that most people thought the idea of cobbling together an enduring republic out of Britain's thirteen American colonies was pretty flaky, too. The colonies seemed too incompatible for that sort of thing: too many ethnic groups (English, Scots-Irish, Germans, and African slaves), too many religions (Calvinists, Lutherans, and Catholics), incompatible economic interests, too many square miles. Ten years before the American Revolutionary War began, the animosity among the colonies was notorious. Borders were constantly in dispute. New York wouldn't even send help when Indians raided Massachusetts, and vice versa.[19] In 1765, the Massachusetts attorney James Otis predicted that "were these colonies left to themselves tomorrow, America would be a mere shambles of blood and confusion."[20] The colonists had every reason to be dubious: there was no precedent for such a thing in world history. But today, we take for granted that such a superorganism can happen because it did happen.

THE OLIVE BRANCH, OR, OUT OF MANY, ONE

On July 4, 1776, the day the Continental Congress ordered the printing and publication of the Declaration of Independence, more mundane items of business also required their attention. In between an order to devise a continental system for the manufacture of gunflints and an order to sell twenty-five pounds of gunpowder to a John Garrison of North Carolina, the Continental

Congress appointed Benjamin Franklin, John Adams, and Thomas Jefferson to supervise the design of a great seal for the United States.

Six years and three committees later, the great seal was completed, and none too soon: the war with Britain was over, and a seal would be needed to ratify the peace treaty. On the obverse side of that seal is an American bald eagle. In the left talon the eagle holds thirteen arrows, symbolizing the nation's power to make war. In the right talon, the eagle holds an olive branch— an ancient symbol of peace with both classical and biblical provenance. The eagle faces to its right, in the direction of peace.[21]

At war's end, with American independence secure, it was time to forgive. The young nation had too much to gain from cooperating with its neighbors on the other side of the Atlantic. The new complex life form that had arisen from the thirteen colonies was still in its infancy, but even then, the urge to put old resentments away in light of new opportunities to establish productive, cooperative relations with the old enemy was irresistible.

For thousands of years, Western civilization has entertained a series of myths about revenge and forgiveness. Revenge is a disease. Forgiveness is the cure. Revenge is nothing more than wanton, nihilistic violence. Revenge is the product of sick minds and sick societies. Forgiveness is completely foreign to human nature. Somebody somewhere "discovered" or "invented" forgiveness. Revenge comes easily. Forgiveness is hard.

It's time to put these myths to rest. Our propensity for revenge and our ability to forgive are both innate, they're both governed by an elegant adaptive logic, they're both receptive to changes in our social and ecological circumstances, they're both naturally evoked by specific environmental inputs, and they're both sensitive to cultural forces. And, they're both intimately human.

To comprehend our species' readiness for revenge and our willingness to forgive is to understand a story about who we are and how we got to be that way. *Homo sapiens, Homo ignoscens,* and *Homo ultor* are one. Evolution has made us *Homo ultor* and, as a result, we'll use vengeful aggression to protect ourselves, our loved ones, our cooperative social institutions, and the other things we cherish, as the need arises. Evolution has also made us

Homo ignoscens, and, as a result, we're willing to put resentment and ill will behind us, once we're convinced that it's safe and worthwhile to do so. Evolution has also made us *Homo sapiens,* and, as a result, we've already discovered many of the secrets of how to help *Homo sapiens* display more of its forgiveness and less of its vengeance.

Notes

Introduction

1. Details of the Gregory Biggs-Chante Mallard story were taken from R. Blumenthal, "Victim's son is given award for forgiving father's murderer,"*New York Times,* October 23, 2003, p. A26; "Timeline of events in the Chante Mallard windshield death case," retrieved June 23, 2007, from www.foxnews. com/story/0,2933,90498,00.html; "Doctors agree windshield victim bled to death, as testimony ends," retrieved June 23, 2007, from http://courttv.com/trials/mallard/062503_ctv. html; and a transcript of Mallard's sentencing hearing, retrieved June 23, 2007, from http://transcripts.cnn.com/ TRANSCRIPTS/0306/26/bn.06.html.
2. Bud Welch's story was taken from "Bud Welch," retrieved April 18, 2007, from www.theforgivenessproject.com/stories/ bud-welch; and "More forgiveness: A shared mourning," retrieved April 18, 2007, from www.science-spirit.org/article_ detail.php?article_id=423.

Chapter One: Putting Vengeance and Forgiveness Back into Human Nature

1. de Waal 1996, p. 5.
2. Wrangham and Peterson 1996.
3. Wrangham and Peterson 1996.
4. For a review, see Hewstone, Rubin, and Willis 2002.
5. K. Curtis, "Chimpanzees' attack leads to investigation," *Miami Herald,* March 6, 2005, p. 16A.
6. Jacoby 1983, p. 1. Pinker 2002 also writes about how the public health field has erroneously used the language of disease to understand human violence more generally.

7. For a review of the teachings of the world's major religions on forgiveness, see Rye and others 2000.

8. Jacoby 1983; Marongiu and Newman 1987; Murphy 2003.

9. Horney 1948, p. 5.

10. Parkes 1993.

11. Cardozo, Vergara, Agani, and Gotway 2000. Derek Summerfield 2002 does a good job of laying bare the Western assumption that revenge creates psychological problems, and how this assumption has predominated professional attempts to promote recovery after war.

12. American Psychiatric Association 1994.

13. N. R. Kleinfield, "Before deadly rage, a life consumed by a troubling silence,"*New York Times,* April 22, 2007, retrieved April 23, 2007, from www.nytimes.com/2007/04/22/us/22vatech.html?ex=1177905600&en=599cdd0e7ef887ac&ei=5070&emc=eta1.

14. McCullough, Emmons, Kilpatrick, and Mooney 2003.

15. Lawler and others, 2003; Witvliet, Ludwig, and Vander Laan 2001.

16. Miller, Smith, Turner, Guijarro, and Hallet 1996.

17. R. D. Enright and G. Reed, "Process Model," retrieved October 21, 2007, from www.forgiveness-institute.org/html/process_model.htm.

18. Jampolsky and Walsch 1999.

19. Tooby and Cosmides 1992.

20. Pinker 2002.

21. Brown 1991, Pinker 2002.

22. Butler 1970 [1726], p. 74.

23. Smith 1976 [1790], p. 71.

24. Darwin 1952 [1871], p. 294.

25. Richerson and Boyd 2005.

26. Wright 1994, p. 339.

27. Frijda 1994, p. 283.

28. Wilson, Dietrich, and Clark 2003.

29. Thornhill and Palmer 2000.

30. Allport 1950.

31. Seligman and Csikszentmihalyi 2000, p. 12.

32. Aureli 1997; Karremans, Van Lange, Ouwerkerk, and Kluwer 2003; Schino 1998.

33. Bradfield and Aquino 1999; McCullough, Rachal, Sandage, Worthington, Brown, and Hight 1998; Wohl and Branscombe 2005.
34. de Waal 2001.
35. Details on Finnegan and Giselle were taken from "Pregnant dog adopts hurt squirrel," retrieved April 23, 2007, from www.cbsnews.com/stories/2005/10/14/earlyshow/living/petplanet/printable943873.shtml; "Finnegan the squirrel," retrieved April 23, 2007, from www.snopes.com/photos/animals/finnegan.asp?print=y; and "Finnegan," retrieved April 23, 2007, from www.animalliberationfront.com/News/AnimalPhotos/Animals_31-40/Squirrel-dog.htm.
36. Krishnan 1993.

Chapter Two: Revenge Is a Problem
1. I assembled these details from several sources, including "Bulldozer rampage ends in Granby," CBS 4 Denver, June 4, 2004, retrieved from http://news4colorado.com/topstories/local_story_156173524.html; J. Aguilar, "I never got caught," *Rocky Mountain News,* June 9, 2004, retrieved from www.rockymountainnews.com/drmn/state/article/0,1299,DRMN_21_2949388,00.html; J. Aguilar, "Heemeyer lists found," *Rocky Mountain News,* June 8, 2004, retrieved from www.rockymountainnews.com/drmn/state/article/0,1299,DRMN_21_2946605,00.html; D. Montero and O. S. Good, "Rage fueled man's assault on Granby," *Rocky Mountain News,* June 7, 2004, retrieved from www.rockymountainnews.com/drmn/state/article/0,1299,DRMN_21_2944165,00.html; T. Fong, B. D. Creccente, and C. Brennan, "Acquaintances describe two different sides to Heemeyer, "*Rocky Mountain News,* June 5, 2004, retrieved from www.rockymountainnews.com/drmn/state/article/0,1299,DRMN_21_2940402,00.html; C. Brennan, O. S. Good, and J. Poppen, "Rampage guts Granby," *Rocky Mountain News,* June 5, 2004, retrieved from www.rockymountainnews.com/drmn/state/article/0,1299,DRMN_21_2940309,00.html; and J. Aguilar, "Armored dozer was bad to go," *Rocky Mountain News,* June 25, 2004, retrieved from www.rockymountainnews.com/drmn/state/article/0,1299,DRMN_21_2989657,00.html. I retrieved them all on August 13, 2004.

2. Frijda 1994, p. 266.
3. Rokeach and Ball-Rokeach 1989.
4. Gorsuch and Hao 1993.
5. Kadiangandu, Mullet, and Vinsonneau 2001; Mullet, Houdbine, Laumonier, and Girard 1998.
6. Van Biema 1999.
7. Davis, Smith, and Marsden 2002.
8. Crombag, Rassin, and Horselenberg 2003.
9. Crombag, Rassin, and Horselenberg 2003.
10. Cardozo, Vergara, Agani, and Gotway 2000.
11. Cardozo, Kaiser, Gotway, and Agani 2003.
12. Anderson and Bushman 1997.
13. On the basis of Carlson and Miller 1988, Richard, Bond, and Stokes-Zoota (2003) reported an effect size for aggression against provokers of r = .51, which converts to a percentile score of 88. They also reported that the effect size for aggression against nonprovokers was r = .06, which converts to a percentile score of 54.
14. Richard, Bond, and Stokes-Zoota 2003.
15. Boehm 1999; Daly and Wilson 1988; Walker 2001.
16. Otterbein and Otterbein 1965; Daly and Wilson 1988.
17. Daly and Wilson 1988.
18. Eisner 2001.
19. Federal Bureau of Investigation 2006.
20. Daly and Wilson 1988.
21. Dooley 2001.
22. Carcach 1997.
23. Gaylord and Galligher 1994.
24. Frijda 1994, p. 266.
25. Wilson and Daly 1985.
26. Kubrin and Weitzer 2003, p. 164.
27. Actually, my 20 percent estimate is probably also too conservative, because many murders that are motivated by sexual jealousy (for example, when a man or woman shoots his or her spouse for sexual unfaithfulness)—which account for many homicides (Daly and Wilson, 1988)—often have a vengeful component to them as well.
28. Cardona and others 2005.

NOTES 243

29. Kubrin and Weitzer 2003, p. 172.
30. Reported in M. Obamscik, "Massacre at Columbine High: Bloodbath leaves 15 dead, 28 hurt,"*Denver Post,* April 21, 1999, retrieved August 19, 2004, from http://63.147.65.175/news/shot0420a.htm.
31. Nansel, Overpeck, Pilla, Ruan, Simons-Morton, and Scheidt 2001.
32. Anderson and others 2001.
33. Anderson and others 2001. See also Kimmel and Mahler 2003; McGee and DeBernardo 1999.
34. Vossekuil, Fein, Reddy, Borum, and Modzeleski 2002.
35. Ember 1978; Keeley 1996; Le Blanc and Register 2003; Ross 1983.
36. See Fry 2006; Kelly 2003.
37. For a review of the anthropology on this point, see Kelly 2003, Chapter 4.
38. Scheff 2000. See also Blainey 1988 and Suganami 1996.
39. Scheff 2000.
40. Moerk 2002.
41. Pape 2005.
42. "Al-Aqsa Brigades claims Jerusalem bombing," Aljazeera.net, January 29, 2004, retrieved April 4, 2005, from http://english.aljazeera.net/NR/exeres/66521E61-8418-4812-99A4-273986B2E82D.htm; and "Israel air strikes hit Gaza City," BBC News, March 15, 2004, retrieved April 4, 2005, from http://news.bbc.co.uk/go/pr/fr/-/1/hi/world/middle_east/3511820.stm.
43. Full text: bin Laden's "Letter to America," retrieved April 25, 2007, from http://observer.guardian.co.uk/worldview/story/0,11581,845725,00.html.
44. This work is summarized and discussed in Speckhard and Ahkmedova 2006.
45. Kaplan, Mintz, Mishal, and Samban 2005.
46. Bombing is another violent and crime that's often motivated by revenge. The Bureau of Alcohol, Tobacco and Firearms (1999) reported that between 1993 and 1997, 7,746 bombing incidents occurred in which the motivation behind the bombing could be discerned (for another 5,764 incidents

it was impossible to discern the motivation). Investigators concluded that 2,122, or 27 percent, of the 7,746 bombings with known motives were committed by someone with a score to settle. These 2,122 bombings caused $8,770,000 in damages.

Chapter Three: Revenge Is a Solution

1. This story is constructed from facts reported in a series of news articles, including "Air crash traffic controller murdered: Victim's husband held,"*London Daily Telegraph,* February 27, 2004, retrieved May 28, 2004, from http://smh. com.au/articles/2004/02/27/1077676949297.html; "Cops: Plane crash-murder link," CBS News.com, February 26, 2004, retrieved June 1, 2004, from www.cbsnews.com/ stories/2004/02/26/world/printable602367.shtml; "Grieving father detained for air controller's murder," *Russia Journal Daily,* February 27, 2004, retrieved June 1, 2004, from www .russiajournal.com/print/russia_news_42711.html; "Russian says he might have killed Skyguide controller," *Russia Journal Daily,* March 17, 2004, retrieved June 1, 2004, from http://russiajournal.com/print/russia_news_42968.html; "Skyguide admits errors in Russian plane crash," *Russia Journal Daily,* May 20, 2004, retrieved June 1, 2004, from www.russiajournal.com/print/russia_news_43853.html; "Skyguide murder suspect makes partial confession," Swissinfo, March 16, 2004, retrieved June 1, 2004, from www .swissinfo.org/sen/Swissinfo.html?siteSect=41&sid=47929 43; "Swiss air traffic controller slain," CNEW, February 25, 2004, retrieved June 1, 2004, from http://cnews.canoe.ca/ CNEWS/World/2004/02/25/pf-360521.html; A. Hall, "Swiss police arrest murder suspect," *Scotsman,* February 27, 2004, retrieved June 11, 2004, from http://thescotsman.scotsman. com/international.cfm?id=228952004; and I. Shmelev, "Swiss court finds Russian man guilty of revenge killing Skyguide's employee,"*Pravda,* October 27, 2005, retrieved May 3, 2007, from http://english.pravda.ru/main/18/88/351/16376_ Skyguide.html.
2. Dobzhansky 1973.
3. Daly and Wilson 1988.

4. Buss, Haselton, Shackelford, Bleske, and Wakefield 1998.
5. Vargha-Khadem, Gadian, Copp, and Mishkin 2005.
6. Plomin, DeFries, Craig, and McGuffin 2003.
7. Buss 1999, p. 34.
8. Wright 1994, p. 26.
9. Pinker 1994.
10. Flaxman and Sherman 2000.
11. Gangestad, Thornhill, and Garver-Apgar 2005.
12. de Waal 2002; Buss, Haselton, Shackelford, Bleske, and Wakefield 1998.
13. Williams 1966, p. 4.
14. Buss, Haselton, Shackelford, Bleske, and Wakefield 1998.
15. Pinker 1997.
16. Simpson and Campbell 2005.
17. Schmitt and Pilcher 2004.
18. Lerner and Keltner 2000; 2001.
19. Öhman and Mineka 2003.
20. McCullough, Bellah, Kilpatrick, and Johnson 2001; Miller 2001.
21. Clutton-Brock and Parker 1995.
22. Diamond 1977.
23. Ford and Blegen 1992.
24. Dunbar 2003. Chimpanzees, for instance, will hide their facial displays of fear in order to deprive potential rivals of strategic information about their own mental states.
25. Brown 1968; Kim, Smith, and Brigham 1998. See also Kurzban, DeScioli, and O'Brien 2007.
26. Felson 1982.
27. Nisbett and Cohen 1996. Chu, Rivera, and Loftin (2000) argued that some of Nisbett and Cohen's findings could have resulted from methodological problems in analyzing national data, but Nisbett and Cohen make their case on the basis of so many types of evidence that it's hard not to take seriously the possibility that white Southerners really do have a greater propensity for retaliatory violence than do whites from other regions of the United States.
28. Black-Michaud 1975.
29. Tindall and Shi 1996.
30. Nisbett and Cohen 1996.

31. Cohen, Nisbett, Bowdle, and Schwarz 1996.
32. Anderson 1999.
33. Kubrin and Weitzer 2003.
34. Anderson 1999, p. 130.
35. Brezina, Agnew, Cullen, and Wright 2004.
36. Topalli, Wright, and Fornango 2002, pp. 342–343.
37. Ridley 1996.
38. Wright 2000.
39. Rousseau 1984 [1754].
40. Boyd, Gintis, Bowles, and Richerson 2003; Boyd and Richerson 1992.
41. Fehr and Gächter 2002.
42. Price, Cosmides, and Tooby 2002.
43. de Quervain and others 2004; Fehr and Gächter 2002.
44. Fehr and Gächter 2002.
45. Gürerk, Irlenbusch, and Rockenbach 2006.

Chapter Four: The Retribution Solution

1. Fletcher 2003, p. 7. A full translation of the original document recounting the feud appears in Morris 1992.
2. Shelley-Tremblay and Rosén 1996.
3. Brody 2001.
4. More on the types of scientific evidence that are relevant to adaptationist hypotheses can be found in Andrews, Gangestad, and Matthews 2002, Buss 1999, Schmitt and Pilcher 2004, and Simpson and Campbell 2005.
5. Handel 1989.
6. Brown 1989.
7. Smale and Spickenheuer 1979. See also Orth, Montada, and Maercker 2006.
8. Rudolph, Roesch, Greitemeyer, and Weiner 2004.
9. Aase 2002b; Black 1998; Crombag, Rassin, and Horselenberg 2003; Miller 2001.
10. J. Simpson (ed.), 1989. *Oxford English Dictionary* (2nd Ed.), retrieved February 11, 2004, from http://iiiprxy.library. miami.edu:2160/cgi/entry/00107749?query_type=word&q ueryword=honor&edition=2e&first=1&max_to_show=10&- sort_type=alpha&result_place=2&search_id=uDhI-90gqWr- 1726&hilite=00107749.

11. Black-Michaud 1975, p. 181.
12. For example, Berger 1970. See Aase 2002a for review.
13. Text from Tim Russert's interview with President George W. Bush, which appeared on NBC's "Meet the Press" on February 8, 2004. I retrieved this transcript from http://msnbc.msn.com/id/4179618/ on February 13, 2004.
14. See Aase 2002b and Daly and Wilson 1988.
15. Jacobs 2004; Kubrin and Weitzer 2003.
16. Jacoby 1983.
17. Bay 2002.
18. Anderson 1999.
19. Boehm 1987; Otterbein and Otterbein 1965.
20. William Shakespeare, *The Merchant of Venice*, Act III, Scene 1.
21. Brown 1991.
22. Westermarck 1898, p. 19.
23. Otterbein and Otterbein 1965.
24. Daly and Wilson 1988.
25. Daly and Wilson 1988, p. 226.
26. Daly and Wilson, 1988, p. 227.
27. Boster, Yost, and Peeke 2004, pp. 472–473.
28. Boster, Yost, and Peeke 2004, p. 476.
29. Henrich and others 2006.
30. Brown 1991.
31. Wilson 2002.
32. Darwin 1952 [1871], p. 289.
33. Westermarck 1924.
34. de Waal and Luttrell 1988.
35. Silk 1992.
36. Donald Black (1998) hypothesized that revenge is difficult to maintain when individuals are in close social proximity; perhaps the same is true of physical proximity as well.
37. Aureli, Cozzolino, Cordischi, and Scucchi 1992.
38. Clutton-Brock and Parker 1995.
39. Hoover and Robinson 2007.
40. Dugatkin 1991.
41. Dugatkin and Alfieri 1992.
42. O'Steen, Cullum, and Bennett 2002.
43. Dugatkin 1988; 1991; Milinski 1987.

Chapter Five: Family, Friendship, and the Functions of Forgiveness

1. Clutton-Brock and Parker 1995.
2. I know what you're thinking: "What about all of the children who are killed by their parents each year?" This does happen, but it's stepfathers and stepmothers, rather than biological fathers and biological mothers, who are the most likely culprits. Homicide data suggest that living with a stepfather increases somewhere between 800 to 6,000 percent the risk that a child will be murdered (Daly and Wilson, 1994; Weekes-Shackelford and Shackelford, 2004). Even for stepparents, of course, it is very rare.
3. Dunbar, Clark, and Hurst 1995. Daly and Wilson (1988) estimate that somewhere between 2 percent and 6 percent of murderers are blood relatives of their victims.
4. Clutton-Brock and Parker 1995, p. 210.
5. Poundstone 1992, p. 9.
6. Axelrod 1997, p. xi.
7. Ridley 1996. This chapter has benefited greatly from Chapters Three and Four in particular from Ridley's superb book.
8. Poundstone 1992; Ridley 1996.
9. Poundstone 1992.
10. Dugatkin 1988; Milinski 1987.
11. Axelord 1984.
12. Wilson 2002.
13. Axelrod and Dion 1988.
14. Axelrod 1984.
15. Nowak and Sigmund 1992. See also Godfray 1992.
16. Nowak and Sigmund 1993.
17. Wu and Axelord 1995.
18. Frean 1994; Hauert and Schuster 1998; Nowak and Sigmund 1994.
19. Birditt and Fingerman 2005; Birditt, Fingerman, and Almeida 2005.
20. Richerson, Boyd, and Henrich 2003.
21. Grim 1995; 1996.
22. Hruschka and Henrich 2006.
23. Dunbar 1996.
24. Ohtsuki and Iwasa 2004; 2006.
25. Bendor, Kramer, and Stout 1991; Van Lange, Ouwerkerk, and Tazelaar 2002; Wedekind and Milinski 1996.

Chapter Six: The Forgiveness Instinct

1. Arendt 1958, p. 214.
2. Hoppe 2003.
3. de Waal and Pokorny 2005, p. 17.
4. Enright, Freedman, and Rique 1998; Park and Enright 2000.
5. Karremans and Van Lange 2004.
6. McCullough, Worthington, and Rachal 1997.
7. Köhler 1956, p. 261.
8. de Waal 2000, p. 16.
9. de Waal and van Roosmalen 1979.
10. Veenema 2000. Primatologists calculate a primate group's CT by first adding up the number of pairs of animals that have friendly contact after a conflict (say, in the first fifteen minutes post-conflict) more quickly than they do during a peacetime observation period of the same length. These pairs are called attracted pairs. Second, they take that number and subtract from it the number of animal pairs that have friendly contact during peacetime more quickly than they do following a conflict. These pairs are called dispersed pairs. Divide this difference by the total number of conflicts that were observed, and you've got the CT for that group.
11. Aureli and de Waal 2000, see Appendix A.
12. Katsukake and Castles 2004.
13. Aureli and de Waal 2000.
14. de Waal 1989.
15. de Waal 1989.
16. Cheney, Seyfarth, and Silk 1995.
17. Schino 2000.
18. Butovskaya, Verbeek, Ljungberg, and Lunardini 2000.
19. Ljungberg, Horowitz, Jansson, Westlund, and Clarke 2005; Fujisawa, Kutsukake, and Hasegawa 2005.
20. Wilson 2002, p. 195.
21. Brown 1991.
22. The anthropologist Douglas Fry is currently conducting a much larger cross-cultural study of reconciliation in 186 world cultures. His work, when completed, should do much to either confirm or disconfirm what the evidence from the HRAF Probability Sample seems to be saying.
23. Calame-Griaule 1986.

24. Lodge 1941.
25. Chagnon 1988; 1992.
26. Here's documentation of reconciliation at work among the Yanomamö: "Thus, two very hostile settlements might manage to suspend the raids between them. Later, they might agree not to fight any more should they see one another in a friendly settlement. Until they arrive at this accord, a neutral settlement friendly to both, when it is visited by people from one of these settlements hostile to each other, must send a message to the other, warning that they should not come so long as there are visitors from the hostile settlement in it. Still later they might agree to receive the visit of a small group of visitors from the other enemy settlement, for commercial purposes. From this time on the two settlements can undertake their negotiations directly, and friendships begin to form among their respective members. Then, when one settlement, out of good will, gives its own girls as wives to the men of the other settlement, it can be said that they have recovered; they have truly become good friends. While the greater the number of persons involved in a dispute or a fight, the less the probability that the opposing bands will reach an understanding after a short time, the disputes within a settlement itself are in general settled quickly. Within a few months all will have been forgotten. Disputes between settlements which have not gone beyond macana [the use of handheld weapons] fights are usually forgotten in a year or two. Disputes between settlements which have occasion to use arrows, especially if someone has been killed, might require a greater number of years to be reconciled. Disputes which have reached the proportions of regional wars are rarely forgotten within the same generation, since there is hardly any neutral settlement left by means of which peace negotiations can be made" (Barker, 1995 [1953], pp. 48–49).
27. Silk 2000; 2002.
28. Cheney, Seyfarth, and Silk 1995.
29. de Waal and Pokorny 2005.
30. de Waal and Ren 1988.
31. Preuschoft, Wang, Aureli, and de Waal 2002. See also Koski, Koops, and Sterck 2007.

32. Call, Aureli, and de Waal 1999.
33. Cords and Thurnheer 1993.
34. Silk 2002.
35. Aureli 1997; Koski, Koops, and Sterck 2007.
36. Smucny, Price, and Byrne 1997.
37. Haidt 2001.
38. Fujisawa, Kutsukake, and Hasegawa 2005.
39. Butovskaya, Boyko, Selverova, and Ermakova 2005.
40. Witvliet, Ludwig, and Vander Laan 2001.
41. Lawler and others 2003; Orcutt 2006.
42. Karremans, Van Lange, Ouwerkerk, and Kluwer 2003.
43. Wilson 2002, p. 195.

Chapter Seven: The Forgiving Brain
1. Cacioppo, Visser, and Pickett 2006; Panksepp 1998.
2. Panksepp 1998.
3. Knutson and Wimmer 2007.
4. King-Casas, Tomlin, Anen, Camerer, Quartz, and Montague 2005; Rilling, Gutman, Zeh, Pagnoni, Berns, and Kilts 2002.
5. Eisenberger, Lieberman, and Williams 2003; Eisenberger and Lieberman 2004.
6. Sanfey, Rilling, Aronson, Nystrom, and Cohen 2003.
7. Stillwell, Baumeister, and Del Priore 2005; Zechmeister and Romero 2002.
8. Panksepp 1998.
9. Philip McCabe, personal communication, June 5, 2006.
10. William Shakespeare, *The Merchant of Venice*, Act III, Scene I.
11. Knutson 2004.
12. de Quervain and others 2004.
13. Bushman, Baumeister, and Phillips 2001.
14. Harmon-Jones and Sigelman 2001; Harmon-Jones, Vaughn-Scott, Mohr, Sigelman, and Harmon-Jones 2004.
15. Marlatt, Kosturn, and Lang 1975.
16. Giancola 2000.
17. Fallujah details from J. Price, J. Neff, and C. Crain, "Chapter 6: Fury boils to surface," *News and Observer*, November 28, 2004, retrieved June 25, 2007, from www.newsobserver.com/nation_world/blackwater/series/story/237807.html; J. Gettleman, "Enraged mob in Fallujah kills 4 American

contractors," *New York Times,* March 31, 2004, retrieved June 25, 2007, from www.nytimes.com/2004/03/31/international/worldspecial/31CND-IRAQ.html?ex=1183003200&en=dfb7d93 3316d4379&ei=5070; and Perlmutter and Major 2004.

18. Geronimo 1983 [1906], pp. 53–54.
19. Boehm 1987.
20. Anastasia 1991, cited in Baumeister 1996, p. 158.
21. Crombag, Rassin, and Horselenberg 2003; Haidt, Sabini, and Worthington n.d.; Stillwell, Baumeister, and Del Priore 2005.
22. Rolls 2005.
23. Singer, Seymour, O'Doherty, Stephan, Dolan, and Frith 2006.
24. Mark Twain, letter to Olivia, December 27, 1869, from Wechter 1949, p. 132.
25. Clark 2005; Newberg, d'Aquili, Newberg, and deMarici 2000.
26. Korchmaros and Kenny 2001.
27. Rushton 1989.
28. Batson and Powell 2003.
29. McCullough, Worthington, and Rachal 1997; McCullough, Rachal, Sandage, Worthington, Brown, and Hight 1998.
30. Batson, Ahmad, Lishner, and Tsang 2002.
31. McCullough, Worthington, and Rachal 1997; McCullough, Rachal, Sandage, Worthington, Brown, and Hight 1998; Zechmeister and Romero 2002.
32. Berry, Worthington, Wade, Witvliet, and Keifer 2005; Eaton and Struthers 2006; Moeschberger, Dixon, Niens, and Cairns 2005.
33. Batson and Ahmad 2001; Giancola 2003.
34. Harmon-Jones, Vaughn-Scott, Mohr, Sigelman, and Harmon-Jones 2004.
35. Arnold 2003, p. 153.
36. Uganda details taken from M. Lacey, "Atrocity victims in Uganda choose to forgive,"*New York Times,* April 18, 2005, retrieved April 18, 2005, from www.nytimes.com/2005/04/18/international/africa/18uganda.html; J. G. Price, "Ex-child soldiers forced to fight in Northern Uganda's civil war seeking redemption,"*Sudan Tribune,* August 30, 2005, retrieved June 1, 2006, from www.sudantribune.com/article_impr.php3?id_article=11359; "Uganda: Locals want rebel leader forgiven," UN Office for the Coordination of Humanitarian Affairs,

retrieved June 25, 2007, from www.irinnews.org/Report.
aspx?ReportID=59805; and "Uganda: IDPs begin slow journey home amid concerns over peace process," UN Office
for the Coordination of Humanitarian Affairs, retrieved
June 25, 2007, from http://irinnews.org/PrintReport.
aspx?ReportID=72228.

37. King-Casas, Tomlin, Anen, Camerer, Quartz, and Montague
2005; Knutson and Wimmer 2007; Rilling, Gutman, Zeh,
Pagnoni, Berns, and Kilts 2002.
38. Finkel, Rusbult, Kumashiro, and Hannon 2002.
39. Boehm 1987; Bottom, Gibson, Daniels, and Murnighan 2002.
40. Gordon, Burton, and Porter 2004.
41. Butovskaya, Boyko, Selverova, and Ermakova 2005.
42. Bradfield and Aquino 1999; Gordon, Burton, and Porter
2004.
43. Gold and Weiner 2000; Nadler and Liviatan 2006.
44. de Jong, Peters, and de Cremer 2003.
45. Bottom, Gibson, Daniels, and Murnighan 2002; Nadler and
Liviatan 2006.
46. Boehm 1987.

Chapter Eight: "To Promote and to Maintain Friendly Relations"
1. General Accounting Office 2007.
2. United States Department of Defense, May 8, 2007, "News
transcript: DoD news briefing with Col. Nicholson from
Afghanistan," retrieved July 2, 2007, from www.defenselink.
mil/transcripts/transcript.aspx?transcriptid=3959. See also
D. S. Cloud, "U.S. pays and apologizes to kin of Afghans killed by
marines,"*New York Times,* May 9, 2007, retrieved May 9, 2007,
from www.nytimes.com/2007/05/09/world/asia/09afghan.
html?ex=1336363200&en=4829c8e94ab32cfb&ei=5088&part
ner=rssnyt&emc=rss.
3. Combined Joint Task Force-82, May 12, 2007, "Allies: Coalition
delivers 'solatia' payments to Nangarhar families," retrieved
July 2, 2007, from www.blackanthem.com/News/Allies_
20/Coalition_delivers_solatia_payments_to_Nangarhar_
families6615.shtml.
4. United States Department of Defense, May 8, 2007, "News
transcript: DoD news briefing with Col. Nicholson from

Afghanistan," retrieved July 2, 2007, from www.defenselink. mil/transcripts/transcript.aspx?transcriptid=3959.

5. Nowak and Sigmund 1993.
6. To hear a pant-grunt, visit http://webdrive.service.emory. edu/groups/research/chimpanzee-cognition/CCL/etho-gram.htm.
7. Tabak, McCullough, Root, Bono, and Berry 2007. See also Blum-Kulka and Olshtain 1984; Butovskaya, Verbeek, Ljungberg, and Lunardini 2000; Fry 2000; Fujisawa, Kutsukake, and Hasegawa 2005; Keltner, Young, and Buswell 1997.
8. For example, see Exline, DeShea, and Holeman 2007; Ohbuchi, Kameda, and Agarie 1989.
9. Allan, Allan, Kaminer, and Stein 2006.
10. Cohen 2004.
11. Blum-Kulka and Olshtain 1984; Olshtain 1989.
12. Lazare 2004, p. 74.
13. Scher and Darley 1997.
14. Schönbach 1990.
15. Shaw, Wild, and Colquitt 2003.
16. Hareli 2005, p. 361.
17. "1998: Clinton denies affair with intern," retrieved July 21, 2006, from http://news.bbc.co.uk/onthisday/hi/dates/ stories/january/26/newsid_2672000/2672291.stm.
18. P. Baker and J. F. Harris, "Clinton admits to Lewinsky relation-ship, challenges Starr to end personal prying,"*Washington Post*, August 18, 1998, p. A01, retrieved July 21, 2006, from www. washingtonpost.com/wp-srv/politics/special/clinton/stories/ clinton081898.htm.
19. "Clinton's evolving apology for the Lewinsky affair," CNN. com, February 12, 1999, retrieved July 21, 2006, from www. cnn.com/ALLPOLITICS/stories/1999/02/12/apology/.
20. T. B. Edsall, "Lott decried for part of salute to Thurmond," *Washington Post*, December 7, 2002, p. A06, retrieved July 19, 2006, from www.washingtonpost.com/ac2/wp-dyn?pagename= article&node=&contentId=A20730-2002Dec6.
21. "Beyond the pale," *Economist*, December 7, 2002, retrieved July 19, 2006, from www.economist.com/World/na/displayStory. cfm?story_id=1493020.

22. A. York, "A whole Lott of trouble," Salon.com, December 12, 2002, retrieved July 19, 2006, from http://archive.salon.com/politics/feature/2002/12/12/lott/print.html.

23. "Lott: Apology no. 4," Salon.com, December 12, 2002, retrieved July 19, 2006, from http://archive.salon.com/politics/feature/2002/12/14/apology/print.html.

24. Lazare 2004.

25. McCullough, Worthington, and Rachal 1997; Singer, Seymour, O'Doherty, Stephan, Dolan, and Frith 2006.

26. For review, see Petrucci 2002.

27. Dunbar 2003; Pinker 1994.

28. Hickson 1986.

29. Keltner, Young, and Buswell 1997.

30. Twain 1897, p. 170.

31. Keltner, Young, and Buswell 1997.

32. Kuschel 1988.

33. Rovinskii 1901, quoted in Boehm 1987, p. 136.

34. Lazare 2004.

35. Details and quotations regarding the Bertuzzi-Moore incident are from "Bertuzzi: I wish that day never happened," August 15, 2005, retrieved August 15, 2006, from http://sports.espn.go.com/nhl/news/story?id=2134946; the Todd Bertuzzi entry in Wikipedia, retrieved August 15, 2006, from http://en.wikipedia.org/wiki/Todd_Bertuzzi; and D. Cox, "An NHL dream lives on," *Toronto Star,* March 8, 2007, retrieved March 8, 2007, from www.thestar.com/printArticle/189616.

36. Bottom, Gibson, Daniels, and Murnighan 2002.

37. Daly and Wilson 1988.

38. For example, see Boehm 1987; Kelly 2003; and Kuschel 1988.

39. Strang 2002.

40. Bottom, Gibson, Daniels, and Murnighan 2003.

41. Strang and Sherman 2003.

42. Strang 2002, p. 1.

43. Roche 2006. Quotation is from p. 217.

44. Strang and others 2006.

45. Sherman and others 2005.

46. Strang and others 2006.

47. Sherman and others 2005; Strang and others 2006.

48. Sapolsky 2004.
49. Exline, DeShea, and Holeman 2007.
50. Cohen 2004.
51. Baumeister, Stillwell, and Wotman 1990.

Chapter Nine: From Neurons to Nations
 1. Staub, Pearlman, Gubin, and Hagengimana 2005; see also Nadler and Liviatan 2006.
 2. "Main points of Iraq's peace plan," BBC News, June 25, 2006, retrieved July 12, 2007, from http://news.bbc.co.uk/2/low/middle_east/5114932.stm.
 3. L. Beehner, "Impediments to national reconciliation in Iraq," January 5, 2007, retrieved July 12, 2007 from www.cfr.org/publication/12347.
 4. "IRA statement in full," BBC News, July 16, 2002, retrieved November 28, 2006, from http://news.bbc.co.uk/1/low/northern_ireland/2132113.stm; "The IRA says sorry sort of." *Economist,* July 20, 2000, *364* (8282), pp. 25–29.
 5. Elias 1969, p. 235.
 6. Eisner 2001.
 7. See also Keeley 1996.
 8. Burnham, Lafta, Doocy, and Roberts 2006. But see also Iraq Family Health Survey Study Group 2008.
 9. S. Tavernise, "Cycle of revenge fuels a pattern of Iraqi killings,"*New York Times,* November 20, 2006, retrieved November 20, 2006, from www.nytimes.com/2006/11/20/world/middleeast/20revenge.htm.
10. Tavernise, "Cycle of revenge," 2006.
11. Aebi 2004; see also Europol 2005.
12. Long and Brecke 2003.
13. For example, see Daye 2004; Tutu 1999.
14. Long and Brecke 2003, pp. 70, 71.
15. Long and Brecke 2003, p. 71.
16. Moerk 2002; Scheff 2000.
17. Boehm (2003) provides an excellent diagnosis of the structural limitations that prevent the UN from fostering and restoring peace as effectively as it might if it were structured differently.
18. Long and Brecke 2003.
19. Lindskold and Aronoff 1980.

20. Auerbach 2004; Rouhana 2004.
21. Long and Brecke 2003, p. 114.
22. Cohen 2004.
23. Kurzban, Tooby, and Cosmides 2001.
24. Darwin 1952 [1871], p. 317.
25. Wright 2000.
26. Singer 1981.
27. Hewstone, Rubin, and Willis 2002; Pagel and Mace 2004; Wrangham and Peterson 1996.
28. Hewstone, Cairns, Voci, McLernon, Niens, and Noor 2004.
29. Sherif, Harvey, White, Hood, and Sherif 1961.
30. Hewstone, Rubin, and Willis 2002.
31. Kurzban, Tooby, and Cosmides 2001.
32. Hewstone, Cairns, Voci, Hamberger, and Niens 2006; Hewstone, Cairns, Voci, McLernon, Niens, and Noor 2004; Moeschberger, Dixon, Niens, and Cairns 2005.
33. Richerson, Boyd, and Henrich 2003.
34. Keeley 1996, p. 181.
35. Wohl and Branscombe 2005.
36. Gaertner, Dovidio, Banker, Houlette, Johnson, and McGlynn 2000; see also Hewstone, Rubin, and Willis 2002 and Pettigrew 1998.
37. H. S. Wong, "Youth program sows hope for conflict areas,"*Washington Times,* November 8, 2006, retrieved November 30, 2006, from www.seedsofpeace.org/site/News2?page=NewsArticle&id=8147.

Chapter Ten: Divine Forgiveness and Righteous Revenge
1. Hostetler 1993.
2. D. B. Kraybill, "Forgiving is woven into life of Amish,"*Philadelphia Inquirer,* October 8, 2006, retrieved February 26, 2007, from www.philly.com/mld/inquirer/15698632.htm.
3. R. Hampson, "Amish community unites to mourn slain schoolgirls,"*USA Today,* November 5, 2006, retrieved November 19, 2006, from www.usatoday.com/news/nation/2006-10-04-amish-shooting_x.htm.
4. Kraybill, "Forgiving is woven into life of Amish."
5. Details about and quotations from Brandon Biggs come from R. Blumenthal, "Victim's son is given award for forgiving

father's murderer,"*New York Times,* October 23, 2003, p. A26; and "Son forgives father's murderer in windshield case," retrieved February 28, 2007, from www.cbn.com/700club/ features/amazing/forgive_brandon_biggs_112003.aspx.

6. Rye and others 2000.
7. Davis and Smith 1998.
8. For a review of some of these studies, see McCullough, Bono, and Root 2005; and Tsang, McCullough, and Hoyt 2005.
9. David and Choi 2006.
10. Nisbet and Shanahan 2004.
11. Smith 1991.
12. "Osama bin Laden's letter to America," retrieved February 5, 2007, from http://observer.guardian.co.uk/print/0,,4552895-110490,00.html.
13. Kohut 2005.
14. By-product theorists include Atran 2002, Boyer 2001, and Kirkpatrick 2005.
15. I'm making some fine distinctions here. For a more in-depth (and technical) discussion of secondary adaptation, see Andrews, Gangestad, and Matthews 2002.
16. Bering and Johnson 2005; Irons 2001; Sosis 2003; Wilson 2002.
17. Even as I crib heavily from David Sloan Wilson 2002 in some of what's coming next, I'm going to completely gloss over Wilson's major conceptual tool for this sort of thinking, namely, the idea that natural selection can work on groups in the same way that it can work on individuals. This idea itself relies on yet another idea—that it's meaningful to think of a group of individuals as a sort of "superorganism" or a "group mind" that has an ontological and even biological integrity that's not reducible to the sum of its parts. To make these issues properly intelligible would require many more words than are at my disposal at this late point in the book, so I'll be driving around this whole crevasse—slowly enough so that you can have a look at it out your window, but quickly enough and far enough back that we don't have to risk getting sucked into it.
18. The task of extracting the historical Jesus from the Gospels has occupied many great minds, and yet we still don't know exactly what happened and what didn't happen. We may be

on the firmest ground by assuming that these first-century documents reflect the early Christians' beliefs about Jesus and his priorities rather than assuming that they are, strictly speaking, historical documents.

19. All quotations from the Bible come from the New International Version.
20. Bond 1998.
21. Wilson 2002, p. 216.
22. Shriver 1995.
23. Boster, Yost, and Peeke 2004.
24. Boster, Yost, and Peeke 2004, p. 182.
25. Boster, Yost, and Peeke 2004, p. 481.
26. A. Warren, "Waorani—the saga of Ecuador's secret people: A historical perspective," 2002, retrieved August 2, 2007, from www.lastrefuge.co.uk/data/articles/waorani/waorani_page1.htm.
27. Bushman, Ridge, Das, Key, and Busath 2007.
28. Greer, Berman, Varan, Bobrycki, and Watson 2005.
29. For instance, Homerin 2006; Smith 1991.
30. Juergensmeyer 2003; Smith 1991.
31. Juergensmeyer 2003.
32. See Asani 2003.
33. Homerin 2006; Juergensmeyer 2003.
34. J. Mann and R. L. Jackson, "Motive behind Trade Center bombing remains a mystery," *Los Angeles Times,* March 20, 1993, p. 16.
35. Niebuhr 1937, p. 1391.

Chapter Eleven: *Homo ignoscens*
1. R. Conniff, "A vast garden of knowledge, still blooming today," *New York Times,* May 13, 2007, retrieved August 31, 2007, from http://travel.nytimes.com/2007/05/13/travel/13Footsteps.html?pagewanted=print.
2. Richerson and Boyd 2005.
3. Pagel and Mace 2004, p. 275.
4. Richerson and Boyd 2005, p. 5.
5. de Waal and Johanowicz 1993.
6. Richerson and Boyd 2005.
7. Weaver and de Waal 2003.

8. Ljungberg and Westlund 2000.
9. Schijman 2005.
10. Hayner 1994. See also Gibson 2006; Long and Brecke 2003; and United States Institute of Peace, "Truth commissions digital collection," May 5, 2005, retrieved August 22, 2007, from www.usip.org/library/truth.html#tc.
11. Richerson and Boyd 2005.
12. Cohen, Nisbett, Bowdle, and Schwarz 1996.
13. Cohen, Malka, Rozin, and Cherfas 2006.
14. Nowak 2006.
15. Nowak 2006, p. 1560.
16. Wilson 2007.
17. Michod and Nedelcu 2003.
18. Michod and Nedelcu 2003.
19. Morgan 1992; Ashli White, personal communication, August 24, 2007.
20. Quoted in Morgan 1992, p. 6.
21. United States Department of State 1996; *Journals of the Continental Congress, 1774—1789,* Thursday, July 4, 1776, retrieved August 28, 2007, from http://memory.loc.gov/cgi-bin/query/r?ammem/hlaw:@field(DOCID+@lit(jc00525)).

BIBLIOGRAPHY

Aase, T. (2002a). Introduction: Honor and revenge in the contemporary world. In T. Aase (Ed.), *Tournaments of power: Honor and revenge in the contemporary world* (pp. 1–17). Burlington, VT: Ashgate.

Aase, T. (Ed.). (2002b). *Tournaments of power: Honor and revenge in the contemporary world.* Burlington, VT: Ashgate.

Aebi, M. (2004). Crime trends in Western Europe from 1990 to 2000. *European Journal on Criminal Policy and Research, 10,* 163–186.

Allan, A., Allan, M. M., Kaminer, D., and Stein, D. J. (2006). Exploration of the association between apology and forgiveness amongst victims of human rights violations. *Behavioral Sciences and the Law, 24,* 87–102.

Allport, G. W. (1950). A psychological approach to the study of love and hate. In P. A. Sorokin (Ed.), *Explorations in altruistic love and behavior* (pp. 145–164). Boston: Beacon Press.

American Psychiatric Association. (1994). *Diagnostic and statistical manual of mental disorders* (4th ed.). Washington, DC: American Psychiatric Association.

Anastasia, G. (1991). *Blood and honor: Inside the Scarfo mob—the Mafia's most violent family.* New York: Morrow.

Anderson, C. A., and Bushman, B. J. (1997). External validity of "trivial" experiments: The case of laboratory aggression. *Review of General Psychology, 1,* 19–41.

Anderson, E. (1999). *Code of the street.* New York: Norton.

Anderson, M., and others. (2001). School-associated violent deaths in the United States, 1994–1999. *Journal of the American Medical Association, 286,* 2695–2702.

Andrews, P. W., Gangestad, S. W., and Matthews, D. (2002). Adaptationism—How to carry out an exaptationist program. *Behavioral and Brain Sciences, 25,* 489–504.

Arendt, H. (1958). *The human condition.* Chicago: University of Chicago Press.

Arnold, J. C. (2003). *Why forgive?* Retrieved June 1, 2006, from www.jesus.org.uk/vault/library/arnold_jc_why_forgive.pdf.

Asani, A. S. (2003). "So that you may know one another": A Muslim American reflects on pluralism and Islam. *Annals, AAPSS, 588,* 40–51.

Atran, S. (2002). *In gods we trust: The evolutionary landscape of religion.* New York: Oxford University Press.

Auerbach, Y. (2004). The role of forgiveness in reconciliation. In Y. Bar-Simian-Tov (Ed.), *From conflict resolution to reconciliation* (pp. 146–175). New York: Oxford University Press.

Aureli, F. (1997). Post-conflict anxiety in nonhuman primates: The mediating role of emotion in conflict resolution. *Aggressive Behavior, 23,* 315–328.

Aureli, F., Cozzolino, R., Cordischi, C., and Scucchi, S. (1992). Kin-oriented redirection among Japanese macaques: An expression of a revenge system? *Animal Behaviour, 44,* 283–291.

Aureli, F., and de Waal, F.B.M. (2000). *Natural conflict resolution.* Berkeley: University of California Press.

Axelrod, R. (1984). *The evolution of cooperation.* New York: Basic Books.

Axelrod, R. (1997). *The complexity of cooperation: Agent-based models of competition and collaboration.* Princeton, NJ: Princeton University Press.

Axelrod, R., and Dion, D. (1988). The further evolution of cooperation. *Science, 242,* 1385–1390.

Barker, J. (1995). Memoir on the culture of the Waica. New Haven, CT: Human Relations Area Files. Originally published in *Boletín Indigenista Venezolano,* 1953, *1,* 433–489.

Batson, C. D., and Ahmad, N. (2001). Empathy-induced altruism in a prisoner's dilemma II: What if the target of empathy has defected? *European Journal of Social Psychology, 31,* 25–36.

Batson, C. D., Ahmad, N., Lishner, D. A., and Tsang, J. (2002). Empathy and altruism. In C. R. Snyder and S. J. Lopez (Eds.), *Handbook of positive psychology* (pp. 485–498). New York: Oxford University Press.

Batson, C. D., and Powell, A. A. (2003). Altruism and prosocial behavior. In T. Millon and M. J. Lerner (Eds.), *Handbook of psychology; Vol. 5. Personality and social psychology* (pp. 463–484). Hoboken, NJ: John Wiley & Sons.

Baumeister, R. F. (1996). *Evil: Inside human violence and cruelty.* New York: Freeman.

Baumeister, R. F., Stillwell, A., and Wotman, S. R. (1990). Victim and perpetrator accounts of interpersonal conflict: Autobiographical narratives about anger. *Journal of Personality and Social Psychology, 59,* 994–1005.

Bay, J. (2002). Honor and revenge in the culture of Danish outlaw bikers. In T. Aase (Ed.), *Tournaments of power: Honor and revenge in the contemporary world* (pp. 49–60). Burlington, VT: Ashgate.

Bendor, J., Kramer, R. M., and Stout, S. (1991). When in doubt . . . Cooperation in a noisy prisoner's dilemma. *Journal of Conflict Resolution, 35,* 691–719.

Berger, P. (1970). On the obsolescence of the concept of honor. *European Journal of Sociology, 11,* 339–347.

Bering, J. M., and Johnson, D.D.P. (2005). "O Lord . . . You perceive my thoughts from afar": Recursiveness and the evolution of supernatural agency. *Journal of Cognition and Culture, 5,* 118–142.

Berry, J. T., Worthington, E. L., Wade, N. G., Witvliet, C. v. O., and Keifer, R. (2005). Forgiveness, moral identity, and perceived justice in crime victims and their supporters. *Humboldt Journal of Social Relations, 29,* 136–162.

Birditt, K. S., and Fingerman, K. L. (2005). Do we get better at picking our battles? Age group differences in descriptions of behavioral reactions to interpersonal tensions. *Journal of Gerontology: Psychological Sciences, 60B,* P121–P128.

Birditt, K. S., Fingerman, K. L., and Almeida, D. M. (2005). Age differences in exposure and reactions to interpersonal tensions: A daily diary study. *Psychology and Aging, 20,* 330–340.

Black, D. (1998). *The social structure of right and wrong* (Rev. ed.). San Diego, CA: Academic Press.

Black-Michaud, J. (1975). *Cohesive force: Feud in the Mediterranean and the Middle East.* Oxford, U.K.: Basil Blackwell.

Blainey, G. (1988). *The causes of war.* New York: Free Press.

Blum-Kulka, S., and Olshtain, E. (1984). Requests and apologies: A cross-cultural study of speech act realization patterns (CCSARP). *Applied Linguistics, 5,* 196–212.

Boehm, C. (1987). *Blood revenge: The enactment and management of conflict in Montenegro and other tribal societies* (2nd ed.). Philadelphia: University of Pennsylvania Press.

Boehm, C. (1999). *Hierarchy in the forest: The evolution of egalitarian behavior.* Cambridge, MA: Harvard University Press.

Boehm, C. (2003). Global conflict resolution: An anthropological diagnosis of problems with world governance. In R. W. Bloom and N. Dess (Eds.), *Evolutionary psychology and violence: A primer for policymakers and public policy advocates* (pp. 203–237). Westport, CT: Praeger.

Bond, H. K. (1998). *Pontius Pilate in history and interpretation.* New York: Cambridge University Press.

Boster, J. S., Yost, J., and Peeke, C. (2004). Rage, revenge, and religion: Honest signaling of aggression and nonaggression in Waorani coalitional violence. *Ethos, 31,* 471–494.

Bottom, W. P., Gibson, K., Daniels, S. E., and Murnighan, J. K. (2002). When talk is not cheap: Substantive penance and expressions of intent in rebuilding cooperation. *Organization Science, 13,* 497–513.

Boyd, R., Gintis, H., Bowles, S., and Richerson, P. J. (2003). The evolution of altruistic punishment. *Proceedings of the National Academy of Sciences, 100,* 3531–3535.

Boyd, R., and Richerson, P. J. (1992). Punishment allows the evolution of cooperation (or anything else) in sizable groups. *Ethology and Sociobiology, 13,* 171–195.

Boyer, P. (2001). *Religion explained: The evolutionary origins of religious thought.* New York: Basic Books.

Bradfield, M., and Aquino, K. (1999). Effects of blame attributions and offender likeableness on forgiveness and revenge in the workplace. *Journal of Management, 25,* 607–631.

Brezina, T., Agnew, R., Cullen, F. T., and Wright, J. P. (2004). The code of the street: A quantitative assessment of Elijah Anderson's subculture of violence thesis and its contribution to youth violence research. *Youth Violence and Juvenile Justice, 2,* 303–328.

Brody, J. F. (2001). Evolutionary recasting: ADHD, mania and its variants. *Journal of Affective Disorders, 65,* 197–205.

Brown, B. R. (1968). The effects of need to maintain face on interpersonal bargaining. *Journal of Experimental Social Psychology, 4,* 107–122.

Brown, C. H. (1989). The acoustic ecology of East African primates and the perception of vocal signals by grey-cheeked mangabeys and blue monkeys. In R. J. Dooling and S. H. Hulse (Eds.), *The comparative psychology of audition: Perceiving complex sounds* (pp. 201–239). Hillsdale, NJ: Lawrence Erlbaum Associates.

Brown, D. E. (1991). *Human universals.* Boston: McGraw-Hill.

Bureau of Alcohol, Tobacco and Firearms. (1999). *Arson and explosives incidents report, 1997* (No. ATF P 3320.4).

Burnham, G., Lafta, R., Doocy, S., and Roberts, L. (2006). Mortality after the 2003 invasion of Iraq: A cross-sectional cluster sample survey. *Lancet, 368,* 1421–1428.

Bushman, B. J., Baumeister, R. F., and Phillips, C. M. (2001). Do people aggress to improve their mood? Catharsis beliefs, affect regulation opportunity, and aggressive responding. *Journal of Personality and Social Psychology, 81,* 17–32.

Bushman, B. J., Ridge, R. D., Das, E., Key, C. W., and Busath, G. M. (2007). When God sanctions killing: Effect of scriptural violence on aggression. *Psychological Science, 18,* 204–207.

Buss, D. M. (1999). Human nature and individual differences: The evolution of human personality. In L. A. Pervin and O. P. John (Eds.), *Handbook of personality: Theory and research* (2nd ed., pp. 31–56). New York: Guilford.

Buss, D. M., Haselton, M. G., Shackelford, T. K., Bleske, A. L., and Wakefield, J. C. (1998). Adaptations, exaptations, and spandrels. *American Psychologist, 53,* 533–548.

Butler, J. (1970). *Fifteen sermons preached at Rolls Chapel.* London: SPCK. Originally published in 1726.

Butovskaya, M. L., Boyko, E. Y., Selverova, N. B., and Ermakova, I. V. (2005). The hormonal basis of reconciliation in humans. *Journal of Physiological Anthropology and Applied Human Science, 24,* 333–337.

Butovskaya, M., Verbeek, P., Ljungberg, T., and Lunardini, A. (2000). A multicultural view of peacemaking among young children. In F. Aureli and F.B.M. de Waal (Eds.), *Natural conflict resolution* (pp. 243–258). Berkeley: University of California Press.

Cacioppo, J. T., Visser, P. S., and Pickett, C. L. (2006). *Social neuroscience: People thinking about people.* Cambridge, MA: MIT Press.

Calame-Griaule, G. (1986). *Words and the Dogon world.* Philadelphia: Institute for the Study of Human Issues.

Call, J., Aureli, F., and de Waal, F.B.M. (1999). Reconciliation patterns among stumptailed macaques: A multivariate approach. *Animal Behaviour, 58,* 165–172.

Carcach, C. (1997). *Youth as victims and offenders of homicide* (No. 73). Canberra: Australian Institute of Criminology.

Cardona, M., and others. (2005). Homicides in Medellín, Colombia, from 1990 to 2002: Victims, motives, and circumstances. *Cadernos de Salude Publica, Rio de Janeiro, 21,* 840–851.

Cardozo, B. L., Kaiser, R., Gotway, C. A., and Agani, F. (2003). Mental health, social functioning, and feelings of hatred and revenge of Kosovar Albanians one year after the war in Kosovo. *Journal of Traumatic Stress, 16,* 351–360.

Cardozo, B. L., Vergara, A., Agani, F., and Gotway, C. A. (2000). Mental health, social functioning, and attitudes of Kosovar Albanians following the war in Kosovo. *Journal of the American Medical Association, 284,* 569–577.

Carlson, M., and Miller, N. (1988). Bad experiences and aggression. *Sociology and Social Research, 72,* 155–158.

Chagnon, N. (1988). Life histories, blood revenge, and warfare in a tribal population. *Science, 239,* 985–992.

Chagnon, N. (1992). *Yanomamö: The fierce people* (4th ed.). Fort Worth, TX: Harcourt Brace Jovanovich College Publishers.

Cheney, D. L., Seyfarth, R. M., and Silk, J. B. (1995). The role of grunts in reconciling opponents and facilitating interactions among adult female baboons. *Animal Behaviour, 50,* 249–257.

Chu, R., Rivera, C., and Loftin, C. (2000). Herding and homicide: An examination of the Nisbett-Reaves hypothesis. *Social Forces, 78,* 971–987.

Clark, A. J. (2005). Forgiveness: A neurological model. *Medical Hypotheses, 65,* 649–654.

Clutton-Brock, T. H., and Parker, G. A. (1995). Punishment in animal societies. *Nature, 373,* 209–216.

Cohen, A. B., Malka, A., Rozin, P., and Cherfas, L. (2006). Religion and unforgivable offenses. *Journal of Personality, 74,* 85–117.

Cohen, D., Nisbett, R. E., Bowdle, B. F., and Schwarz, N. (1996). Insult, aggression, and the Southern culture of honor: An "experimental ethnography." *Journal of Personality and Social Psychology, 70,* 945–960.

Cohen, R. (2004). Apology and reconciliation in international relations. In Y. Bar-Simian-Tov (Ed.), *From conflict resolution to reconciliation* (pp. 177–195). New York: Oxford University Press.

Cords, M., and Thurnheer, S. (1993). Reconciliation with valuable partners by long-tailed macaques. *Ethology, 93,* 315–325.

Crombag, H., Rassin, E., and Horselenberg, R. (2003). On vengeance. *Psychology, Crime and Law, 9,* 333–344.

Daly, M., and Wilson, M. (1988). *Homicide.* New York: Aldine de Gruyter.

Daly, M., and Wilson, M. I. (1994). Some differential attributes of lethal assaults on small children by stepfathers versus genetic fathers. *Ethology and Sociobiology, 15,* 207–217.

Darwin, C. (1952). *The descent of man, and selection in relation to sex.* Chicago: University of Chicago Press. Originally published in 1871.

David, R., and Choi, S.Y.P. (2006). Forgiveness and transitional justice in the Czech Republic. *Journal of Conflict Resolution, 50,* 339–367.

Davis, J. A., and Smith, T. W. (1998). General Social Survey. Retrieved December 30, 2002, from www.thearda.com/archive/codebooks/gss1998cb.html.

Davis, J. A., Smith, T. W., and Marsden, P. V. (2002). *General Social Survey 2000.* Chicago: National Opinion Research Center.

Daye, R. (2004). *Political forgiveness: Lessons from South Africa.* Maryknoll, NY: Orbis.

de Jong, P. J., Peters, M. L., and de Cremer, D. (2003). Blushing may signify guilt: Revealing effects of blushing in ambiguous social situations. *Motivation and Emotion, 27,* 225–249.

de Quervain, D. J.-F., and others. (2004). The neural basis of altruistic punishment. *Science, 305,* 1254–1258.

de Waal, F.B.M. (1989). *Peacemaking among primates.* Cambridge, MA: Harvard University Press.

de Waal, F.B.M. (1996). *Good natured: The origins of right and wrong in humans and other animals.* Cambridge, MA: Harvard University Press.

de Waal, F.B.M. (2000). The first kiss: Foundations of conflict resolution research in animals. In F. Aureli and F.B.M. de Waal (Eds.), *Natural conflict resolution* (pp. 15–33). Berkeley: University of California Press.

de Waal, F.B.M. (2001). *The ape and the sushi master: Cultural reflections of a primatologist.* New York: Basic Books.

de Waal, F.B.M. (2002). Evolutionary psychology: The wheat and the chaff. *Current Directions in Psychological Science, 11,* 187–191.

de Waal, F.B.M., and Johanowicz, D. L. (1993). Modification of reconciliation behavior through social experience: An experiment with two macaque species. *Child Development, 64,* 897–908.

de Waal, F.B.M., and Luttrell, L. M. (1988). Mechanisms of social reciprocity in three primate species: Symmetrical relationship characteristics or cognition? *Ethology and Sociobiology, 9,* 109–118.

de Waal, F.B.M., and Pokorny, J. J. (2005). Primate conflict and its relation to human forgiveness. In E. L. Worthington (Ed.), *Handbook of forgiveness* (pp. 17–32). New York: Routledge.

de Waal, F.B.M., and Ren, R. (1988). Comparison of the reconciliation behavior of stumptail and rhesus macaques. *Ethology, 78,* 129–142.

de Waal, F.B.M., and van Roosmalen, A. (1979). Reconciliation and consolation among chimpanzees. *Behavioral Ecology and Sociobiology, 5,* 55–66.

Diamond, S. R. (1977). The effect of fear on the aggressive responses of anger aroused and revenge motivated subjects. *Journal of Psychology, 95,* 185–188.

Dobzhansky, T. (1973). Nothing in biology makes sense except in the light of evolution. *American Biology Teacher, 35,* 125–129.

Dooley, E. (2001). *Homicide in Ireland 1992–1996* (No. 9435). Dublin: Government of Ireland.

Dugatkin, L. A. (1988). Do guppies play tit-for-tat during predator inspection visits? *Behavioral Ecology and Sociobiology, 25,* 395–399.

Dugatkin, L. A. (1991). Dynamics of the TIT FOR TAT strategy during predator inspection in the guppy (Poecilia reticulata). *Behavioral Ecology and Sociobiology, 29,* 127–132.

Dugatkin, L. A., and Alfieri, M. (1992). Interpopulation differences in the use of the tit-for-tat strategy during predator inspection in the guppy, Poecilia reticulata. *Evolutionary Ecology, 6,* 519–526.

Dunbar, R.I.M. (1996). *Grooming, gossip, and the evolution of language.* Cambridge, MA: Harvard University Press.

Dunbar, R.I.M. (2003). The social brain: Mind, language, and society in evolutionary perspective. *Annual Review of Anthropology, 32,* 163–181.

Dunbar, R.I.M., Clark, A., and Hurst, N. L. (1995). Conflict and cooperation among the Vikings: Contingent behavioral decisions. *Ethology and Sociobiology, 16,* 233–246.

Eaton, J., and Struthers, C. W. (2006). The reduction of psychological aggression across varied interpersonal contexts through repentance and forgiveness. *Aggressive Behavior, 32,* 195–206.

Eisenberger, N. I., and Lieberman, M. D. (2004). Why rejection hurts: A common neural alarm system for physical and social pain. *TRENDS in Cognitive Sciences, 8,* 294–300.

Eisenberger, N. I., Lieberman, M. D., and Williams, K. D. (2003). Does rejection hurt? An fMRI study of social exclusion. *Science, 302,* 290–292.

Eisner, M. (2001). Modernization, self-control, and lethal violence. *British Journal of Criminology, 41,* 618–638.

Elias, N. (1969). *The civilizing process* (Vol. 2, E. Jephcott, Trans.). New York: Pantheon.

Ember, C. R. (1978). Myths about hunter-gatherers. *Ethnology, 17,* 439–448.

Enright, R. D., Freedman, S. R., and Rique, J. (1998). The psychology of interpersonal forgiveness. In R. D. Enright and J. North (Eds.), *Exploring forgiveness* (pp. 46–62). Madison: University of Wisconsin Press.

Europol. (2005). *2005 EU organized crime report: Public version.* The Hague: Council of the European Union.

Exline, J. J., DeShea, L., and Holeman, V. T. (2007). Is apology worth the risk? Predictors, outcomes, and ways to avoid regret. *Journal of Social and Clinical Psychology, 26,* 479–504.

Federal Bureau of Investigation. (2006). *Crime in the United States: Uniform crime reports for the United States 2005.* Washington, DC: Federal Bureau of Investigation.

Fehr, E., and Gächter, S. (2002). Altruistic punishment in humans. *Nature, 415,* 137–140.

Felson, R. B. (1982). Impression management and the escalation of aggression and violence. *Social Psychology Quarterly, 45,* 245–254.

Finkel, E. J., Rusbult, C. E., Kumashiro, M., and Hannon, P. A. (2002). Dealing with a betrayal in close relationships: Does commitment promote forgiveness? *Journal of Personality and Social Psychology, 82,* 956–974.

Flaxman, S. M., and Sherman, P. W. (2000). Morning sickness: A mechanism for protecting mother and embryo. *Quarterly Review of Biology, 75,* 113–148.

Fletcher, R. (2003). *Bloodfeud: Murder and revenge in Anglo-Saxon England.* New York: Oxford University Press.

Ford, R., and Blegen, M. A. (1992). Offensive and defensive use of punitive tactics in explicit bargaining. *Social Psychology Quarterly, 55,* 351–362.

Frean, M. R. (1994). The prisoner's dilemma without synchrony. *Proceedings of the Royal Society of London, Series B—Biological Sciences, 257,* 75–79.

Frijda, N. H. (1994). The lex talionis: On vengeance. In S.H.M. van Goozen, N. E. Van de Poll, and J. A. Sargeant (Eds.), *Emotions: Essays on emotion theory* (pp. 263–289). Hillsdale, NJ: Lawrence Erlbaum Associates.

Fry, D. P. (2000). Conflict management in cross-cultural perspective. In F. Aureli and F.B.M. de Waal (Eds.), *Natural conflict resolution* (pp. 334–351). Berkeley: University of California Press.

Fry, D. P. (2006). *The human potential for peace.* New York: Oxford University Press.

Fujisawa, K. K., Kutsukake, N., and Hasegawa, T. (2005). Reconciliation pattern after aggression among Japanese preschool children. *Aggressive Behavior, 31,* 138–152.

Gaertner, S. L., Dovidio, J. F., Banker, B. S., Houlette, M., Johnson, K. M., and McGlynn, E. A. (2000). Reducing intergroup conflict: From superordinate goals to decategorization, recategorization, and mutual differentiation. *Group dynamics: Theory, research, and practice, 4,* 98–114.

Gangestad, S. W., Thornhill, R., and Garver-Apgar, C. E. (2005). Adaptations to ovulation. In D. M. Buss (Ed.), *Handbook of evolutionary psychology* (pp. 344–371). Hoboken, NJ: John Wiley & Sons.

Gaylord, M. S., and Galligher, J. F. (1994). Death penalty politics and symbolic law in Hong Kong. *International Journal of the Sociology of Law, 22,* 19–37.

General Accounting Office. (2007). *Military operations: The Department of Defense's uses of solatia and condolence payments in Iraq and Afghanistan* (No. GAO-07-699). Washington, DC: United States Government Accounting Office.

Geronimo. (1983). *Geronimo's story of his life.* New York: Irvington. Originally published in 1906.

Giancola, P. R. (2000). Executive functioning: A conceptual framework for alcohol-related aggression. *Experimental and Clinical Psychopharmacology, 8,* 576–597.

Giancola, P. R. (2003). The moderating effects of dispositional empathy on alcohol-related aggression in men and women. *Journal of Abnormal Psychology, 112,* 275–281.

Gibson, J. L. (2006). The contributions of truth to reconciliation: Lessons from South Africa. *Journal of Conflict Resolution, 50,* 409–432.

Godfray, H.C.J. (1992). The evolution of forgiveness. *Nature, 355,* 206–207.

Gold, G. J., and Weiner, B. (2000). Remorse, confession, group identity, and expectancies about repeating a transgression. *Basic and Applied Social Psychology, 22,* 291–300.

Gordon, K. C., Burton, S., and Porter, L. (2004). Predicting the intentions of women in domestic violence shelters to return to partners: Does forgiveness play a role? *Journal of Family Psychology, 18,* 331–338.

Gorsuch, R. L., and Hao, J. Y. (1993). Forgiveness: An exploratory factor analysis and its relationships to religious variables. *Review of Religious Research, 34,* 333–347.

Greer, T., Berman, M., Varan, V., Bobrycki, L., and Watson, S. (2005). We are a religious people; we are a vengeful people. *Journal for the Scientific Study of Religion, 44,* 45–57.

Grim, P. (1995). The greater generosity of the spatialized prisoner's dilemma. *Journal of Theoretical Biology, 173,* 353–359.

Grim, P. (1996). Spatialization and greater generosity in the stochastic prisoner's dilemma. *BioSystems, 37,* 3–17.

Gürerk, O., Irlenbusch, B., and Rockenbach, B. (2006). The competitive advantage of sanctioning institutions. *Science, 312,* 108–111.

Haidt, J. (2001). The emotional dog and its rational tail: A social intuitionist approach to moral judgment. *Psychological Review, 108,* 814–834.

Haidt, J., Sabini, J., and Worthington, E. L. (n.d.). *What exactly makes revenge sweet?* Unpublished manuscript, Charlottesville, VA.

Handel, S. (1989). *Listening: An introduction to the perception of auditory events.* Cambridge, MA: MIT Press.

Hareli, S. (2005). Accounting for one's behavior: What really determines its effectiveness? Its type or its content? *Journal for the Theory of Social Behavior, 35,* 359–372.

Harmon-Jones, E., and Sigelman, J. (2001). State anger and prefrontal brain activity: Evidence that insult-related relative left prefrontal activity is associated with experienced anger and aggression. *Journal of Personality and Social Psychology, 80,* 797–803.

Harmon-Jones, E., Vaughn-Scott, K., Mohr, S., Sigelman, J., and Harmon-Jones, C. (2004). The effect of manipulated sympathy and anger on left and right frontal cortical activity. *Emotion, 4,* 95–101.

Hauert, C., and Schuster, H. G. (1998). Extending the iterated prisoner's dilemma without synchrony. *Journal of Theoretical Biology, 192,* 155–166.

Hayner, P. B. (1994). Fifteen truth commissions—1974–1994: A comparative study. *Human Rights Quarterly, 16,* 597–655.

Henrich, J., and others. (2006). Costly punishment across human societies. *Science, 312,* 1767–1770.

Hewstone, M., Cairns, E., Voci, A., Hamberger, J., and Niens, U. (2006). Intergroup contact, forgiveness, and experience of "the troubles" in Northern Ireland. *Journal of Social Issues, 62,* 99–120.

Hewstone, M., Cairns, E., Voci, A., McLernon, F., Niens, U., and Noor, M. (2004). Intergroup forgiveness and guilt in Northern Ireland: Social psychological dimensions of "the troubles." In N. R. Branscombe and B. Doosje (Eds.), *Collective guilt: International perspectives* (pp. 193–215). New York: Cambridge University Press.

Hewstone, M., Rubin, M., and Willis, H. (2002). Intergroup bias. *Annual Review of Psychology, 53,* 575–604.

Hickson, L. (1986). The social contexts of apology in dispute settlement: A cross-cultural study. *Ethnology, 25,* 283–294.

Homerin, T. E. (2006). Islam: What it is and how it has interacted with Western civilization. In J. Neusner (Ed.), *Religious foundations of Western civilization* (pp. 105–158). Nashville: Abingdon Press.

Hoover, J. P., and Robinson, S. K. (2007). Retaliatory mafia behavior by a parasitic cowbird favors host acceptance of parasitic eggs. *Proceedings of the National Academy of Sciences, 104,* 4479–4483.

Hoppe, D. (2003). Still Vonnegut after all these years. *Utne Reader,* May-June, pp. 86–89.

Horney, K. (1948). The value of vindictiveness. *American Journal of Psychoanalysis, 8,* 3–12.

Hostetler, J. A. (1993). *Amish society* (4th ed.). Baltimore: Johns Hopkins University Press.

Hruschka, D. J., and Henrich, J. (2006). Friendship, cliquishness, and the emergence of cooperation. *Journal of Theoretical Biology, 239,* 1–15.

Iraq Family Health Survey Study Group (2008). Violence-related mortality in Iraq from 2002 to 2006. *New England Journal of Medicine, 358,* 484–493.

Irons, W. (2001). Religion as a hard-to-fake sign of commitment. In R. M. Nesse (Ed.), *The evolution of commitment* (pp. 292–309). New York: Russell Sage Foundation.

Jacobs, B. A. (2004). A typology of street criminal retaliation. *Journal of Research in Crime and Delinquency, 41,* 295–323.

Jacoby, S. (1983). *Wild justice: The evolution of revenge.* New York: Harper and Row.

Jampolsky, G. G., and Walsch, N. D. (1999). *Forgiveness: The greatest healer of all.* Hillsboro, OR: Beyond Words.

Juergensmeyer, M. (2003). *Terror in the mind of God: The global rise of religious violence* (3rd ed.). Berkeley: University of California Press.

Kadiangandu, J. K., Mullet, É., and Vinsonneau, G. (2001). Forgivingness: A Congo-France comparison. *Journal of Cross-Cultural Psychology, 32,* 504–511.

Kaplan, E. H., Mintz, A., Mishal, S., and Samban, C. (2005). What happened to suicide bombings in Israel? Insights from a terror stock model. *Studies in Conflict and Terrorism, 28,* 225–235.

Karremans, J. C., and Van Lange, P.A.M. (2004). Back to caring after being hurt: The role of forgiveness. *European Journal of Social Psychology, 34,* 207–227.

Karremans, J. C., Van Lange, P.A.M., Ouwerkerk, J. W., and Kluwer, E. S. (2003). When forgiving enhances psychological well-being: The role of interpersonal commitment. *Journal of Personality and Social Psychology, 84,* 1011–1026.

Katsukake, N., and Castles, D. L. (2004). Reconciliation and post-conflict third-party affiliation among wild chimpanzees in the Mahale Mountains, Tanzania. *Primates, 45,* 157–165.

Keeley, L. H. (1996). *War before civilization.* New York: Oxford University Press.

Kelly, R. C. (2003). *Warless societies and the origin of war.* Ann Arbor: University of Michigan Press.

Keltner, D., Young, R. C., and Buswell, B. N. (1997). Appeasement in human emotion, social practice, and personality. *Aggressive Behavior, 23,* 359–374.

Kim, S. H., Smith, R. H., and Brigham, N. L. (1998). Effects of power imbalance and the presence of third parties on reactions to harm: Upward and downward revenge. *Personality and Social Psychology Bulletin, 24,* 353–361.

Kimmel, M. S., and Mahler, M. (2003). Adolescent masculinity, homophobia and violence: Random school shootings, 1982–2001. *American Behavioral Scientist, 46,* 1439–1458.

King-Casas, B., Tomlin, D., Anen, C., Camerer, C. F., Quartz, S. R., and Montague, P. R. (2005). Getting to know you: Reputation and trust in a two-person economic exchange. *Science, 308,* 78–83.

Kirkpatrick, L. A. (2005). *Attachment, evolution, and the psychology of religion.* New York: Guilford.

Knutson, B. (2004). Sweet revenge? *Science, 305,* 1246–1247.

Knutson, B., and Wimmer, G. E. (2007). Reward: Neural circuitry for social valuation. In E. Harmon-Jones and P. Winkielman (Eds.), *Fundamentals of social neuroscience* (pp. 157–175). New York: Guilford.

Köhler, W. (1956). *The mentality of apes.* New York: Vintage Books.

Kohut, A. (2005). *Support for terror wanes among Muslim publics.* Washington, DC: Pew Global Attitudes Project.

Korchmaros, J. D., and Kenny, D. A. (2001). Emotional closeness as a mediator of the effect of genetic relatedness on altruism. *Psychological Science, 12,* 262–265.

Koski, S. E., Koops, K., and Sterck, E.H.M. (2007). Reconciliation, relationship quality, and postconflict anxiety: Testing the integrated hypothesis in captive chimpanzees. *American Journal of Primatology, 69,* 158–172.

Krishnan, V. (1993). Religious homogamy and voluntary childlessness in Canada. *Sociological Perspectives, 36,* 83–93.

Kubrin, C. E., and Weitzer, R. (2003). Retaliatory homicide: Concentrated disadvantage and neighborhood culture. *Social Problems, 50,* 157–180.

Kurzban, R., DeScioli, P., and O'Brien, E. (2007). Audience effects on moralistic punishment. *Evolution and Human Behavior, 28,* 75–84.

Kurzban, R. O., Tooby, J., and Cosmides, L. (2001). Can race be erased? Coalitional computation and social categorization. *Proceedings of the National Academy of Sciences, 98,* 15387–15392.

Kuschel, R. (1988). *Vengeance is their reply: Blood feuds and homicides on Bellona Island, part I: Conditions underlying generations of bloodshed.* Copenhagen: Dansk Psykologisk Forlag.

Lawler, K. A., and others. (2003). A change of heart: Cardiovascular correlates of forgiveness in response to interpersonal conflict. *Journal of Behavioral Medicine, 26,* 373–393.

Lazare, A. (2004). *On apology.* New York: Oxford University Press.

Le Blanc, S. A., and Register, K. E. (2003). *Constant battles: The myth of the peaceful, noble savage.* New York: St. Martin's Press.

Lerner, J. S., and Keltner, D. (2000). Beyond valence: Toward a model of emotion-specific influences on judgement and choice. *Cognition and Emotion, 14,* 473–493.

Lerner, J. S., and Keltner, D. (2001). Fear, anger, and risk. *Journal of Personality and Social Psychology, 81,* 146–159.

Lindskold, S., and Aronoff, J. (1980). Conciliatory strategies and relative power. *Journal of Experimental Social Psychology, 16.*

Ljungberg, T., Horowitz, L., Jansson, L., Westlund, K., and Clarke, C. (2005). Communicative factors, conflict progression, and use of reconciliatory strategies in pre-school boys—a series of random events or a sequential process? *Aggressive Behavior, 31,* 303–323.

Ljungberg, T., and Westlund, K. (2000). Impaired reconciliation in rhesus macaques with a history of early weaning and disturbed socialization. *Primates, 41,* 79–88.

Lodge, O. (1941). *Peasant life in Jugoslavia.* London: Seeley, Service and Co.

Long, W. J., and Brecke, P. (2003). *War and reconciliation: Reason and emotion in conflict resolution.* Cambridge, MA: MIT Press.

Marlatt, G. A., Kosturn, C. F., and Lang, A. R. (1975). Provocation to anger and opportunity for retaliation as determinants of alcohol consumption in social drinkers. *Journal of Abnormal Psychology, 84,* 652–659.

Marongiu, P., and Newman, G. R. (1987). *Vengeance: The fight against injustice.* Totowa, NJ: Rowman and Littlefield.

McCullough, M. E., Bellah, C. G., Kilpatrick, S. D., and Johnson, J. L. (2001). Vengefulness: Relationships with forgiveness, rumination, well-being, and the Big Five. *Personality and Social Psychology Bulletin, 27,* 601–610.

McCullough, M. E., Bono, G. B., and Root, L. M. (2005). Religion and forgiveness. In R. Paloutzian and C. Park (Eds.), *Handbook of the psychology of religion and spirituality* (pp. 394–411). New York: Guilford.

McCullough, M. E., Emmons, R. A., Kilpatrick, S. D., and Mooney, C. N. (2003). Narcissists as "victims": The role of narcissism in the perception of transgressions. *Personality and Social Psychology Bulletin, 29,* 885–893.

McCullough, M. E., Rachal, K. C., Sandage, S. J., Worthington, E. L., Brown, S. W., and Hight, T. L. (1998). Interpersonal forgiving in close relationships. II: Theoretical elaboration and measurement. *Journal of Personality and Social Psychology, 75,* 1586–1603.

McCullough, M. E., Worthington, E. L., and Rachal, K. C. (1997). Interpersonal forgiving in close relationships. *Journal of Personality and Social Psychology, 73,* 321–336.

McGee, J. P., and DeBernardo, C. R. (1999). The classroom avenger. *Forensic Examiner, 8,* 16–18.

Michod, R. E., and Nedelcu, A. M. (2003). On the reorganization of fitness during evolutionary transitions in individuality. *Integrative and Comparative Biology, 43,* 64–73.

Milinski, M. (1987). Tit-for-tat in sticklebacks and the evolution of cooperation. *Nature, 325,* 433–435.

Miller, D. T. (2001). Disrespect and the experience of injustice. *Annual Review of Psychology, 52,* 527–553.

Miller, T. Q., Smith, T. W., Turner, C. W., Guijarro, M. L., and Hallet, A. J. (1996). A meta-analytic review of research on hostility and physical health. *Psychological Bulletin, 119,* 322–348.

Moerk, E. L. (2002). Scripting war-entry to make it appear unavoidable. *Peace and Conflict: Journal of Peace Psychology, 8,* 229–248.

Moeschberger, S. L., Dixon, D. N., Niens, U., and Cairns, E. (2005). Forgiveness in Northern Ireland: A model for peace in the midst of the "troubles." *Peace and Conflict: Journal of Peace Psychology, 11,* 199–124.

Morgan, E. S. (1992). *The birth of the republic: 1763–89* (3rd ed.). Chicago: University of Chicago Press.

Morris, C. J. (1992). *Marriage and murder in eleventh-century Northumbria: A study of "De Obsessione Dunelmi" (Borthwick Paper No. 82)*. York, England: Borthwick Institute of Historical Research, University of York.

Mullet, É., Houdbine, A., Laumonier, S., and Girard, M. (1998). "Forgivingness": Factor structure in a sample of young, middle-aged, and elderly adults. *European Psychologist, 3,* 289–297.

Murphy, J. G. (2003). *Getting even: Forgiveness and its limits.* New York: Oxford University Press.

Nadler, A., and Liviatan, I. (2006). Intergroup reconciliation: Effects of adversary's expressions of empathy, responsibility, and recipients' trust. *Personality and Social Psychology Bulletin, 32,* 459–470.

Nansel, T. R., Overpeck, M., Pilla, R. S., Ruan, W. J., Simons-Morton, B., and Scheidt, P. (2001). Bullying behaviors among U.S. youth: Prevalence and association with psychosocial adjustment. *Journal of the American Medical Association, 285,* 2094–2100.

Newberg, A. B., d'Aquili, E. G., Newberg, S. K., and deMarici, V. (2000). The neuropsychological correlates of forgiveness. In M. E. McCullough, K. I. Pargament, and C. E. Thoresen (Eds.), *Forgiveness: Theory, research, and practice* (pp. 91–110). New York: Guilford.

Niebuhr, R. (1937, November 10). Japan and the Christian conscience. *Christian Century,* 1390–1391.

Nisbet, E. C., and Shanahan, J. (2004). *MSRG special report: Restrictions on civil liberties, views of Islam, and Muslim Americans.* Ithaca, NY: Media and Society Research Group.

Nisbett, R. E., and Cohen, D. (1996). *Culture of honor: The psychology of violence in the South.* Boulder, CO: Westview.

Nowak, M. (2006). Five rules for the evolution of cooperation. *Science, 314,* 1560–1563.

Nowak, M., and Sigmund, K. (1992). Tit for tat in heterogeneous populations. *Nature, 355,* 250–252.

Nowak, M., and Sigmund, K. (1993). A strategy of win-stay, lose-shift that outperforms tit-for-tat in the prisoner's dilemma game. *Nature, 364,* 56–58.

Nowak, M., and Sigmund, K. (1994). The alternating prisoner's dilemma. *Journal of Theoretical Biology, 168,* 219–226.

O'Steen, S., Cullum, A. J., and Bennett, A. F. (2002). Rapid evolution of escape ability in Trinidadian guppies (Poecilia reticulata). *Evolution, 56,* 776–784.

Ohbuchi, K., Kameda, M., and Agarie, N. (1989). Apology as aggression control: Its role in mediating appraisal of and response to harm. *Journal of Personality and Social Psychology, 56,* 219–227.

Öhman, A., and Mineka, S. (2003). The malicious serpent: Snakes as a prototypical stimulus for an evolved module of fear. *Current Directions in Psychological Science, 12,* 5–9.

Ohtsuki, H., and Iwasa, Y. (2004). How should we define goodness?— Reputation dynamics in indirect reciprocity. *Journal of Theoretical Biology, 231,* 107–120.

Ohtsuki, H., and Iwasa, Y. (2006). The leading eight: Social norms that can maintain cooperation by indirect reciprocity. *Journal of Theoretical Biology, 239,* 435–444.

Olshtain, E. (1989). Apologies across languages. In S. Blum-Kulka, J. House, and G. Kasper (Eds.), *Cross-cultural pragmatics: Requests and apologies* (pp. 155–173). Norwood, NJ: Ablex.

Orcutt, H. K. (2006). The prospective relationship of interpersonal forgiveness and psychological distress symptoms among college women. *Journal of Counseling Psychology, 53,* 350–361.

Orth, U., Montada, L., and Maercker, A. (2006). Feelings of revenge, retaliation motive, and posttraumatic stress reactions in crime victims. *Journal of Interpersonal Violence, 21,* 229–243.

Otterbein, K. F., and Otterbein, C. S. (1965). An eye for an eye, a tooth for a tooth: A cross-cultural study of feuding. *American Anthropologist, 67,* 1470–1482.

Pagel, M., and Mace, R. (2004). The cultural wealth of nations. *Nature, 428,* 275–278.

Panksepp, J. (1998). *Affective neuroscience: The foundations of human and animal emotions.* New York: Oxford University Press.

Pape, R. A. (2005). *Dying to win: The strategic logic of suicide terrorism.* New York: Random House.

Park, S., and Enright, R. D. (2000). Forgiveness across cultures. In F. Aureli and F.B.M. de Waal (Eds.), *Natural conflict resolution* (pp. 359–361). Berkeley: University of California Press.

Parkes, C. M. (1993). Psychiatric problems following bereavement by murder or manslaughter. *British Journal of Psychiatry, 162,* 49–54.

Perlmutter, D. D., and Major, L. H. (2004). Images of horror from Fallujah. *Nieman Reports, 58*(2), 71–74.

Petrucci, C. J. (2002). Apology in the criminal justice setting: Evidence for including apology as an additional component in the legal system. *Behavioral Sciences and the Law, 20,* 337–362.

Pettigrew, T. F. (1998). Intergroup contact theory. *Annual Review of Psychology, 49,* 65–85.

Pinker, S. (1994). *The language instinct: How the mind creates language.* New York: William Morrow.

Pinker, S. (1997). *How the mind works.* New York: Norton.

Pinker, S. (2002). *The blank slate: The modern denial of human nature.* New York: Viking.

Plomin, R., DeFries, J. C., Craig, I. W., and McGuffin, P. (Eds.). (2003). *Behavioral genetics in the postgenomic era.* Washington, DC: American Psychological Association.

Poundstone, W. (1992). *Prisoner's dilemma.* New York: Doubleday.

Preuschoft, S., Wang, X., Aureli, F., and de Waal, F.B.M. (2002). Reconciliation in captive chimpanzees: A reevaluation with controlled methods. *International Journal of Primatology, 23,* 29–50.

Price, M. E., Cosmides, L., and Tooby, J. (2002). Punitive sentiment as an anti-free rider psychological device. *Evolution and Human Behavior, 23,* 203–231.

Richard, F. D., Bond, C. F., Jr., and Stokes-Zoota, J. J. (2003). One hundred years of social psychology quantitatively described. *Review of General Psychology, 7,* 331–363.

Richerson, P. J., and Boyd, R. (2005). *Not by genes alone: How culture transformed human evolution.* Chicago: University of Chicago Press.

Richerson, P. J., Boyd, R. T., and Henrich, J. (2003). Cultural evolution of human cooperation. In P. Hammerstein (Ed.), *Genetic and cultural evolution of cooperation* (pp. 357–388). Cambridge, MA: MIT Press.

Ridley, M. (1996). *The origins of virtue: Human instincts and the evolution of cooperation.* New York: Penguin.

Rilling, J. K., Gutman, D. A., Zeh, T. R., Pagnoni, G., Berns, G. S., and Kilts, C. D. (2002). A neural basis for social cooperation. *Neuron, 35,* 395–405.

Roche, D. (2006). Dimensions of restorative justice. *Journal of Social Issues, 62,* 217–238.

Rokeach, M., and Ball-Rokeach, S. J. (1989). Stability and change in American value priorities, 1968–1981. *American Psychologist, 44,* 775–784.

Rolls, E. T. (2005). *Emotion explained.* Oxford, UK: Oxford University Press.

Ross, M. H. (1983). Political decision making and conflict: Additional cross-cultural codes and scales. *Ethnology, 22,* 169–192.

Rouhana, N. N. (2004). Group identity and power asymmetry in reconciliation processes: The Israeli-Palestinian case. *Peace and Conflict: Journal of Peace Psychology, 10,* 33–52.

Rousseau, J. J. (1984). *Discourse on the origin of inequality.* Chicago: University of Chicago Press. Originally published in 1754.

Rovinskii, P. (1901). *Chrnogoriia v eia proshlom i nastoiashchem* [Montenegro in its past and present] (Vol. 2, Part 2). St. Petersburg: Printing Office of the Imperial Academy of Sciences.

Rudolph, U., Roesch, S. C., Greitemeyer, T., and Weiner, B. (2004). A meta-analytic review of help giving and aggression from an attributional perspective: Contributions to a general theory of motivation. *Cognition and Emotion, 18,* 815–848.

Rushton, J. P. (1989). Genetic similarity, human altruism, and group selection. *Behavioral and Brain Sciences, 12,* 503–559.

Rye, M. S., and others. (2000). Religious perspectives on forgiveness. In M. E. McCullough, K. I. Pargament, and C. E. Thoresen (Eds.), *Forgiveness: Theory, research, and practice* (pp. 17–40). New York: Guilford.

Sanfey, A. G., Rilling, J. K., Aronson, J. A., Nystrom, L. E., and Cohen, J. D. (2003). The neural basis of economic decision-making in the ultimatum game. *Science, 300,* 1755–1758.

Sapolsky, R. M. (2004). Social status and health in humans and other animals. *Annual Review of Anthropology, 33,* 393–418.

Scheff, T. J. (2000). *Bloody revenge: Emotions, nationalism and war.* Lincoln, NE: iUniverse.

Scher, S. J., and Darley, J. M. (1997). How effective are the things that people say to apologize? Effects of the realization of the apology speech act. *Journal of Psycholinguistic Research, 26,* 127–140.

Schijman, E. (2005). Artificial cranial deformation in newborns in the pre-Columbian Andes. *Child's Nervous System, 21,* 945–950.

Schino, G. (1998). Reconciliation in domestic goats. *Behaviour, 135,* 343–356.

Schino, G. (2000). Beyond the primates: Expanding the reconciliation horizon. In F. Aureli and F.B.M. de Waal (Eds.), *Natural conflict resolution* (pp. 225–242). Berkeley: University of California Press.

Schmitt, D. P., and Pilcher, J. J. (2004). Evaluating evidence of psychological adaptation: How do we know one when we see one? *Psychological Science, 15,* 643–649.

Schönbach, P. (1990). *Account episodes: The management or escalation of conflict.* New York: Cambridge University Press.

Seligman, M.E.P., and Csikszentmihalyi, M. (2000). Positive psychology: An introduction. *American Psychologist, 55,* 5–14.

Shaw, J. C., Wild, E., and Colquitt, J. A. (2003). To justify or excuse? A meta-analytic review of the effects of explanations. *Journal of Applied Psychology, 88,* 444–458.

Shelley-Tremblay, J. F., and Rosén, L. A. (1996). Attention deficit hyperactivity disorder: An evolutionary perspective. *Journal of Genetic Psychology, 157,* 443–453.

Sherif, M., Harvey, O. J., White, B. J., Hood, W. R., and Sherif, C. W. (1961). *Intergroup conflict and cooperation: The Robbers Cave experiment.* Norman: University of Oklahoma Book Exchange.

Sherman, L. W., and others. (2005). Effects of face-to-face restorative justice on victims of crime in four randomized, controlled trials. *Journal of Experimental Criminology, 1,* 367–395.

Shriver, D. W., Jr. (1995). *An ethic for enemies: Forgiveness in politics.* New York: Oxford University Press.

Silk, J. B. (1992). The patterning of intervention among male bonnet macaques: Reciprocity, revenge, and loyalty. *Current Anthropology, 33,* 318–325.

Silk, J. B. (2000). The function of peaceful post-conflict interactions: An alternate view. In F. Aureli and F.B.M. de Waal (Eds.), *Natural conflict resolution* (pp. 179–181). Berkeley: University of California Press.

Silk, J. B. (2002). The form and function of reconciliation in primates. *Annual Review of Anthropology, 31,* 21–44.

Simpson, J. A., and Campbell, L. (2005). Methods of evolutionary sciences. In D. M. Buss (Ed.), *Handbook of evolutionary psychology* (pp. 119–144). Hoboken, NJ: John Wiley & Sons.

Singer, P. (1981). *The expanding circle: Ethics and sociobiology.* New York: Farrar, Straus and Giroux.

Singer, T., Seymour, B., O'Doherty, J. P., Stephan, K. E., Dolan, R. J., and Frith, C. D. (2006). Empathic neural responses are modulated by the perceived fairness of others. *Nature, 439,* 466–469.

Smale, G.J.A., and Spickenheuer, H.L.P. (1979). Feelings of guilt and need for retaliation in victims of serious crimes against property and persons. *Victimology: An International Journal, 4,* 75–85.

Smith, A. (1976). *The theory of moral sentiments* (6th ed.). Oxford, UK: Clarendon Press. Originally published in 1790.

Smith, H. (1991). *The world's religions.* New York: HarperCollins.

Smucny, D. A., Price, C. S., and Byrne, E. A. (1997). Post-conflict affiliation and stress reduction in captive rhesus macaques. *Advances in Ethology, 32,* 157.

Sosis, R. (2003). Why aren't we all Hutterites? Costly signaling theory and religious behavior. *Human Nature, 14,* 91–127.

Speckhard, A., and Ahkmedova, K. (2006). The making of a martyr: Chechen suicide terrorism. *Studies in Conflict and Terrorism, 29,* 429–492.

Staub, E., Pearlman, L. A., Gubin, A., and Hagengimana, A. (2005). Healing, reconciliation, forgiving, and the prevention of violence after genocide or mass killing: An intervention and its experimental evaluation in Rwanda. *Journal of Social and Clinical Psychology, 24,* 297–334.

Stillwell, A., Baumeister, R. F., and Del Priore, R. E. (2005). *We're all victims here: Toward a psychology of revenge.* Unpublished manuscript.

Strang, H. (2002). *Repair or revenge: Victims and restorative justice.* Oxford, UK: Clarendon Press.

Strang, H., and Sherman, L. W. (2003). Repairing the harm: Victims and restorative justice. *Utah Law Review, 15,* 15–42.

Strang, H., and others. (2006). Victim evaluations of face-to-face restorative justice conferences: A quasi-experimental analysis. *Journal of Social Issues, 62,* 281–306.

Suganami, H. (1996). *On the causes of war.* New York: Oxford University Press.

Summerfield, D. (2002). Effects of war: Moral knowledge, revenge, reconciliation, and medicalised concepts of "recovery."*British Medical Journal, 325,* 1105–1107.

Tabak, B., McCullough, M. E., Root, L. M., Bono, G., and Berry, J. T. (2007). *Conciliatory gestures facilitate forgiveness by making offenders seem more agreeable* (Manuscript submitted for publication).

Thornhill, R., and Palmer, C. T. (2000). *A natural history of rape: Biological bases of sexual coercion.* Cambridge, MA: MIT Press.

Tindall, G. B., and Shi, D. E. (1996). *America: A narrative history* (4th ed.). New York: Norton.

Tooby, J., and Cosmides, L. (1992). Psychological foundations of culture. In J. Barkow, L. Cosmides, and J. Tooby (Eds.), *The adapted mind: Evolutionary psychology and the generation of culture* (pp. 19–136). New York: Oxford University Press.

Topalli, V., Wright, R., and Fornango, R. (2002). Drug dealers, robbery, and retaliation. *British Journal of Criminology, 42,* 337–351.

Tsang, J., McCullough, M. E., and Hoyt, W. T. (2005). Psychometric and rationalization accounts for the religion-forgiveness discrepancy. *Journal of Social Issues, 61,* 785–805.

Tutu, D. M. (1999). *No future without forgiveness.* New York: Doubleday.

Twain, M. (1897). *More tramps abroad.* London: Chatto and Windus.

United States Department of State. (1996). *The Great Seal of the United States* (No. 10411). Washington, DC: United States Department of State.

Van Biema, D. (1999, April 5). Should all be forgiven? *Time, 153,* 54–58.

Van Lange, P.A.M., Ouwerkerk, J. W., and Tazelaar, M.J.A. (2002). How to overcome the detrimental effects of noise in social interaction: The benefits of generosity. *Journal of Personality and Social Psychology, 82,* 768–780.

Vargha-Khadem, F., Gadian, D. G., Copp, A., and Mishkin, M. (2005). FOXP2 and the neuroanatomy of speech and language. *Nature Reviews Neuroscience, 6,* 131–138.

Veenema, H. C. (2000). Methodological progress in post-conflict research. In F. Aureli and F.B.M. de Waal (Eds.), *Natural conflict resolution* (pp. 21–23). Berkeley: University of California Press.

Vossekuil, B., Fein, R. A., Reddy, M., Borum, R., and Modzeleski, W. (2002). *The final report and findings of the Safe School Initiative: Implications for the prevention of school attacks in the United States.* Washington, DC: U.S. Department of Education, Office of Elementary and Secondary Education, Safe and Drug-Free Schools Program and U.S. Secret Service, National Threat Assessment Center.

Walker, P. L. (2001). A bioarchaeological perspective on the history of violence. *Annual Review of Anthropology, 30,* 573–596.

Weaver, A., and de Waal, F.B.M. (2003). The mother-offspring relationship as a template in social development: Reconciliation in captive brown capuchins (Cebus apella). *Journal of Comparative Psychology, 117,* 101–110.

Wechter, D. (Ed.). (1949). *The love letters of Mark Twain.* New York: Harper and Brothers.

Wedekind, C., and Milinski, M. (1996). Human cooperation in the simultaneous and the alternating prisoner's dilemma: Pavlov versus Generous tit-for-tat. *Proceedings of the National Academy of Sciences, 93,* 2686–2689.

Weekes-Shackelford, V. A., and Shackelford, T. K. (2004). Methods of filicide: Stepparents and genetic parents kill differently. *Violence & Victims, 19,* 75–81.

Westermarck, E. (1898). The essence of revenge. *Mind,* 7(27), 289–310.

Westermarck, E. (1924). *The origin and development of the moral ideas.* London: MacMillan.

Williams, G. C. (1966). *Adaptation and natural selection: A critique of some current evolutionary thought.* Princeton, NJ: Princeton University Press.

Wilson, D. S. (2002). *Darwin's cathedral: Evolution, religion, and the nature of society.* Chicago: University of Chicago Press.

Wilson, D. S. (2007). *Evolution for everyone.* New York: Delacorte Press.

Wilson, D. S., Dietrich, E., and Clark, A. B. (2003). On the inappropriate use of the naturalistic fallacy in evolutionary psychology. *Biology and Philosophy, 18,* 669–682.

Wilson, M., and Daly, M. (1985). Competitiveness, risk taking, and violence: The young male syndrome. *Ethology and Sociobiology, 6,* 59–73.

Wilson, M. L., and Wrangham, R. W. (2003). Intergroup relations in chimpanzees. *Annual Review of Anthropology, 32,* 363–392.

Witvliet, C. v. O., Ludwig, T. E., and Vander Laan, K. L. (2001). Granting forgiveness or harboring grudges: Implications for emotion, physiology, and health. *Psychological Science, 12,* 117–123.

Wohl, M.J.A., and Branscombe, N. R. (2005). Forgiveness and collective guilt assignment to historical perpetrator groups depend on level of social category inclusiveness. *Journal of Personality and Social Psychology, 88,* 288–303.

Wrangham, R. W., and Peterson, D. (1996). *Demonic males: Apes and the origins of human violence.* New York: Houghton Mifflin.

Wright, R. (1994). *The moral animal: Evolutionary psychology and everyday life.* New York: Pantheon.

Wright, R. (2000). *Nonzero: The logic of human destiny.* New York: Pantheon.

Wu, J., and Axelrod, R. (1995). How to cope with noise in the iterated prisoner's dilemma. *Journal of Conflict Resolution, 39,* 183–189.

Zechmeister, J. S., and Romero, C. (2002). Victim and offender accounts of interpersonal conflict: Autobiographical narratives of forgiveness and unforgiveness. *Journal of Personality and Social Psychology, 84,* 675–686.

The Author

Michael E. McCullough is a professor of psychology at the University of Miami in Coral Gables, Florida, where he directs the Laboratory for Social and Clinical Psychology. His research is focused upon human moral sentiments such as forgiveness, the desire for revenge, and gratitude. He also conducts research on religion and its links to health, well-being, and social behavior. The author or editor of five previous books, this is his first sole-authored book for a general audience. He lives in Miami with his wife and their two children.

INDEX